PERFECT
RECIPES
FOR
HAVING
PEOPLE
OVER

PERFECT RECIPES FOR HAVING PEOPLE OVER

PAM ANDERSON

PHOTOGRAPHS BY RITA MAAS

HOUGHTON MIFFLIN COMPANY
Boston   New York

For information about permission to reproduce selections from
this book, write to Permissions, Houghton Mifflin Company,
215 Park Avenue South, New York, New York 10003.

Visit our Web site: www.houghtonmifflinbooks.com.

Library of Congress Cataloging-in-Publication Data
Anderson, Pam.
    Perfect recipes for having people over / Pam Anderson ;
photographs by Rita Maas.
        p.   cm.
    Includes index.
    ISBN 0-618-32972-2
    1. Cookery. 2. Entertaining. I. Title.
    TX714.A524 2005
    641.5—dc22   2005046370

Book design by Anne Chalmers
Typefaces: Filosofia, ITC Officina Sans
Food styling by Michael Pederson
Prop styling by Bette Blau

Printed in the United States of America
QWT 10 9 8 7 6 5 4 3 2

TO DAN,
FAITHFUL COLLEAGUE
ON THIS PROJECT,

AND TO DAVID,
FAITHFUL PARTNER FOR LIFE,

AND TO THE MEMORY OF
ANNE BLANCHARD

CONTENTS

THE BIG STUFF

ALL THE REST

ACKNOWLEDGMENTS

I'm grateful to

My editor, Rux Martin, for never taking her eyes off the book

My agent, Sarah Jane Freymann, for always looking out for me

Rita Maas, the photographer, Michael Pederson, the food stylist, Bette Blau, the prop stylist, and Anne Chalmers, the designer, for capturing this book's message

Judith Sutton, the copy editor, for asking the right questions

Deborah DeLosa, the publicist, for getting me to all the right places

My colleagues at *USA Weekend*, especially my editors, Connie Kurz and Brenda Turner

My colleagues at *Fine Cooking*

INTRODUCTION

When I first started cooking, back in the late 1970s, entertaining was a production. I starched and ironed the tablecloth and napkins, polished each glass, and set the table at least a day before the big event. I slavishly followed menus, trekking from store to store to find the exact ingredients. No recipe was too long, no meal too elaborate. In fact, I thrived on multistep dishes that required days of attention and care: puff pastry, layered pâtés and vegetable terrines, miniature sweet and savory tarts.

I still love to have friends over, but something happened along the way. First one daughter was born, then a second. Part-time work evolved into a full-time job. Casual hobbies became passionate avocations. With all these activities fighting for my time, I had to change the way I cooked.

My menus are simple and flexible now, and my parties mostly spur-of-the-moment. I love potlucks and shared suppers, and kids are always welcome. The food's fun, the atmosphere's casual, and family and friends always gravitate to the kitchen.

My standards haven't slipped — great food helps make a great party — but great food doesn't have to be difficult. My Rosemary-Scented Roast Pork Loin is succulent, juicy, beautiful, and utterly simple. Molten Chocolate Cakes are wonderfully oozy and chocolaty — many people think they're better than a chocolate layer cake. Made in muffin pans, they can be assembled in just a few minutes and then baked in the time it takes to clear the dinner dishes and put on a pot of coffee.

Because it's so easy, Chicken Chili (red or white) always makes it onto my short list when I host a crowd. Although it tastes authentic and long-simmered, it's made with convenience items — rotisserie chickens, store-bought chicken broth, and canned beans — and it cooks in less than forty-five minutes.

Whether you're sharing a meal with family, kicking back with a few friends, or hosting half the neighborhood, having a set of simple, foolproof recipes makes it easy to focus on the all-important goal of bringing people together around the table.

Sharing a Meal

The greater end of table fellowship was brought home to me forcefully a few years back. I had just arrived home from a months-long book tour. Since I was teaching in a different city nearly every day, my life had become strangely unreal. I was feeling depleted and altogether uninspired on my return home, when our friends Monty and Anne invited us for an impromptu lunch. Monty said they were grilling chicken breasts, with a black bean and corn salad. He suggested I bring a dessert that would go with fruit. I didn't have the energy to make anything, so I sped to the grocery store and grabbed a container of sliced pound cake and a can of whipped cream.

"Even with such short notice, they're expecting more from me," I thought. I should have known better. Anne had wrestled with cancer. Staring down Medusa-eyed death until it blinked, Anne was the realest person I knew.

We arrived as one of her friends was cutting up the grilled chicken to add to the black bean and corn salad. The six of us carried the meal—including plates, flatware, and glasses—to an outdoor table. That shared meal was a timeless moment of simplicity and plain beauty. We spooned the black bean salad from a metal mixing bowl, and we picked up salad greens with our hands straight from the salad spinner. We ate from plastic plates, sipped ice tea from an array of plastic cups collected from fast-food restaurants, and talked.

We changed into swimsuits for a quick dip in the pool, then ended with dessert—my store-bought pound cake, lightly toasted, with a salad of fresh plums, peaches, strawberries, and blueberries, flavored with mint from Anne's garden. My husband and I had arrived harried and bickering. We left calm and relaxed.

Stop Entertaining

We all understand the importance of gathering with friends and family. So why don't we do it more often? It's fear—fear that we don't have the time or skill to pull off a meal that will be good enough.

That's why it's important to stop entertaining and just have people over. The very word "entertain" makes most people cringe. A recent Gallup poll found that Americans rank entertaining—along with filing tax returns and visiting the dentist—as the number-one stress-related event in their lives. Entertaining scored even higher on the stress chart than childbirth.

How could something so ultimately satisfying cause so much anxiety?

It's because "entertaining" doesn't imply simply making a nice dinner for a few of your friends. It means you have to cook something fancy — something you've probably never made before. You've got to head to the wine store and hope the salesperson knows his stuff. You've got to buy candles and a flower arrangement. You have to iron the tablecloth and napkins. You can't just pick up the house, you have to scrub it. By the time the guests arrive, you'll be in no mood for a party.

If you're entertaining, in short, you've got to have your place looking as if the photo crew from *Architectural Digest* is about to drop in. But if you're having people over, all that can wait.

At our house, the chores still have to get done, of course, but my husband and I have succeeded in unhooking these from food and friends. If there's time to clean up and organize the stacks of magazines, catalogues, and unpaid bills, fine. If not, we just straighten them. If the garden was worked over last week, fine. If not, my husband picks out the towering weeds, and we let it go.

Deciding when to have people over can be a little like waiting for the perfect time to get married or have a baby or buy a house: you may never get around to doing it if you delay until all the conditions are right. It takes courage to invite them, ready or not, but it's powerful when you do.

And here's the reality: most people cook so infrequently that any home-cooked meal is special. In fact, I've found the more down-home the food and the more casual the setting, the livelier and happier the party.

A Menu That Works

There are two different ways to have people over. The first way — preferable to most cooks — is to plan a menu that can be prepared almost completely ahead, so there's very little to do (and very little that can go wrong) during the party. Really Good Lasagna, for instance, is an uncomplicated crowd-pleaser, refined enough for a formal dinner party yet right at home at a potluck. Oven-Barbecued Pork has all the flavor and appearance of meat that's been lovingly tended over an outdoor fire all day, but it literally cooks while you sleep. Simple Cassoulet is robust and rustic, and unlike the traditional version, which must be started a day or two in advance, it can be made in a few hours.

The second way to have people over is to do a little of the cooking during the party. Easy Baked Risotto and Roast Rack of Lamb with Vinegar-Mint Pan Sauce are impressive dinners that demand very little up-front time or effort and can cook unattended while you enjoy cocktail hour.

Better yet, have guests do some of the cooking—they may not even realize that you've enlisted them to do half the work! For Shish Kebabs—the perfect meal for satisfying both strict vegetarians and ravenous carnivores—set out bowls of marinated meat and cut-up vegetables and let your friends skewer their own.

Get Comfortable with the Meal You've Chosen

Because the rest of the meal follows naturally after you've picked a main course, I've organized the book by placing the main courses ("The Big Stuff") first, followed by the appetizers, soups, salads, side dishes, breads, desserts, and drinks ("All the Rest"). To help you quickly find what you need, I've divided the main-course recipes into those suitable for casual get-togethers, warm-weather events, more formal affairs, and morning fare.

So you can get comfortable with your choice and make sure it's right for the occasion, each recipe is accompanied by a shaded box with answers to important questions. When should I serve it? How can I vary it? Any shortcuts? What should I serve with it? How far ahead can I make it? What about leftovers?

For instance, when you've decided to have a sit-down dinner for eight people and you're considering rack of lamb for the main course, if you scan the box, you'll be reminded that this cut is expensive and also demands last-minute cooking and carving. That's not what you had in mind, so you look for another main course.

You want to have a couple dozen friends over for drinks and appetizers. Since you're short on time and money and it's a group with mixed tastes, you think about the appetizer bar (see page 126). This attractive hors d'oeuvre buffet of breads, spreads, and colorful toppings really makes a splash. The box tells you it offers incredible variety, is relatively inexpensive, and, since guests assemble their own nibbles, requires minimal preparation. Bingo! The question about shortcuts lets you know that you could also use store-bought pita and tortilla chips and grocery-store salad bar items for some of the toppings.

Sensible Steps—Shop, Set, Cook

Before you go any further, be sure you're being realistic about the time you can devote to shopping and cooking. Make up your mind to be flexible—at the store, in the kitchen, at the table. If the recipe calls for watercress but the bunch you see in the market looks ready for the compost heap, let the market keep it. Buy a baby lettuce blend or arugula instead. Or consider a head of mild butter lettuce mixed with assertive radicchio. If the grocery store flowers look unexceptional and you don't have time to arrange them anyway, head back to the produce department and pick up some apples or lemons or strawberries for a centerpiece bowl.

Setting the table in advance sends guests the welcome message that you're ready—even if you're not. And if you're behind when they arrive, it's easier to ask for help slicing a cucumber or topping toasts than to send someone off to try to set the table.

After the table is ready, you can relax a little. From here on out, it's just cooking. With a decently stocked kitchen, you can pull things together by the time your company comes—even if it's not everything that you planned.

If you find yourself running behind, stay calm and rely on backup ingredients in the cupboards. When there's no time to make the quesadilla appetizers or smoked salmon toasts after all, don't fret. Proudly set out a big bowl of pistachios and cherry tomatoes. Or just skip the toasts and serve the smoked salmon with some nice crackers, and let your friends assemble their own. Instead of the dessert you planned on, put a couple of scoops of sorbet in nice goblets and garnish with a little fresh fruit. You don't have beautiful berries? Thinly slice or mince an apple for a handsome garnish.

Planning for Big Get-Togethers

If you find yourself frequently hosting dinners for two or three dozen people, it may be time to buy a few things for such occasions. I invested in a couple dozen nice but inexpensive white plates, cheap wineglasses that work for any beverage, and a few sets of silverware. This way, I don't have to call the rental company or try to piece together enough from my cupboards every time I have a buffet. I store all of these in the basement, separate from my everyday dishes and china, bringing them up when it's time to prepare and returning them to their place after I've cleaned them.

Whenever possible, mix disposable tableware with the real stuff to lend an air of substance. Plates and silverware are easy to pop in the dishwasher, so you could pair them with disposable plastic glasses. Or consider real dishes for the main course and paper ones for dessert.

For glasses, be sure to figure on about one third more than the number of guests you've invited, to take into account people who'll lose theirs or switch drinks between cocktails and dinner. If you don't have enough glassware, put out what you have with a stack of disposables as backup. You'll also need an ice bucket and a metal tub (or a large cooler) for icing down beer, wine, and sodas.

You may want to invest in a small folding table to serve as a bar (which frees up the dining room and kitchen tables for dinner seating) and a thirty-cup coffeepot. Since most buffets include a big salad, you'll want a gigantic salad bowl.

Two large roasting pans will save you hours of kitchen time. Here's how: You've decided to make beef stew for your dinner for twenty-four. For a crowd that size, you will need to brown at least nine pounds of beef cubes, which would take you more than an hour in a Dutch oven (eight batches at eight minutes per batch). Instead, heat up those roasting pans over two burners and reduce your number to two batches per pan, or a total of sixteen minutes. You've saved forty-eight minutes.

Roasting pans work for other cooking techniques as well—sautéing onions, simmering chili, or steaming green beans for a crowd. The larger the surface is, the more you can cook at a time, and the more time you can spend relaxing with your guests.

Large disposable roasting pans can also be used. Although they're a little thin for browning and searing meat, they work beautifully for sautéing, steaming, and simmering. Just watch the heat a little more carefully and stir a little more frequently.

Going with the Flow

No matter how organized you may be, though, there are times when life intervenes to thwart your plans. Not long ago, my husband and I commissioned our artist nephew to do two large paintings. As part of the deal, he would deliver them, and we'd use the occasion to host a mini family reunion. When the time came for him to make the trip, he talked his father into driving out with him for the Memorial Day weekend. A few days before they arrived, he called to say they were able to get away a day earlier. Since I had to work that day, I didn't get around to figuring out a menu until midafternoon. I had enough sense to plan a simple grocery store menu of Perfect Roast Chicken served with Lemon-Artichoke Sauce with Garlic and Parsley, but I didn't get home from shopping until late afternoon.

I had managed to fry the tortillas for the Tortilla Sundaes and ready the chickens for the oven when the doorbell rang—two hours early. We broke open a bottle of bubbly to celebrate and spent the next hour chatting and admiring the paintings. A piece of me was enjoying the moment, but deep down I was panicked. At 7:30, just as

I was heading back to the kitchen, my brother- and sister-in-law and their three kids pulled into the driveway. I was living my worst anxiety dream.

Sharing anxiety does wonders for stress, and in a moment my sister-in-law and her kids were helping me assemble Easy Butternut Squash Ravioli for the first course. My niece and nephews seemed to be having fun. The guys carried in the luggage and made up the guest room while my sister-in-law set the table.

I put the chickens in the oven, refilled the nut bowl, and opened some more sparkling wine. When apocalypse threatens, let them sip champagne! There was so much family bonding going on that no one cared that dinner was delayed.

Finally the chickens were roasted, and I made the sauce. We cooked the ravioli, put them on plates, and garnished them. After the first course, I piled the carved chickens and bright green asparagus on a platter, and we passed it around family-style. I was beginning to unwind. The conversation was lively, and our usually quiet niece and nephews were especially talkative. The platter was passed again, and we devoured all the food. It worked its magic around the table.

I often think back on that dinner. More than the embarrassment of being caught unprepared, what I remember is my sister-in-law's satisfaction at being able to help someone who was usually well prepared. I recall the pride in my niece's and nephews' faces as they made a real contribution to dinner. And I won't forget my brother-in-law's comment a few months later. "You're always so relaxed when you have people over," he said. "You just seem to roll with whatever happens."

I would prefer not to preside over that kind of dinner party often, but it was a good reminder that having people over is a selfless act. Even if things aren't perfect —and often precisely because, blessedly, they're not—people appreciate your gift of time and self. As much as I care about food, dinners like that remind me that the food is not the ultimate point—the people are. And when I remember that, it is much easier to have people over.

THE BIG STUFF: MAIN COURSES

When

planning a meal,

decide on the main course first.

Once you've nailed that,

the rest will fall

into place.

KITCHEN GATHERINGS

These are the dishes to
consider when you want to
keep it casual and friendly.
Most of the recipes in
this section are completely
do-ahead — even ones that
are traditionally made at
the last minute.

CHICKEN SOUP FOR COZY NIGHTS

MAKES
3½ TO 4 QUARTS;
SERVES 8

The first spoonful of this soup evokes an ahhh. I often make it the night houseguests arrive, and it's on the short list of dishes my daughters request when they come home from college. Light yet satisfying and nourishing, it's perfect for people who are tired, road-weary, and unsettled from snacking on junk all day. It's also great the next day, when you've been playing tour guide and there's no time to make lunch. Pull out the soup and heat up an honest loaf of bread. Serve some apple chunks, maybe some cookies. Or drop off a pot of soup for someone who has just moved, had a baby, or is feeling under the weather.

From-scratch chicken soup doesn't have to start with a raw chicken. Soup made from a store-bought roast chicken is just as flavorful and oh-so-simple. By shredding the meat and simmering the bones and skin with cartoned or canned chicken broth, you knock hours off the cooking time but end up with soup that tastes as good as if you'd started from scratch.

WHEN SHOULD I SERVE IT?
For weekend houseguests
As one of the offerings at a soup party
For casual suppers and potlucks
For low-budget entertaining
For intergenerational gatherings

ANY SHORTCUTS?
Although the soup will lack that rich, full-bodied broth, you can skip simmering the bones in the broth.
Stick with the basic chicken noodle and chicken rice versions.

WHAT SHOULD I SERVE WITH IT?
You've got a complete meal in a bowl. If you'd like to serve a first course before the soup (or another course after it), consider one of the salads (pages 165–93).
Desserts:
One of the cakes made from the recipe for Simple, Tender Yellow Cake (pages 257–61)
Saucer-Size Oatmeal Cookies (page 238)

HOW FAR AHEAD CAN I MAKE IT?
The soup base can be refrigerated for up to 3 days. Return it to a simmer and add the ingredients for the individual soups, along with the peas, fresh herbs, and seasoning.

WHAT ABOUT LEFTOVERS?
Although the peas and herbs will fade and the noodles swell, the soup will still be very satisfying for at least 3 or 4 days.

I've given you a formula so you can make a simple chicken noodle soup or more elaborate soups—from tortellini to pasta and white beans—using the same proportions and method. These soups are warm and comforting enough to heal the sick, but they're also meant for tired cooks who need to prepare a soul-satisfying meal in a bowl—quickly. Before adding the extras, you can split the broth mixture and make different kinds of soup. Just remember to halve the added ingredients.

For even more impromptu gatherings, make a store-bought broth doctored with Asian or southwestern flavorings, lay out an array of ingredients and condiments, and let guests finish making the soups themselves to their liking. (See the recipes on pages 8 and 9.)

2   quarts chicken broth
1   store-bought roast chicken, meat picked from bones and pulled into bite-size pieces, bones and skin reserved
3   tablespoons vegetable oil
2   large onions, cut into medium dice
2   large carrots, peeled and cut into rounds or half rounds, depending on size
2   large celery stalks, sliced ¼ inch thick
    Additional ingredients from the soup of your choice (recipes follow)
1   cup (5 ounces) frozen green peas
½   cup chopped fresh herbs (see recipes)
    Salt and freshly ground black pepper

Bring broth and 4 cups water to a simmer in a large pot over medium-high heat. Add reserved chicken bones and skin, reduce heat to low, partially cover, and simmer until bones release their flavor, 20 to 30 minutes. Strain broth into a large bowl; discard bones and skin.

Return pot to burner set on medium-high. Add oil, then onions, carrots, and celery, and sauté until soft, 8 to 10 minutes. Add chicken and broth and bring to a simmer.

Add ingredients from soup of choice. Simmer until tender, 10 to 20 minutes more, depending on starch (if any). Stir in peas and herbs, and adjust seasonings, adding salt and pepper to taste. Serve.

CLASSIC CHICKEN NOODLE SOUP

- 3 cups egg noodles
- 1 teaspoon dried thyme leaves
  Chopped fresh parsley

CLASSIC CHICKEN AND RICE SOUP

- ¾ cup long-grain white rice
- 1 teaspoon dried thyme leaves
  Chopped fresh parsley

CHICKEN TORTELLINI SOUP WITH ZUCCHINI AND TOMATOES

- 1 package (9 ounces) refrigerated small cheese tortellini or 1 bag (8½ ounces) dried
- 1 can (14.5 ounces) diced tomatoes
- 2 medium zucchini, cut into medium dice
- 1 teaspoon dried basil
  Chopped fresh parsley

Serve with grated Parmesan cheese.

CHICKEN SOUP WITH BLACK BEANS AND CORN

- 2 cans (16 ounces each) black beans, drained and rinsed
- 1 package (10 ounces) frozen corn
- 1 can (14.5 ounces) diced tomatoes
- 1 jalapeño, seeded and minced
- 2 tablespoons ground cumin
- 2 teaspoons chili powder
  Chopped fresh cilantro

Omit peas. Serve with tortilla chips, grated Monterey Jack cheese, and lime wedges.

CURRIED CHICKEN SOUP WITH CHICKPEAS AND CAULIFLOWER

- 2 cans (16 ounces each) chickpeas, drained and rinsed
- 1 can (13.5 ounces) coconut milk (optional, but very good)
- 2 cups bite-size cauliflower florets
- 2 tablespoons curry powder
  Chopped fresh cilantro

CHICKEN SOUP WITH PASTA AND WHITE BEANS

- 1 can (14.5 ounces) diced tomatoes
- 2 cans (16 ounces each) white beans, drained and rinsed
- 1 cup small pasta, such as ditalini
- 2 teaspoons minced fresh rosemary
  Chopped fresh parsley

Serve with grated Parmesan cheese.

CHICKEN SOUP WITH ASIAN FLAVORINGS

This soup gives your guests a chance to assemble their own meal in a bowl, choosing from a wide assortment of colorful possibilities. Since the ingredients will be at room temperature, it's important for the broth to be piping hot. Keep it simmering on the stove or a hot plate, if you've got one. Don't use large shallow soup bowls; they will make the soup cool too quickly. Instead, use small deep bowls. Smaller bowls also encourage guests to come back for a second round, with a new set of flavoring ingredients. After they've helped themselves, ladle the simmering broth into each bowl.

SERVES 18 TO 20

6 quarts chicken broth

9 thin slices fresh ginger

18 2-inch cilantro stems

9 scallions, trimmed to white part only

6 strips lime zest, removed with a vegetable peeler

Combine all ingredients in a large pot, bring to a simmer, and simmer to blend flavors, about 10 minutes. Strain, return to pot, and if not serving immediately, cover and keep warm; return to a simmer before serving.

POSSIBLE ADDITIONS

2 cups shredded cooked chicken

1/2 pound cooked shrimp, cut into bite-size pieces

1/4 pound thinly sliced rare roast beef

1/4 pound firm tofu, patted dry and cut into 1/2-inch cubes

1 bag (6 ounces) radishes, thinly sliced and cut into thin strips

6 ounces (about 2 cups) fresh bean sprouts, rinsed and drained

1/4 pound shiitake or white mushrooms, stemmed and thinly sliced

1 can (8 ounces) water chestnuts, drained and rinsed

1/4 pound bok choy, thinly sliced

2 packages (3 ounces each) ramen noodles, flavoring packet discarded, noodles broken into bite-size pieces

3 ounces (2 cups) chow mein noodles

1 cup roasted unsalted peanuts, coarsely chopped

1 bunch scallions, thinly sliced

1 handful each fresh basil leaves, fresh mint leaves, and cilantro sprigs

1 lime, cut into 8 wedges

1 jalapeño, sliced into thin rounds

Soy sauce

Thai or Vietnamese fish sauce

CHICKEN SOUP WITH SOUTHWESTERN FLAVORINGS

6 quarts chicken broth

18 2-inch cilantro stems

9 sun-dried tomato halves

6 garlic cloves

6 strips lime zest, removed with a
    vegetable peeler

1 jalapeño

Combine all ingredients in a large pot, bring to a simmer, and simmer to blend flavors, about 10 minutes. Strain, return to pot, and if not serving immediately, cover and keep warm; return to a simmer before serving.

POSSIBLE ADDITIONS

2 cups shredded cooked chicken

½ pound cooked shrimp, cut into bite-size pieces

4 ounces pepper Jack cheese, grated

1 jar (8 ounces) nacho cheese sauce

1 bag (12 ounces) Fritos (original strip shape)

1 bag (12 ounces) tortilla chips

1 each red and green bell pepper, cut into thin strips and sautéed (see page 127)

1 cup frozen corn kernels, thawed

1 bag (6 ounces) radishes, thinly sliced and cut into thin strips

1 cup chopped tomatoes

1 can (4.5 ounces) chopped mild green chiles

1 can (2.25 ounces) sliced black olives

1 can (16 ounces) pinto or black beans, drained

1 bunch scallions, thinly sliced

1 handful cilantro sprigs

1 lime, cut into 8 wedges

1 jalapeño pepper, minced

1 jar (8 ounces) green salsa

1 jar (8 ounces) red salsa

1 bottle each green and red hot pepper sauce

SAUSAGE AND WHITE BEAN SOUP

Most of us enjoy a good pot of ham and bean soup, but often we don't have a ham bone on hand or the time to soak and simmer dried beans. Minced prosciutto instantly transforms chicken broth into a ham-flavored soup base. Italian sausage reinforces the pork flavor and makes the soup satisfying and substantial. Canned beans work as well as dried ones, and mashing some of them thickens the soup and gives it body.

SERVES 8

2	tablespoons olive oil
1½	pounds Italian sausages
2	ounces thinly sliced prosciutto, minced
2	medium onions, cut into medium dice
2	medium carrots, peeled and cut into medium dice
2	medium celery stalks, cut into medium dice

WHEN SHOULD I SERVE IT?
Fall picnics or tailgate parties
A fall or winter lunch or casual supper — especially when time's short

HOW CAN I VARY IT?
Substitute smoked cooked sausage: kielbasa or chorizo.
Other varieties of canned beans can be substituted as well.

WHAT SHOULD I SERVE WITH IT?
Breads:
Moist, Savory Corn Muffins (page 226) or other interesting breads
Salads:
Carrot Salad with Cumin Vinaigrette (page 178), served before the soup

1   teaspoon dried thyme leaves
1   quart chicken broth
3   cans (16 ounces each) canned great northern or other white beans, undrained

Heat oil in a large deep pot over medium-high heat until hot. Add sausages and cook, turning once or twice, until well browned on all sides, about 5 minutes (sausage will not be fully cooked). Remove with a slotted spoon; when cool enough to handle, cut into ¼-inch-thick slices.

Meanwhile, add prosciutto, onions, carrots, celery, and thyme to pot and cook, stirring frequently, until vegetables are well browned, 8 to 10 minutes.

Add broth and sausage. Smash 1 can of beans with a fork, then add to soup with remaining beans. Cover, and bring to a simmer, then reduce heat to medium-low and simmer, partially covered, to blend flavors, about 20 minutes. Turn off heat and let sit for 10 minutes to let flavors develop.

Return soup to a simmer and serve.

Pear Halves with Blue Cheese and
   Toasted Nuts (page 166),
   served after the soup
Cheeses and fall fruits, like
   apples, pears, and grapes,
   served after the soup

Desserts:
   Saucer-Size Oatmeal Cookies
      (page 238)
   Perfectly Simple Pumpkin
      Cheesecake (page 274)
   Moist, Tender Spice Cake
      (page 259)

HOW FAR AHEAD CAN I MAKE IT?
   The cooled soup can be refrigerated up to 3 days.

WHAT ABOUT LEFTOVERS?
   Leftover soup can be refrigerated up to 3 days, and it freezes well.

CHICKEN CHILI—RED OR WHITE

SERVES 12

If you want a chili that brings people back for seconds and always makes them ask for the recipe, try one of these. Chicken gives chili the broadest possible appeal when you're serving a big group.

Both the red and white versions have the look and flavor of serious chili, yet they are easy to prepare. The meat of rotisserie chicken is perfect for this dish—it's deeply seasoned, tender, and easy to shred, and using it shaves a couple hours off the cooking process. Adding garlic at the end makes the chili pleasantly potent. If you'd prefer a chunky beef or pork chili, consider Stew with Southwestern Flavorings (page 52).

QUICK RED CHICKEN CHILI

This may seem like a lot of chili powder, but the chocolate rounds out the flavor, resulting in a rich, full-bodied stew. You can make it in a large pot instead of a roasting pan, but allow extra time for the onions to sauté and the chili to simmer.

2 store-bought roast chickens, meat picked from bones and pulled into bite-size pieces, bones and skin reserved

2 quarts chicken broth

6 tablespoons vegetable oil

2 large onions, cut into medium dice

²/₃ cup chili powder

1¹/₂ tablespoons ground cumin

1¹/₂ tablespoons dried oregano

2 cans (28 ounces each) crushed tomatoes

2 cans (16 ounces each) pinto beans, drained and rinsed

6 medium garlic cloves, minced

1¹/₂ ounces bittersweet or semisweet chocolate, chopped

3 tablespoons cornmeal

Accompaniments: See page 14 for suggestions

Combine chicken bones and skin, chicken broth, and 4 cups water in a large pot and bring to a boil over medium-high heat. Reduce heat to low, partially cover, and simmer until bones release their flavor, about 30 minutes. Strain broth into a large bowl; discard bones and skin.

WHEN SHOULD I SERVE IT?

At casual parties like Super Bowl Sunday or other sports gatherings, Halloween, family reunions, or potlucks

At large gatherings with lots of guests who don't eat red meat

For a casual lunch or supper, especially when you have house-guests

ANY SHORTCUTS?

Simmering the bones in the chicken broth gives the chili a more homemade flavor, but skip this step if you're short on time.

Use ready-peeled garlic.

HOW CAN I VARY IT?

Substitute leftover turkey or chicken (7 to 8 cups) for the rotisserie chicken.

For the white chili, substitute canned white beans, such as great northern or cannellini, for the hominy.

WHAT SHOULD I SERVE WITH IT?
Drinks:

Instant Frozen Margaritas (page 287)

Sparkling Coolers (page 283), especially limeade

Beer

Appetizers and Salads:

Quesadillas for a Crowd (page 138)
Salads:

Chopped Caesar Salad (page 172)

Boston Lettuce and Baby Spinach Salad (page 176)
Accompaniments:

Fried Corn Tortilla Triangles (page 123–24) or 1 bag each tortilla and corn chips

Shredded sharp cheese (two 12-ounce bags)

1 bunch scallions, thinly sliced

1 cup fresh cilantro leaves

1 jar (12 ounces) sliced jalapeños

1 bottle each red and green hot pepper sauce

1 container (24 ounces) sour cream

2 cans (2.25 ounces each) sliced black olives

1 jar (8 ounces) red or green salsa (improve the flavor by stirring in 1 to 2 tablespoons chopped fresh cilantro and squeezing in a little fresh lime juice)

1 lime, cut into wedges
Guacamole:

Peel and seed 4 avocados, mash with a fork, then season gener-ously with a couple pinches each salt and pepper and ¼ cup fresh lime juice.
Sides:

Moist, Savory Corn Muffins (page 226–27)
Desserts:

Tortilla Sundaes with Minted Mango Salsa (page 241)

Hot Fudge Brownie Sundaes (page 244)

HOW FAR AHEAD CAN I MAKE IT?

You can pick and shred the chicken and simmer the broth the day before making the chili.

The chili can be made up to 3 days ahead.

WHAT ABOUT LEFTOVERS?

The chili freezes very well for 2 months.

Heat oil in a large roasting pan set over two burners on medium-high heat. Add onions and sauté until soft, 4 to 5 minutes. Add chili powder, cumin, and oregano, reduce heat to medium-low, and cook, stirring, until spices are fragrant, 1 to 2 minutes. Stir in chicken, tomatoes, and broth and bring to a simmer. Reduce heat to low and simmer uncovered, stirring occasionally, to blend flavors, 25 to 30 minutes.

Stir in beans, garlic, and chocolate and simmer to blend flavors, about 5 minutes. Sprinkle cornmeal over chili, stir in, and simmer to thicken chili, 1 to 2 minutes longer. Turn off heat, cover, and let stand for 5 minutes.

Ladle into bowls and serve with accompaniments of your choice.

QUICK WHITE CHICKEN CHILI WITH HOMINY

Their pale color and mild corn flavor make hominy and shoepeg corn the perfect replacement for pinto beans in this white variation. Hominy (soft, chewy corn kernels from which the hull and germ have been removed) is found in the canned-vegetable aisle in supermarkets. Frozen white shoepeg corn is more delicate than yellow corn.

2	store-bought roast chickens, meat picked from bones and pulled into bite-size pieces, bones and skin reserved
2	quarts chicken broth
6	tablespoons vegetable oil
1/4	cup ground cumin
4	teaspoons dried oregano
1/2	teaspoon cayenne pepper
2	large onions, cut into medium dice
2	jars or cans (4.5 ounces each) diced mild green chiles
2	cans (20 ounces each) hominy, rinsed (about 6 cups)
6	medium garlic cloves, minced
2	cups frozen corn, preferably white shoepeg

Accompaniments: See page 14 for suggestions

Combine chicken bones and skin, chicken broth, and 4 cups water in a large pot and bring to a boil over medium-high heat. Reduce heat to low and simmer until bones release their flavor, about 30 minutes. Strain broth into a large bowl; discard bones and skin.

Meanwhile, heat oil in a large roasting pan set over two burners (or a large pot) on medium-low heat. Add cumin, oregano, and cayenne and cook, stirring, until spices sizzle and are fragrant, about 1 minute. Add onions, increase heat to medium, and sauté until soft, 4 to 5 minutes. Add chicken and chiles and stir to coat. Add 4 cups hominy and all but 1 cup broth and bring to a simmer. Reduce heat to low and simmer, stirring occasionally, to blend flavors, 25 to 30 minutes.

In a food processor, process remaining 2 cups hominy and reserved 1 cup broth until silky smooth. Stir into simmering soup. Stir in minced garlic and corn and simmer to blend flavors, about 5 minutes. Turn off heat, cover, and let stand for 5 minutes.

Ladle into bowls and serve with accompaniments of your choice.

OVEN-BARBECUED PORK FOR SANDWICHES OR CARNITAS

I love pulled pork, but I don't have time to spend all day standing at a charcoal grill, coddling a pork shoulder to fall-off-the-bone tenderness. I've discovered, however, that you can pat the shoulder with a dry rub, shove it into the oven, and let it slow-roast for 10 to 12 hours overnight. The next morning, the pork emerges tender and mahogany-colored. Once the meat cools, pull it into bite-size shreds and moisten it with the pan drippings. The pulled pork can be spooned onto buns for barbecue sandwiches or wrapped in corn tortillas for a carnita party. Few dishes allow you to serve such a large group with so little effort.

A whole pork shoulder consists of the front part of the leg, called the picnic, and the butt, also known as Boston butt roast or Boston-style butt. Either cut is good here. If choosing the picnic, however, pull off the thick rind before brushing the meat with mustard, using a sharp knife to facilitate the process. Once the roast reaches 165 degrees, you can increase the oven temperature to 325 degrees to speed up the cooking process if you like.

- 3 tablespoons packed light or dark brown sugar
- 3 tablespoons paprika
- 1½ teaspoons salt, plus more for sprinkling
- 1½ tablespoons coarsely ground black pepper
- 1½ tablespoons garlic powder
- 1 bone-in pork shoulder butt roast or fresh picnic shoulder (8–9 pounds)
- ½ cup Dijon mustard

Adjust oven rack to lowest position and heat oven to 250 degrees.

Mix brown sugar, paprika, salt, pepper, and garlic powder in a small bowl. Pat roast dry and place on a rack set over a foil-lined shallow baking sheet. Lightly sprinkle top and sides of roast with salt, brush with half the mustard, and sprinkle with half the spice rub. Carefully turn roast over. Sprinkle with a little salt, brush with remaining mustard, and sprinkle with remaining spice rub.

Roast until a meat thermometer registers 170 degrees, 9 to 11 hours, depending on size. Transfer pork to a platter and let cool enough to handle, about 1 hour.

Meanwhile, if making sandwiches or if pork needs a little more moisture, pour off any fat and scrape pan drippings into a small saucepan, add 1 cup water, and bring to a simmer. Remove from heat.

Cut roast into 1- to 2-inch chunks and shred meat into a large bowl. Add enough pan drippings to moisten pork and stir to combine.

WHEN SHOULD I SERVE IT?

For any large casual event—Super Bowl party, pre- or post-sports meals, family reunions

ANY SHORTCUTS?

Roast 2 smaller pork shoulder roasts rather than one big one. You'll save a couple of hours of roasting and cooling time.

Buy a good spice rub instead of making your own.

HOW CAN I VARY IT?

Add a couple tablespoons of cumin to the spice rub if you like —especially if you're making carnitas.

Make Pulled Chicken Barbecue Sandwiches instead. For about 15 sandwiches, to serve 10 people, pick and shred the meat from 2 to 3 rotisserie or roast chickens (see Perfect Roast Chicken, page 38) to yield 10 to 12 cups shredded meat. Reserve the chicken juices, and add

enough chicken broth to equal 1 cup. Heat the shredded chicken, 1¾ to 2 cups of your favorite barbecue sauce, and chicken broth in a large covered pot over medium-low heat until hot. Serve on sandwich buns.

WHAT SHOULD I SERVE WITH IT?
Drinks:

Distinctive bottled beers and sodas (cream and black cherry soda, root or birch beer) or Sparkling Coolers (page 283), lemonade, and iced tea

Appetizers:

Peanuts in the shell
Curried Popcorn (page 116)
Perfect Deviled Eggs (page 120)
For carnitas, Quesadillas for a Crowd (page 138)

Sides and Salads:

For barbecue sandwiches,
Slaw with Creamy American Dressing (page 181)

Fresh Corn Salad with Cabbage and Bell Peppers (page 184)
Quick Southern-Style Baked Beans (page 218)
For carnitas,
Fresh Corn Salad with Cabbage and Bell Peppers (page 184), doubled

Desserts:

Hot Fudge Brownie Sundaes (page 244)
S'more Bars (page 236)

HOW FAR AHEAD CAN I MAKE IT?

Roast and shred the pork up to 3 days ahead; refrigerate. Reheat in a roasting pan set over two burners over low heat, adding a little water if necessary.

WHAT ABOUT LEFTOVERS?

Leftovers can be packaged in freezer bags and frozen for up to 3 months.

PULLED PORK SANDWICHES

SERVES 18 TO 20

Oven-Barbecued Pork (page 17)
1 cup barbecue sauce of your choice, plus (optional) extra for serving
18–20 large sandwich buns

Heat pulled pork and barbecue sauce in a large covered pot over low heat, stirring frequently. Serve with buns and extra barbecue sauce, if desired.

CARNITAS

SERVES 12

Oven-Barbecued Pork (page 17)
24 corn tortillas
Slaw with Salsa Verde Dressing or Orange Cumin Dressing (page 181), doubled
Scant 3 cups Guacamole (page 14)
1 container (24 ounces) sour cream

Twenty to 30 minutes before serving, adjust oven rack to middle position and heat oven to 350 degrees.

Slowly heat pulled pork in a roasting pan set over two burners over low heat, stirring frequently, adding a little water if necessary.

Meanwhile, lay a damp paper towel on a 24-by-18-inch piece of heavy-duty foil. Set 2 stacks of 4 corn tortillas each side by side on towel. Cover with another damp paper towel. Seal foil completely. Make 2 more foil packets. Bake until steamy, about 5 minutes.

Pull tortillas from oven as needed, and let guests fill them with pork, slaw, guacamole, and sour cream, as they like.

GROWN-UP SLOPPY JOES

I make these sloppy joes, along with a salad, for family reunions. After the guests arrive in the afternoon, a team of us can put together dinner for forty people in about half an hour. Everyone loves the meal—toddlers and teen cousins, middle-aged siblings, even Grandpa. Those who are watching carbohydrates skip the buns. One of my nephews says he's never had sloppy joes as good as these.

MAKES ABOUT 30 SANDWICHES; SERVES 20

½	cup vegetable oil
5	medium-large onions, chopped
5	pounds lean ground beef or turkey
4	cups (1 quart) ketchup
1¼	cups Dijon mustard
⅔	cup soy sauce
¼	cup Worcestershire sauce
1	tablespoon hot pepper sauce
⅔	cup packed light or dark brown sugar
1	tablespoon garlic powder
30	sandwich buns

WHEN SHOULD I SERVE IT?

For casual suppers, including family reunions

For kids' and teen parties

For a quick main course that can be made in advance or at the last minute

ANY SHORTCUTS?

If you use a disposable roasting pan, cleanup is a breeze. Make sure to reduce heat to medium.

HOW FAR AHEAD CAN I MAKE IT?

The sloppy joe mixture can be made up to 3 days ahead. Reheat slowly in a roasting pan set over two burners, stirring frequently and adding water if necessary to keep it from burning.

Heat oil in a large roasting pan over two burners on medium-high heat. Add onions and cook, stirring, until tender, 5 to 7 minutes. Add ground meat and cook, stirring frequently to break up large clumps, until no longer pink. Drain or spoon off any excess fat.

Mix remaining ingredients, except buns, in a medium bowl and stir them into meat. Continue to cook, stirring frequently, until mixture is thick, 5 to 8 minutes.

To warm sandwich buns, heat oven to 325 degrees. Place 1 bun per person in a single layer on a baking sheet. Bake until buns are warm throughout, 8 to 10 minutes. Warm more as needed.

Spoon a portion of meat onto each bun and serve.

WHAT SHOULD I SERVE WITH IT?
Drinks:
  Beer and soda
Appetizers:
  Baskets of chips and pretzels
Salads:
  Any of the salads (pages 165–93)
  For a large crowd, set up a salad
    bar.

Desserts:
  Hot Fudge Brownie Sundaes
    (page 244)
  S'more Bars (page 236)
  Saucer-Size Oatmeal Cookies
    (page 238)

WHAT ABOUT LEFTOVERS?
  The sloppy joe mixture freezes
well for 1 month. Thaw and then
reheat as directed above.

BAKE-AHEAD PIZZA FOR A CROWD

MAKES 4 PIZZAS;
SERVES 6

The word "party" just naturally follows pizza. Making it from scratch for a crowd is difficult, though. The problem is oven space—the crust has to be baked on the bottom rack so it will brown, which means you have to bake the pizzas one at a time.

I've found two tricks that make it possible to serve pizza for a crowd. First, change the shape. If you form the pizzas into long rectangles, you can bake two at a time. The smaller sizes of dough are easier to manage than a large one, and the centers will crisp up better. You can also sauce the pizzas and bake them several hours ahead. Then, shortly before serving, top them (or better yet, let guests do it), and reheat them at the last minute in a low-temperature oven to melt the cheese and recrisp the crust.

Like good French and Italian bread, a good pizza crust is made with bread flour, which is available in health food stores and many supermarkets. If you use bleached all-purpose flour, the crust will be tough and less crisp. You can, however, substitute a higher-protein unbleached all-purpose flour, such as King Arthur.

WHEN SHOULD I SERVE IT?

For a casual party, especially for young people

As an appetizer

ANY SHORTCUTS?

Here are some ideas, but if you take too many shortcuts, something very special will turn ordinary.

The dough will rise more quickly in an oven that's been preheated to about 100 degrees, then turned off. Set the covered bowl of dough on the oven rack with a dish towel beneath to protect it from the direct heat of the rack.

If you don't have time to make pizza dough, buy it. Many grocery stores sell it in the refrigerated section.

Although grating fresh Parmesan cheese (preferably Parmigiano-Reggiano) makes a remarkable difference in flavor, you can use a good packaged grated cheese.

Use packaged grated mozzarella cheese.

Use as many no-prep toppings as possible (see page 28).

Make just one sauce. If you're hosting a pizza party, however, it's nice, and more festive, to have a second type.

HOW CAN I VARY IT?

If you like barbecue chicken or ham and pineapple, for example, on your pizza, follow the dough and sauce recipes, then create your own toppings.

WHAT SHOULD I SERVE WITH IT?
Drinks:

Zippy red wines, such as Zinfandel or Chianti

Beer and soda

1	package (2¼ teaspoons) active dry yeast
¼	cup extra-virgin olive oil
4	cups bread flour
2	teaspoons salt
	Red and/or White Sauce for Pizza (recipes follow)
	Toppings of choice (see page 28)
1	cup (4 ounces) grated part-skim mozzarella (or other soft cheese, such as Fontina or even pepper Jack; crumbled feta is nice too)
½	cup grated Parmesan cheese
	Cornmeal for dusting pan

Pour ¼ cup warm tap water into a 2-cup Pyrex measuring cup or a small bowl. Sprinkle in yeast and let stand until yeast swells, about 5 minutes. Add cool tap water to the 1½-cup line (1¼ cups water if using bowl), then add olive oil to the 1¾-cup line (¼ cup oil if using bowl), and whisk to mix.

Pour flour and salt in a food processor and pulse to mix. Add yeast mixture and process to form a soft, supple, dough ball; pulse in another tablespoon or so of water if dough feels tight, like clay. Process until smooth, 20 to 30 seconds longer.

Appetizers:
Keep it simple. Set out a dish of roasted pistachios and serve a green salad before or with the pizza.

Salads:
Chopped Caesar Salad (page 172)
Mixed Green Salad with Fresh Herbs (page 168)

Desserts:
Frozen Tiramisu with Coffee Mascarpone Sauce (page 250)
Sorbet- or Ice Cream–Filled Crisp Cinnamon Cups (page 246)
S'more Bars (page 236)

HOW FAR AHEAD CAN I MAKE IT?
The white sauce can be made up to 3 days ahead; since the tomato sauce is so easy, throw it together at the last minute.

The sauced pizzas can be baked up to 2 hours before topping.

Most of the topping ingredients can be prepared 1 to 2 days ahead.

WHAT ABOUT LEFTOVERS?
If you heat it up right, pizza is almost as good the second time around. To reheat a few slices, set a large skillet or griddle over medi-um heat. While the skillet heats, microwave the pizzas just enough to take the chill off (not too much, or you'll end up toughening the crust). Set the slices in a single layer in the skillet and heat until the bottom crisps up and the pizza is heated through. You can heat larger quantities of leftovers in a low-temperature oven, setting the slices directly on an oven rack.

Toss leftover pizza sauce with pasta or spoon over polenta.

Turn dough out onto a lightly floured work surface and knead for a few seconds to form a ball. Place in a large bowl coated with cooking spray. Cover with plastic wrap and let stand in a warm place until doubled in size, 1½ to 2 hours.

Meanwhile, make sauce(s), prepare toppings, and grate cheese.

About 30 minutes before baking, adjust oven rack to lowest position and heat oven to 450 degrees. Lightly sprinkle cornmeal onto each of two parchment-lined cookie sheets, at least 18 by 12 inches. (Do not use insulated cookie sheets, which would prevent crusts from crisping.)

Without punching it down, turn dough onto a lightly floured surface. (It's fine if dough deflates; just don't work or knead it, because that will make stretching more difficult.) Quarter dough with a dough scraper or sharp knife.

Working with 1 portion of dough at a time, stretch each into a rough 18-by-5-inch rectangle. (Don't sweat the shape. You just want 2 pizzas per sheet.) Transfer to a prepared pan; spread with ½ cup sauce. Repeat with another portion of dough, and bake pizzas until bottoms are a crisp golden brown, about 15 minutes. Stretch and sauce remaining 2 portions pizza dough, then bake when first pizzas come out of oven. Set aside at room temperature.

When ready to serve, adjust oven racks to middle and top positions and preheat oven to 325 degrees.

Top pizzas as desired, sprinkle with mozzarella, and bake directly on oven racks until crisp and hot, 7 to 10 minutes. Transfer to a cutting board, sprinkle with Parmesan cheese, and bring to the table. Cut with kitchen shears and serve.

RED SAUCE FOR PIZZA

MAKES ABOUT 2 CUPS (ENOUGH FOR 4 PIZZAS)

- 3 tablespoons extra-virgin olive oil
- 2 large garlic cloves, minced
- 1 can (16 ounces) crushed tomatoes
  Salt to taste

Mix all ingredients together and spread on pizza.

COOKED RED SAUCE

You can also cook the tomato sauce. Add olive oil and garlic to a 10-inch skillet and cook until garlic starts to sizzle. Add tomatoes and salt and bring to a boil, then simmer to blend flavors, about 10 minutes. Spread on pizza.

WHITE SAUCE FOR PIZZA

MAKES ABOUT 2 CUPS (ENOUGH FOR 4 PIZZAS)

1¼   cups 2% or whole milk
¾   cup chicken broth or vegetable broth
2   large garlic cloves, minced
2   tablespoons butter
3   tablespoons all-purpose flour
¼   cup grated Parmesan cheese
     Salt

Combine milk, broth, and garlic in a 1-quart Pyrex measuring cup or a microwave-safe bowl (or a medium saucepan) and microwave (or slowly heat in a medium saucepan) until very hot and steamy. Let stand for 5 minutes to soften garlic.

Meanwhile, melt butter in a large saucepan over medium-high heat. When butter starts to sizzle, whisk in flour. Add milk mixture all at once, then whisk until smooth. Cook until thick and bubbly (since milk is hot, this will take only a minute). Stir in cheese and season with salt. Pour mixture back into measuring cup or bowl and cover with plastic wrap, placed directly on surface of sauce, for up to 2 hours, or until ready to use. Spread on pizza.

POSSIBLE PIZZA TOPPINGS

SIMPLE TOPPINGS:

Canned chopped clams—½ cup drained clams per pizza (from a 6½-ounce can)
Sliced pepperoni or prosciutto
Canadian bacon or ham, cut into small dice
Your favorite olives, pitted
Canned artichokes, drained, quartered, and tossed with a little extra-virgin olive oil
Jarred roast peppers
Jarred pesto

VEGETABLE TOPPINGS (1 POUND PER 4 PIZZAS):

Vegetables that need to be sautéed:

Heat 1 tablespoon oil in a large skillet over medium-high heat. When oil starts to shimmer, add one of the following vegetables and a sprinkling of salt. Cook, stirring often, until soft, about 5 minutes.
Onions, halved and thinly sliced
Bell peppers, stem removed, cored, seeded, then thinly sliced into ¼-inch-thick strips
Mushrooms, sliced ¼ inch thick (or buy packaged sliced)

Vegetables that need to be steam-sautéed:

Place one of the following prepared vegetables, ⅓ cup water (omit water if using spinach), a scant ½ teaspoon salt, and 2 teaspoons olive oil in a deep skillet or Dutch oven. Cover and steam over high heat until vegetables are bright colored and just tender, 3 to 4 minutes. Turn out onto a plate to cool.
Broccoli, florets cut into bite-size pieces; stalks peeled and cut into ¼-inch-thick coins
Asparagus (medium-thick), tough end of stalks trimmed, spears cut into 1-inch lengths
Spinach (buy triple-washed), stems removed

Vegetables that need to be broiled:

Adjust oven rack to highest position and preheat broiler. Lightly brush both sides of vegetables with oil and sprinkle with salt. Broil, turning once, until spotty brown on each side, 7 to 10 minutes.
Zucchini or yellow squash, cut into ⅓-inch-thick rounds
Eggplant, cut into ⅓-inch-thick rounds

MEAT TOPPINGS (1 POUND PER 4 PIZZAS):

Ground sausage, beef, or turkey, browned
Bacon, cut into ½-inch-wide pieces and cooked until crisp

BUTTERMILK-HONEY FRIED CHICKEN FINGERS

Chicken fingers often overcook before they brown. To solve the problem, I add a little honey to the buttermilk bath, which makes them brown more quickly, and they turn out juicy.

SERVES 8

4	teaspoons honey
	Salt
½	teaspoon freshly ground black pepper
	Flavoring of choice (pages 29 and 31)
1⅓	cups buttermilk
2½	pounds boneless, skinless chicken breast halves (about 6 large), each cut crosswise into 8 or 9 strips
1	quart oil (vegetable, canola, peanut, or corn)
3	cups all-purpose flour

In a large bowl or shallow baking dish, mix honey, 1 teaspoon salt, pepper, and flavoring into buttermilk. Add chicken and turn to coat.

Preheat oven to 200 degrees. Heat oil in a large (12-inch) skillet over high heat to 375 degrees.

Meanwhile, mix flour and 1 tablespoon salt in a doubled paper bag. Drop about 8 chicken strips into flour, close bag, and shake to coat chicken. Place chicken pieces on a wire rack set over a baking sheet (or newspaper for easy cleanup). Repeat with remaining chicken.

Working in 4 batches, drop chicken pieces into hot oil and fry until golden brown, turning if necessary to ensure even browning, about 3 minutes. Transfer to another wire rack set over a baking sheet to drain. Keep first batches warm in oven while you cook remaining chicken, returning oil to 375 degrees after each batch.

CLASSIC FLAVORING

1   teaspoon garlic powder

MARYLAND-STYLE FLAVORING

1   tablespoon Old Bay or other Maryland-style spice blend

CURRY FLAVORING

1　tablespoon curry powder

CUMIN FLAVORING

2　teaspoons ground cumin

2　teaspoons paprika

1　teaspoon garlic powder

WHEN SHOULD I SERVE IT?

For gatherings of kids and adults when you're comfortable enough to fry in front of guests

For children's and teen parties

At a picnic (served at room temperature)

As a substantial hors d'oeuvre before a light main course

ANY SHORTCUTS?

Buy chicken already cut into strips.

HOW CAN I VARY IT?

Choose from five different garnishes:

Sprinkle hot chicken with a big handful of chopped fresh herbs — basil, chives, and parsley. Serve with lemon wedges, which guests can squeeze over the chicken.

Sprinkle hot chicken generously with toasted sesame seeds and sliced scallion greens. Serve with hoisin dipping sauce (1 cup hoisin sauce, ¼ cup rice wine vinegar, and 2 tablespoons soy sauce).

Sprinkle hot chicken generously with chopped peanuts and sliced scallion greens. Serve with your favorite Thai peanut sauce.

Sprinkle hot chicken generously with chopped fresh cilantro or

parsley and sliced scallion greens. Serve with curry chutney dipping sauce (1 cup Major Grey chutney, ¼ cup rice wine vinegar, and 2 teaspoons curry powder, heated and served warm, or served at room temperature).

Sprinkle hot chicken generously with chopped fresh cilantro and sliced scallion greens. Serve with lime wedges, which guests can squeeze over chicken, and your favorite jarred salsa or salsa verde.

WHAT SHOULD I SERVE WITH IT?
Drinks:

A playful cocktail — A Pitcher of Mojitos (page 290), Instant Frozen Margaritas (page 287), or Cosmopolitans by the Pitcher (page 288)

A crisp, fruity white wine, such as a Sauvignon Blanc

Iced tea and lemonade

Appetizers:

Curried Popcorn (page 116)

Perfect Deviled Eggs (page 120)

First Courses and Salads:

Year-Round Classic Gazpacho (page 162)

Boston Lettuce and Baby Spinach Salad (page 176)

Mixed Green Salad with Fresh Herbs (page 168)

Baby Spinach Salad with Shaved Parmesan and Garlic Vinaigrette (page 170)

Carrot Salad with Cumin Vinaigrette (page 178)

Sides:

Any of the slaws (pages 180–81)

Creamy Baked Macaroni and Cheese (page 32)

Broiled or Grilled Asparagus (page 195)

Slow-Roasted Plum Tomatoes with Pesto-Flavored Crumbs (page 204)

Desserts:

Hot Fudge Brownie Sundaes (page 244)

S'more Bars (page 236)

Saucer-Size Oatmeal Cookies (page 238)

HOW FAR AHEAD CAN I MAKE IT?

The chicken can soak overnight in the buttermilk.

WHAT ABOUT LEFTOVERS?

Toss leftover warmed chicken fingers with mixed greens for a satisfying lunch salad.

CREAMY BAKED MACARONI AND CHEESE

In groups, young people tend to snub anything but plain cheese pizza, macaroni and cheese, and fried chicken fingers. Why not serve up the best versions of their favorites? And when you offer a perfect dinner, you need only one menu. Adults will enjoy this classic comfort dish as much as the kids do.

1	tablespoon salt, or to taste
1	pound elbow macaroni or other bite-size pasta shape
32	saltine crackers, crushed
2	tablespoons butter, melted
2	cans (12 ounces each) evaporated milk
1	cup chicken broth
3	tablespoons butter
$\frac{1}{3}$	cup all-purpose flour
$1\frac{1}{2}$	tablespoons Dijon mustard
$\frac{1}{2}$	cup grated Parmesan cheese
16	ounces extra-sharp cheddar cheese, grated
	Freshly ground black pepper

WHEN SHOULD I SERVE IT?
For any meal with children
At potluck suppers or other do-ahead meals
For a casual meal

ANY SHORTCUTS?
Use packaged grated cheese.

HOW CAN I VARY IT?
Depending on the crowd, stir in sliced olives, canned chopped green chiles, and/or diced tomatoes.

For a more sophisticated mac and cheese, replace some of the sharp cheddar with one or a mix of the following: Gouda, Fontina, goat cheese, or Parmesan. Kids may prefer it made with mild rather than extra-sharp cheddar.

HOW FAR AHEAD CAN I MAKE IT?
The unbaked macaroni and cheese, minus the cracker crumbs, can be covered with plastic wrap and refrigerated for up to 1 day.

WHAT ABOUT LEFTOVERS?
The macaroni and cheese keeps for 3 days, though the crumbs won't be crisp. Warm the dish in a heavy saucepan over low heat, adding water or milk as necessary to loosen the pasta.

Bring 2 quarts water to a boil in a large pot. Add salt and pasta and cook until pasta is al dente. Drain and immediately pour onto a large rimmed baking sheet to cool.

Mix crackers and melted butter in a small bowl; set aside.

Adjust oven rack to middle position and heat oven to 350 degrees.

Combine milk and chicken broth in a 2-quart Pyrex measuring cup or microwave-safe bowl and microwave (or slowly heat in a large saucepan) until hot and steamy. Meanwhile, melt butter in a Dutch oven or large pot over medium-high heat and whisk in flour. Add hot milk mixture all at once and continue to whisk until thick and bubbly, 3 to 4 minutes. Whisk in mustard and Parmesan. Remove from heat and whisk in cheddar cheese until melted. Stir in pasta and season to taste with salt and pepper.

Turn pasta into a 13-by-9-inch baking pan. Top with cracker crumbs. Bake until hot and bubbly, about 20 minutes. Serve.

WHAT SHOULD I SERVE WITH IT?
Drinks:
  Before the meal, Cosmopolitans by the Pitcher (page 288) for the adults
  Beer, a young red wine such as a Beaujolais, or a rich full-bodied white, such as Chardonnay
Appetizer:
  Curried Popcorn (page 116)

Salads:
  Mixed Green Salad with Fresh Herbs (page 168)
  Chopped Caesar Salad (page 172)
  Carrot Salad with Cumin Vinaigrette (page 178)
  Baby Spinach Salad with Shaved Parmesan and Garlic Vinaigrette (page 170)
Sides:
  Slow-Roasted Plum Tomatoes

with Pesto-Flavored Crumbs (page 204)
  Sautéed Cherry Tomatoes with Garlic and Basil (page 202)
  For a buffet, serve it with a baked ham that's been slowly reheated.
Desserts:
  Roasted Peaches with Caramel Sauce (page 254)
  Apple Crostata (page 278)

REALLY GOOD LASAGNA

I've developed a lasagna that's simple yet exceptional: casual enough to serve at a potluck, friendly enough to take to a neighbor, refined enough to serve as part of a sit-down dinner.

SERVES 12

Instead of having the usual overbearing red sauce and blobs of ricotta cheese, it's layered with two sauces—a rich, meaty Bolognese and a bold white sauce punched up with garlic and Parmesan cheese. And the more assertive Fontina takes the place of the mozzarella. The lasagna may be easy to make, but it's hardly ordinary.

WHEN SHOULD I SERVE IT?

When do-ahead is important

For an impressive dinner at little expense

For friendly gatherings, large or small

ANY SHORTCUTS?

Use ready-peeled garlic and good packaged grated Parmesan.

Don't be tempted to cheat on the sauces. They're both crucial—and quick.

HOW CAN I VARY IT?

Make vegetarian lasagna by omitting the prosciutto and substituting an equal quantity of sliced mushrooms for the ground meat in the tomato sauce; substitute a good vegetable broth for the chicken broth in the white sauce.

Either sauce can be served over pasta.

WHAT SHOULD I SERVE WITH IT?

Drinks:

Chianti or other light red wine

Appetizer:

Quick Marinated Olives (page 117)

First Courses and Salads:

Chopped Caesar Salad (page 172)

Mixed Green Salad with Fresh Herbs (page 168)

Crab-Stuffed Artichokes (page 150)

Desserts:

Frozen Tiramisu with Coffee Mascarpone Sauce (page 250)

Roasted Peaches (or Pears, Plums, or Apples) with Caramel Sauce (page 254)

For a more formal dinner, Lemon-Raspberry Triflettes (page 262)

HOW FAR AHEAD CAN I MAKE IT?

The lasagna can be assembled ahead, doubled-wrapped in plastic wrap, and refrigerated for a couple of days or frozen for 1 to 3 months. (Thaw before baking.)

WHAT ABOUT LEFTOVERS?

Leftover portions heat beautifully in the microwave. They'll look and taste as good as the first time.

BOLOGNESE-STYLE SAUCE

- 3 tablespoons butter
- 1 small onion, cut into small dice
- 1 small carrot, peeled and cut into small dice
- 1 small celery stalk, cut into small dice
- 2 ounces thinly sliced prosciutto, cut into small dice
- 1 pound meat loaf mix (or ground turkey or ground beef)
  Salt and freshly ground black pepper
- ½ cup dry vermouth or dry white wine
- 1 cup whole milk
- 1 can (28 ounces) crushed tomatoes

PARMESAN WHITE SAUCE

- 2½ cups (2% or whole) milk
- 1 cup chicken broth
- 4 garlic cloves, minced
- 3 tablespoons butter
- ⅓ cup all-purpose flour
- ½ cup grated Parmesan cheese
  Salt and freshly ground black pepper

LASAGNA

- 1½ tablespoons salt
- 15 oven-ready (rippled-style, such as Ronzoni) lasagna noodles (from two 8-ounce packages)
- 8 ounces Fontina cheese, grated (about 2½ cups)
- ¾ cup grated Parmesan cheese

TO MAKE BOLOGNESE SAUCE: Heat butter in a Dutch oven over medium heat. Add onion, carrot, and celery and cook until just soft, about 3 minutes. Add prosciutto and sauté until vegetables are fully softened, 2 to 3 minutes. Add ground meat and cook, seasoning with salt and pepper to taste and stirring frequently, until it loses its raw color, about 3 minutes. Add vermouth and simmer until almost evaporated, about 5 minutes. Add milk and cook until almost evaporated, 5 to 7 minutes longer. Add tomatoes and cook, stirring occasionally and adding water as necessary, until reduced to a thick but not gloppy sauce, about 45 minutes. Remove from heat.

TO MAKE WHITE SAUCE: Combine milk, broth, and garlic in a 2-quart Pyrex measuring cup or a microwave-safe bowl, cover with a small plate, and microwave until steamy hot, 8 to 10 minutes (or heat in a medium saucepan over medium-low heat).

Meanwhile, melt butter in a large saucepan over medium heat. When foaming subsides, whisk in flour until well blended. Pour in hot milk all at once; whisk vigorously until sauce is smooth and starts to bubble and thicken. Stir in Parmesan and season to taste with salt and pepper. Remove from heat and place plastic wrap directly on sauce's surface.

TO ASSEMBLE AND BAKE LASAGNA: Adjust oven rack to upper-middle position and heat oven to 425 degrees.

Dissolve salt in 2 quarts hot tap water in a 13-by-9-inch baking dish. Add noodles and soak until soft, about 10 minutes. Drain noodles and stack loosely. (Noodles may stick together as they dry but will pull apart easily.) Wipe baking dish dry.

Smear ¼ cup white sauce over bottom of baking dish. Top with a layer of 3 noodles, then ⅔ cup white sauce, 1 cup meat sauce, ½ cup Fontina, and 2 tablespoons Parmesan. Repeat 3 times, then make a final layer with remaining noodles, white sauce, and cheeses. Cover with aluminum foil.

Bake until very hot throughout, about 30 minutes. Leaving pan on rack, remove foil and turn oven to broil. Watching carefully, broil lasagna until cheese and sauce are spotty brown. Remove from oven and let stand to set, 10 to 15 minutes.

Cut into portions and serve.

PERFECT ROAST CHICKEN— AND SEVERAL SAUCES

SERVES 4

When you're having people over for dinner, nothing is as simple and classic as roast chicken. And it's easy to turn an ordinary chicken into an extraordinary one just by sprinkling it with a little kosher salt and letting it sit uncovered in the refrigerator to dry its skin. In just a few hours, the salt penetrates the meat, seasoning it throughout. The longer it sits, the crisper the skin will be when you roast it.

Roasting it in a V-shaped rack cradles the bird and keeps it stable. If you bought a roasting pan recently, chances are it came with a V-rack. If not, a good one costs only about $12. Not a bad investment for juicy, succulent chicken (and turkey too). You can, however, roast the chicken on a regular rack set in a roasting pan.

If you need more chicken, roast two small birds. Place them crosswise on the V-rack (or ordinary rack) and increase the cooking time to 30 minutes after you turn them breast side up, for a total of 1 hour. I prefer to carve the chicken in the kitchen and arrange it on a platter, along with the accompanying starch and vegetables, so guests can choose dark or white meat.

WHEN SHOULD I SERVE IT?
For both casual and refined dinners
For a mix of kids and adults — chicken pleases everybody

ANY SHORTCUTS?
You can skip the salting step, but the chicken won't be nearly as tasty.
You can forgo the sauce.

HOW CAN I VARY IT?
Change sauce.

WHAT SHOULD I SERVE WITH IT?
Almost any dish; let the sauce drive your choices.

HOW FAR AHEAD CAN I MAKE IT?
The salted chicken can be refrigerated for 4 hours or up to 4 days.
The chicken can be roasted up to 2 hours ahead and served at room temperature or rewarmed in a 300-degree oven for a few minutes. A piping hot sauce will help warm up the chicken.

You can make the sauce in a skillet before or while you cook the chicken. Simply follow the individual recipes and add the reduced sauce to the roasting pan set over two burners after the chicken has roasted.

WHAT ABOUT LEFTOVERS?
Leftover chicken is gold. Toss into a soup, salad, tacos, quesadillas, or sandwiches.

1   chicken (about 3½ pounds)

2   tablespoons kosher salt

1½   tablespoons olive oil

2   teaspoons sugar

     Freshly ground black pepper

     Sauce of choice (recipes follow)

Sprinkle chicken all over with kosher salt, inside and out. Place on a wire rack set over a plate. Refrigerate uncovered for at least 4 hours, or up to 4 days.

Adjust oven rack to lower-middle position and heat oven to 450 degrees.

Tie chicken legs together, and tuck wings under chicken. Brush top and sides of chicken all over with some oil and sprinkle with 1 teaspoon sugar and a few grinds of pepper. Place chicken breast side down on a V-rack set in a small roasting pan, brush with remaining oil, and sprinkle with ½ teaspoon sugar and a few more grinds of pepper.

Roast breast side down until chicken is deep golden brown, about 30 minutes. Remove from oven and, holding a wad of paper towels in each hand to protect yourself, turn chicken breast side up. Sprinkle chicken with remaining ½ teaspoon sugar and add 1 cup water to pan. (If roasting pan starts smoking before the 30-minute mark, add the water sooner.)

Continue to roast until chicken is mahogany brown and thickest part of leg/thigh registers at least 175 degrees, about 20 minutes longer. (If pan dries out before chicken is done, add a little more water.) Transfer to a cutting board to rest for at least 15 minutes or up to 30 minutes (or for up to 2 hours if serving at room temperature).

For the sauce, remove V-rack and set pan over two burners on medium-high heat. If any juices remain in the pan, simmer until they evaporate. Then proceed with individual sauce recipe.

To serve, carve each whole leg from chicken, and cut into leg and thigh pieces. Remove wings. Carve breast meat from bone and slice crosswise. Place warm sauce in a gravy boat and serve alongside chicken.

MUSHROOM SAUCE WITH TOMATOES AND ROSEMARY

- 1 cup chicken broth
- ½ cup canned diced tomatoes
- ¼ cup dry vermouth
- 2 tablespoons olive oil
- ½ pound mushrooms, sliced
  Salt and freshly ground black pepper
- 4 garlic cloves, minced
- 1 teaspoon minced fresh rosemary
- 3 tablespoons chopped fresh parsley

While chicken roasts, combine broth, tomatoes, and vermouth in a small bowl; set aside. Heat oil in a large (12-inch) skillet over medium-high heat. Add mushrooms, season with salt and pepper to taste, and sauté until nicely browned, about 5 minutes. Remove from heat.

While chicken rests, add garlic and rosemary to hot roasting pan and sauté until fragrant and golden, less than 1 minute. Add mushrooms and sauté until moisture has evaporated, about 1 minute. Add broth mixture and simmer until reduced to about 2 cups, 3 to 5 minutes. Stir in parsley.

LEMON-ARTICHOKE SAUCE WITH GARLIC AND PARSLEY

- 1 cup chicken broth
- ¼ cup fresh lemon juice
- ¼ cup dry vermouth
- 4 garlic cloves, minced
- 1 teaspoon dried oregano
- 1 can (14 ounces) whole artichoke hearts, drained, rinsed, and quartered
- 3 tablespoons chopped fresh parsley

While chicken roasts, combine broth, lemon juice, and vermouth in a small bowl; set aside.

While chicken rests, add garlic and oregano to hot roasting pan and sauté until fragrant and golden, less than 1 minute. Add artichokes and sauté until moisture has evaporated, about 1 minute. Add broth mixture and simmer until reduced to about 2 cups, 3 to 5 minutes. Stir in parsley.

APRICOT-PRUNE SAUCE WITH MOROCCAN SPICES

- 1 cup chicken broth
- ¼ cup frozen orange juice concentrate, thawed
- ¼ cup dry vermouth
- 4 garlic cloves, minced
- 1 teaspoon ground cumin
- 1 teaspoon ground ginger
- ½ teaspoon ground cinnamon
- ⅛ teaspoon ground cloves
- ½ cup dried apricots, halved
- ½ cup pitted prunes, halved
- 3 tablespoons chopped fresh cilantro

While chicken roasts, combine broth, orange juice concentrate, and vermouth in a small bowl and set aside.

While chicken rests, add garlic and spices to hot roasting pan and sauté until fragrant and garlic is golden, less than 1 minute. Add apricots and prunes and sauté to blend flavors, about 1 minute. Add broth mixture and simmer until reduced to about 2 cups, 3 to 5 minutes. Stir in cilantro.

BONELESS COQ AU VIN

For occasions when you need a meal that is easy to cut using a fork with a plate on your lap, this dish is the ticket. Made with boneless, skinless chicken thighs, it offers the richness and flavor of traditional coq au vin in record time.

SERVES 12

4 tablespoons (½ stick) butter

2 pounds mushrooms, quartered if medium, cut into sixths if large

1 pound frozen pearl onions (not thawed)

¾ pound bacon, cut into ½-inch-wide pieces

4½ pounds boneless, skinless chicken thighs (about 24 small)
Salt and freshly ground black pepper

2 medium-large onions, chopped

4 large garlic cloves, minced

½ cup all-purpose flour, plus 2 tablespoons more if needed

2 teaspoons dried thyme leaves

4 bay leaves

1 bottle (750 ml) full-bodied dry red wine, such as Cabernet Sauvignon or Merlot

1 quart chicken broth

½ cup chopped fresh parsley

Melt 2 tablespoons butter in a large heavy roasting pan set over two burners on medium-high heat. Add mushrooms and sauté until liquid evaporates and mushrooms start to brown, 10 to 12 minutes. Transfer to a medium bowl and set aside. Add remaining 2 tablespoons butter to roasting pan, then add pearl onions and sauté until golden brown, about 5 minutes. Transfer to bowl of mushrooms.

Add bacon to roasting pan and fry until crisp, 8 to 10 minutes. With a slotted spoon, transfer to a paper towel–lined plate. (Leave bacon drippings in pan.)

While bacon cooks, lay chicken thighs on a sheet of plastic wrap and season both sides with salt and pepper.

Working in 2 batches, sauté thighs in bacon drippings, about 3 minutes per side. Transfer to a platter as they brown. Add chopped onions and garlic to roasting pan and sauté until soft, about 5 minutes. Whisk in ¼ cup flour and cook until lightly colored, less than 1 minute. Whisk in thyme, bay leaves, wine, broth, and bacon. Bring to a boil, then reduce heat to low, cover with a baking sheet or foil, and simmer to develop flavors, about 20 minutes.

Meanwhile, adjust oven rack to middle position and heat oven to 300 degrees.

Add chicken, mushrooms, and onions to pan, cover with foil, and bake until chicken is cooked through and sauce is rich and flavorful, about 30 minutes. For a thicker sauce, return pan to medium heat. Mix 2 tablespoons flour with ¼ cup water. Slowly whisk in enough flour mixture to thicken as desired. Stir in parsley and serve.

WHEN SHOULD I SERVE IT?

For a large buffet dinner when there's a little chill in the air, or for a small dinner party (halve the recipe)

When you need a do-ahead company dish — perfect for houseguests

ANY SHORTCUTS?

Buy sliced mushrooms.
Use ready-peeled garlic.

WHAT SHOULD I SERVE WITH IT?

Before dinner, Sparkling Wine Cocktails (page 284) or Mulled Cider (page 292)

A hearty red wine, such as Cabernet or Merlot

Appetizers:

Lacy Cheddar Crisps (page 118)
Cheddar Puffs with Scallions and Cayenne (page 131)

Salad:

Baby Greens, Romaine, and Iceberg Lettuce with Blue Cheese, Toasted Pecans, and Dried Cranberries (page 174)

Sides:

Make-Ahead Mashed Potatoes (page 206)
Potato Gratin with Garlic and Thyme (page 211)
Yellow Rice with Green Peas (page 216)

Desserts:

Chocolate or Lemon Tart (page 276)
Perfectly Simple Pumpkin Cheesecake (page 274)
Apple Crostata (page 278)
Yellow Cake with Orange Marmalade Filling and Chocolate Glaze (page 259)

HOW FAR AHEAD CAN I MAKE IT?

The chicken can be cooked up to 3 days in advance.

WHAT ABOUT LEFTOVERS?

Leftovers can be refrigerated for 3 to 4 days or frozen for up to 3 months.

SIMPLE CASSOULET

For a fall or winter buffet, cassoulet is a perfect main course.
Containing lamb, two kinds of sausage, and roast duck breast
(rather than the traditional time- and labor-intensive duck confit),
this one offers wonderful variety without the heaviness of the classic version. The meat is in bite-size chunks, ideal when you're bal-
ancing a plate on your lap. And all this substantial dish needs to
round out the meal is a salad.

Though the recipe may look a little long, I've made it—from
start to finish and in double this quantity—the very afternoon of a
dinner party.

3	pounds boneless lamb shoulder roast, cut into 1½-inch cubes (or a combination of lamb and boneless pork shoulder roast)
3	tablespoons olive oil
	Salt and freshly ground black pepper
1	pound mild Italian sausages
½	pound smoked cooked sausages (such as kielbasa), cut into 6 pieces each
4	boneless duck breast halves (about 1½ pounds)
1	can (14.5 ounces) chicken broth, plus enough water to equal 2 cups
1	cup full-bodied dry red wine, such as Cabernet Sauvignon
2	large onions, cut into medium dice
6	garlic cloves, minced
2	ounces thinly sliced prosciutto, minced
2	teaspoons dried thyme leaves
1	can (14.5 ounces) diced tomatoes
6	cans (16 ounces each) white beans, drained (9 cups)
3	cups fresh bread crumbs
3	tablespoons butter, melted
⅓	cup minced fresh parsley

Adjust oven rack to lower-middle position and heat oven to 450
degrees.

Place lamb cubes in a bowl. Drizzle with 2 tablespoons oil and sprinkle generously with salt and pepper, turning to coat.

Place Italian sausages, 1 cup water, and remaining 1 tablespoon oil in a large heavy roasting pan set over two burners. Cover with heavy-duty foil and turn heat to medium-high. Cook until sausages lose their raw color, about 5 minutes. Remove foil (reserve it) and continue to cook until water evaporates. Add smoked sausages and cook, turning frequently,

WHEN SHOULD I SERVE IT?

For buffet suppers during cooler months

For large sit-down dinners

For a houseful of wintertime guests

As the main course for a potluck

ANY SHORTCUTS?

Buy roast duck instead of cooking the duck breasts. Many grocery stores, Asian markets, and food warehouses carry it. Separate the meat from the bones and skin and shred into bite-size pieces. Add the bones and skin to the pot when stewing the lamb. After the lamb is cooked, strain and discard the bones and skin.

Although the dish won't have the same depth of flavor, you can skip stewing the lamb and make it with quick-cooking meats and poultry. Consider breakfast sausage formed into small, thick patties and browned, as well as other fresh or smoked pork, turkey, or chicken sausages.

HOW CAN I VARY IT?

Use chunks of boneless pork shoulder in place of the lamb.

WHAT SHOULD I SERVE WITH IT?
Drinks:

To start, Sparkling Wine Cocktails (page 284) or Mulled Cider (page 292)

A bold red wine, such as Côtes du Rhône, along with a white wine for those who prefer it

Appetizers:

Quick Marinated Olives (page 117)

Fresh Goat Cheese on Flatbread with Grapes and Rosemary Oil (page 130)

Cheddar Puffs with Scallions and Cayenne (page 131)

Salads:

Baby Greens, Romaine, and Iceberg Lettuce with Blue Cheese, Toasted Pecans, and Dried Cranberries (page 174)

Mixed Green Salad with Fresh Herbs (page 168)

For a dinner party, Pear Halves with Blue Cheese and Toasted Nuts (page 166)

Desserts:

Perfectly Simple Pumpkin Cheesecake (page 274)

Chocolate Tart (page 276)

Apple Crostata (page 278)

For a dinner party, Orange Pudding Cakes with Marmalade Drizzle (page 269) or Molten Chocolate Cakes with Sugar-Coated Raspberries (page 264)

HOW FAR AHEAD CAN I MAKE IT?

The cassoulet can be assembled up to 3 days ahead. Bring to a simmer before baking.

WHAT ABOUT LEFTOVERS?

Leftovers keep well for up to 5 days. Microwave or heat slowly on the stovetop.

until all sausages are browned, 5 to 8 minutes longer. Transfer to a plate. When cool enough to handle, cut Italian sausages into bite-size chunks. Halve smoked sausages lengthwise. Set aside.

Generously sprinkle duck breasts with salt and pepper. Reduce heat under roasting pan and add duck breasts, skin side down. Cook until fat has rendered and skin is mahogany brown, 10 to 12 minutes.

Turn duck breasts over and continue to cook until cooked through, about 5 minutes longer. Remove duck from pan. Drain fat from pan and reserve. Slice each breast crosswise into 4 pieces.

Return roasting pan to medium-high heat. Add lamb cubes and cook, turning once, until a brown crust forms on two sides, 8 to 10 minutes. Transfer lamb to a large ovenproof pot; set roasting pan aside. Add broth mixture and wine to lamb and cover with reserved foil, pressing down so that it almost touches meat, then sealing foil around top of pot, leaving a small opening for steam to escape. Bring to a simmer and simmer for a few minutes to burn off alcohol.

Seal foil completely, then cover pot with lid. Bake, without checking pot, for 1 hour and 15 minutes; meat will be very tender.

Meanwhile, reheat roasting pan over medium-high heat. Add enough reserved duck fat or olive oil to pan to equal 2 tablespoons. Add onions and garlic and sauté until tender, about 5 minutes. Add prosciutto and thyme and sauté to blend flavors, 1 to 2 minutes longer. Add tomatoes and beans and simmer to blend flavors, about 10 minutes. Remove from heat.

Transfer cooked lamb and broth to roasting pan. Add duck, sausages, and enough water to make a soupy, moist casserole. You can let the cassoulet mixture stand at room temperature for up to 2 hours.

An hour before serving, adjust oven rack to lower-middle position and heat oven to 350 degrees. Bring cassoulet to a simmer.

Mix bread crumbs, melted butter, and parsley and sprinkle over cassoulet. Bake until crumbs are golden and stew is bubbly, about 45 minutes. Let stand for 5 minutes, and serve.

ONE STEW, MANY VARIATIONS

This recipe invites creativity. With its simple "3 formula" (3 pounds cubed meat, 3 onions, 3 garlic cloves, 3 tablespoons flour, and 3 cups liquid), you can prepare dishes as different as Lamb Stew with Indian Flavorings, Hungarian-Style Beef Stew, and Pork Stew with Bell Peppers and Olives.

SERVES 6 TO 8

    The cooking technique for the meat is unusual and quick: after browning the meat, you finish it in a blistering-hot 450-degree oven, covered tightly with aluminum foil. (If you don't have a heavy roasting pan, brown the meat in batches in a Dutch oven, making sure not to overcrowd the pot.)

3   pounds boneless beef chuck, lamb leg or shoulder, or pork shoulder, cut into 1½-inch cubes and patted dry
2–3 tablespoons vegetable oil or olive oil
    Salt and freshly ground black pepper
3   medium onions, cut into medium dice
3   garlic cloves, minced

WHEN SHOULD I SERVE IT?
For any cool-weather casual buffet or formal dinner party
For fall, winter, and early-spring houseguests

WHAT SHOULD I SERVE WITH IT?
Drinks:
Red wine — a lighter one for the pork stew, a bolder variety for stews made with beef and lamb — or beer, especially the Hungarian- and southwestern-flavored stews

Appetizers:
Cheddar Puffs with Scallions and Cayenne (page 131) for Classic Stew
Potato Crisps with Smoked Salmon (page 128) for Hungarian-Style Stew
Quesadillas for a Crowd (page 138) for Stew with Southwestern Flavorings
Spicy Asian Lettuce Cups (page 140) or Vegetable Egg Rolls with Lime-Ginger Dipping

Sauce (page 134) for Stew with Indian Flavorings
Fresh Goat Cheese on Flatbread (page 130) for Stew with Bell Peppers and Olives, Stew with Tomatoes and Chickpeas, and Stew with Tomatoes, Rosemary, and White Beans
Hummus (page 123) and Baked Pita Triangles (page 124) for Stew with Moroccan Flavorings and Dried Fruit

Spices and/or dried herbs (recipes follow)

3   tablespoons all-purpose flour
3   cups liquid (see recipes)
    Vegetables and/or fruits (see recipes)
    Fresh herbs (see recipes)

Adjust oven rack to lower-middle position and heat oven to 450 degrees.

Heat a heavy roasting pan set over two burners on low heat. Place meat in a medium bowl. Pour 2 tablespoons oil over it and season with salt and pepper, tossing to coat.

Increase heat to medium-high and heat until wisps of smoke start to rise from the pan. Add meat and sear, turning once, until 2 sides form a dark brown crust, 8 to 10 minutes. Transfer meat to a Dutch oven or other pot measuring 9 to 10 inches in diameter.

Add onions and garlic to roasting pan; add another tablespoon of oil if pan is dry. Sauté until softened, about 5 minutes. Add spices and/or dried herbs and cook until fragrant, 30 seconds for herbs, about 1 minute for spices. Whisk in flour, then liquid, season with salt and pepper, and bring to a simmer.

Salads:
  Slaw with Orange-Cumin Dressing (page 181) for Stew with Indian Flavorings and Stew with Moroccan Flavorings and Dried Fruit
  Boston Lettuce and Baby Spinach Salad (page 176) for Stew with Southwestern Flavorings
  Chopped Caesar Salad (page 172) for Stew with Bell Peppers and Olives, Stew with Tomatoes and Chickpeas, Stew with

Tomatoes, Rosemary, and White Beans
  Baby Greens, Romaine, and Iceberg Lettuce (page 174) for Classic Stew
  Carrot Salad with Cumin Vinaigrette (page 178) for Hungarian-Style Stew
Desserts:
  Roasted Pears with Caramel Sauce (page 254)
  Simple, Tender Yellow Cake (pages 257–61)
  Apple Crostata (page 278)

HOW FAR AHEAD CAN I MAKE IT?
  The stew can be made 2 days ahead up to adding the vegetables.

WHAT ABOUT LEFTOVERS?
  Leftover stew is good for 2 to 3 days. Reheat over low heat. You can also freeze the stew (preferably without the vegetables added).

Pour contents of roasting pan into pot with meat. Place a sheet of heavy-duty foil over pot, pressing foil down so that it just touches stew, and seal foil tightly around edges. Place lid snugly on pot and heat over medium-high heat until you hear juices bubble.

Transfer to oven and bake for 1 hour and 15 minutes.

Meanwhile, cook vegetables, if necessary, as directed in individual recipes. Remove pot from oven, carefully remove foil, and stir in any cooked vegetables or dried fruit, then add any remaining ingredients except fresh herbs. Cover pot with foil and lid again and let sit, off heat, to marry flavors, about 15 minutes. Just before serving, add a little water if necessary to thin gravy, return stew to burner, and add fresh herbs. Heat through and serve.

CLASSIC STEW WITH CARROTS, TURNIPS, AND PEAS

Beef or lamb are especially good with this stew. Serve with Make-Ahead Mashed Potatoes (page 206).

LIQUID:

2   cups chicken broth

1   cup dry red wine

DRIED HERBS:

2   bay leaves

2   teaspoons dried thyme leaves

VEGETABLES:

2   large carrots, peeled and cut into bite-size chunks

2   medium turnips, peeled and cut into medium dice

3/4   cup frozen peas, thawed

FRESH HERBS:

1/4   cup minced fresh parsley

TO COOK CARROTS AND TURNIPS: Bring 1 inch water to a boil in a deep skillet or pot over high heat. Place vegetables in a steamer basket, season generously with salt, and set in pan. Cover and steam until just tender, about 6 minutes. Add peas directly to stew.

HUNGARIAN-STYLE STEW

This stew is best made with beef. Serve over egg noodles.

LIQUID:

1   cup chicken broth

1   cup dry red wine

1   can (14.5 ounces) diced tomatoes

SPICES:

1/4   cup sweet paprika

1 1/2   teaspoons caraway seeds, toasted in a small skillet over low heat until fragrant, then crushed with a rolling pin

VEGETABLES:

3   tablespoons vegetable oil

3   medium bell peppers (mix of green and red), cored, seeded, and cut into thick strips

¼ cup minced fresh parsley

TO COOK PEPPERS: Heat oil in a large (12-inch) skillet over medium-high heat until wisps of smoke start to rise from pan. Add peppers and cook, stirring, until golden brown, about 5 minutes.

STEW WITH INDIAN FLAVORINGS

Make this stew with lamb and serve with basmati rice.

LIQUID:

2 cups canned unsweetened coconut milk
1 cup chicken broth

SPICES:

2 tablespoons curry powder
½ teaspoon ground ginger
½ teaspoon ground cinnamon
¼ teaspoon ground cloves

VEGETABLES:

3 medium sweet potatoes, peeled and cut into bite-size cubes
¾ cup frozen green peas, thawed

FRESH HERBS:

¼ cup minced fresh cilantro

TO COOK VEGETABLES: Bring 1 inch water to a boil in a deep skillet or pot over high heat. Place potatoes in a steamer basket, season generously with salt, and set in pan. Cover and steam until just tender, 6 to 8 minutes. Add peas directly to stew.

STEW WITH SOUTHWESTERN FLAVORINGS

Beef (or a combination of beef and pork) works best for this stew.

LIQUID:

1 cup chicken broth
1 cup dry red wine
1 can (14.5 ounces) diced tomatoes

SPICES AND DRIED HERBS:

¼ cup chili powder
2 teaspoons ground cumin
1 teaspoon dried oregano

VEGETABLES:

2 tablespoons vegetable oil
2 medium bell peppers (1 each red and yellow), cored, seeded, and cut into thick strips
2 cans (16 ounces each) pinto beans, drained and rinsed

FRESH HERBS:

¼ cup minced fresh cilantro

TO COOK PEPPERS: Heat oil in a 10-inch skillet over medium-high heat until wisps of smoke start to rise from pan. Add peppers and cook, stirring, until golden brown, about 5 minutes.

STEW WITH BELL PEPPERS AND OLIVES

Pork is my meat of choice for this stew. Serve with Potato Gratin with Garlic and Thyme (page 211).

LIQUID:

2 cups chicken broth
½ cup dry white or red wine (white if using pork, red if using beef or lamb)
½ cup orange juice

DRIED HERBS:

1 tablespoon herbes de Provence or 1 teaspoon each dried oregano, thyme, and basil

2　tablespoons olive oil

3　bell peppers (yellow, red, and orange), cored, seeded, and cut into thick strips

3/4　cup pitted kalamata olives

TO COOK PEPPERS: Heat oil in a large (12-inch) skillet over medium-high heat until wisps of smoke start to rise from pan. Add peppers and cook, stirring, until golden brown, about 5 minutes.

STEW WITH MOROCCAN FLAVORINGS AND DRIED FRUIT

Lamb is especially good for this stew. Serve with Couscous with Chickpeas and Carrots (page 215).

LIQUID:

2　cups chicken broth

1　cup orange juice

SPICES:

1 1/2　teaspoons ground coriander

1 1/2　teaspoons ground cumin

3/4　teaspoon ground cinnamon

1/2　teaspoon ground ginger

FRUIT:

3/4　pound mixed dried fruit, such as prunes, apricots, peaches, and/or pears

FRESH HERBS:

1/4　cup minced fresh mint or cilantro

STEW WITH TOMATOES AND CHICKPEAS

This stew is equally delicious made with lamb, beef, or pork. Serve alone or with instant polenta. To make polenta for 6 to 8 people, bring 8 cups water to a boil in a large saucepan. Whisk in 1 teaspoon salt and 2 cups instant polenta. Cook, stirring frequently, until water is absorbed, 3 to 4 minutes. Stir in 2 tablespoons butter, 1/2 cup grated Parmesan cheese, and, if desired, 2 cups frozen corn, thawed, and heat through.

LIQUID:

1　cup chicken broth

1　cup dry red wine

1　can (14.5 ounces) diced tomatoes

DRIED HERBS:

2　bay leaves

1　tablespoon dried oregano

VEGETABLES:

2　cans (16 ounces each) chickpeas, drained and rinsed

FRESH HERBS:

1/4　cup chopped fresh parsley

STEW WITH TOMATOES, ROSEMARY, AND WHITE BEANS

Choose lamb, beef, or pork for this stew. Serve with olive bread or a good Italian loaf.

Treat the fresh rosemary like a dried herb and add it at the same time as the bay leaves.

LIQUID:

1　cup chicken broth

1　cup dry red wine

1　can (14.5 ounces) diced tomatoes

DRIED HERBS:

2　bay leaves

1　tablespoon minced fresh rosemary (see above)

VEGETABLES:

2　cans (16 ounces each) white beans, drained and rinsed

FRESH HERBS:

1/4　cup minced fresh parsley

OUTDOOR AFFAIRS

If your gas grill is close to the kitchen, the dishes that follow are year-round possibilities.

Shish Kebabs   56

Mixed Grill with Tandoori Flavorings   62

Grilled Chicken Breasts with Orange-Thyme
Glaze   64

Sear-Ahead Steaks or Salmon   66

SHISH KEBABS

Kebabs are a host's dream: buy just a small amount each of meat, fish, poultry, and vegetables and satisfy every guest, regardless of personal preference or dietary restrictions. Those allergic to shrimp can have chicken. Those who don't eat red meat can opt for fish. Vegetarians can enjoy a colorful, sumptuous meal.

SERVES 4 TO 6

The basic formula consists of equal parts of chicken, meat, and/or seafood and vegetables and/or fruits. For vegetarian kebabs, just omit the meat and increase the vegetables proportionally.

Cut the meat into slightly larger chunks than the vegetables,

WHEN SHOULD I SERVE IT?

At casual warm-weather dinners and buffets

Whenever you want guests to participate in the preparation and cooking

When serving both meat-and-potato-types and vegetarians

For a buy-it-in-the-afternoon, serve-it-in-the-evening kind of party

ANY SHORTCUTS?

Buy peeled shrimp, chicken fingers, and already cubed meats. (Use swordfish, tuna, and salmon scraps, which are sold at some seafood stores.)

WHAT SHOULD I SERVE WITH IT?
Drinks:

To start, a Pitcher of Mojitos (page 290), Instant Frozen

Margaritas (page 287), or one of the Sparkling Coolers (page 283)

To complement the touch of sweetness in the kebabs, a fruity red or white wine — or beer

Appetizers:

One or more of the offerings from Spreads and Crispy Breads and Chips (page 122)

Fresh Goat Cheese on Flatbread with Grapes and Rosemary Oil (page 130)

First Courses and Salads:

Year-Round Classic Gazpacho (page 162)

Mixed Green Salad with Fresh Herbs (page 168)

Boston Lettuce and Baby Spinach Salad (page 176)

Sides:

Yellow Rice with Green Peas (page 216)

Couscous with Chickpeas and Carrots (page 215)

Desserts:

Tortilla Sundaes with Minted Mango Salsa (page 241)

One of the cakes made from the recipe for Simple, Tender Yellow Cake (page 257)

HOW FAR AHEAD CAN I MAKE IT?

The chicken, meat, seafood, and vegetables can be tossed in the flavoring pastes up to 3 hours before cooking.

WHAT ABOUT LEFTOVERS?

Reheat them or serve at room temperature and toss into salad for lunch the next day.

so they can cook together without drying out. The flavoring pastes promote browning, resulting in juicy, tender kebabs with striking grill marks.

Metal skewers with a flat blade hold the meat and vegetables in place and are the first choice for kebabs. Or thread the meat and vegetables onto two wooden skewers. If you use thin round bamboo skewers, thread the ingredients so you leave very little of the wood exposed, to prevent it from charring. Then, to prevent the food from twirling around (which would cause it to cook unevenly), use tongs to grasp as much of each skewer as possible when you turn it.

$1^3/_4$ pounds boneless chicken, meat, and/or seafood (see facing page), cut (except shrimp) into about $1^1/_2$-inch pieces

$1^3/_4$ pounds vegetables and/or fruits (see facing page), cut (except mushrooms) into about 1-inch chunks

$1^1/_4$ teaspoons salt

$^1/_2$ teaspoon freshly ground black pepper
      Flavoring paste of choice (recipes follow)

2   tablespoons chopped fresh parsley or cilantro (optional)
      Lemon or lime wedges (optional)

Sprinkle chicken, meat, and/or seafood and vegetables and/or fruits with salt and pepper, and toss with selected flavoring paste.

Thread (or let guests thread) ingredients on eight 12-inch or six 14-inch skewers, alternating a piece of chicken/meat/seafood with every 2 vegetable/fruit pieces (unless making vegetarian kebabs), making sure not to thread too tightly. If using bamboo skewers, leave as little exposed wood as possible at both ends to keep them from charring.

About 30 minutes before serving, heat a gas grill, with all burners on high, for 10 to 15 minutes. Use a wire brush to clean grill rack, then use tongs to wipe a vegetable-oil-soaked rag over grill grate to prevent sticking. Close lid and return to temperature.

Place skewers on grill, close lid, and grill until spotty brown, about 4 minutes. Turn skewers (if using round skewers, grab as much of each kebab as possible from the side with tongs, preferably the spring-action variety, and turn decisively). Grill until spotty brown on second side and cooked through, about 2 minutes for shrimp, 3 minutes for chicken breasts and seafood, and 4 minutes for chicken thighs, pork, beef, and lamb. Transfer to a platter and let rest for a few minutes.

Sprinkle with parsley and squeeze lemon wedges over, if you like.

CHICKEN/MEAT/SEAFOOD OPTIONS:

Boneless, skinless chicken thighs
Boneless, skinless chicken breasts
Pork tenderloin or pork loin (preferably from
   the rib end)
Beef tenderloin (filet mignon) or boneless New York
   strip or rib-eye steak
Swordfish
Salmon
Tuna
Extra-large shrimp (21–25 count), peeled
Italian sausage (sweet or hot), steamed until fully
   cooked but not browned
Kielbasa

VEGETABLE AND FRUIT OPTIONS:

White mushrooms, halved if large, left whole if small
Zucchini
Yellow squash
Eggplant
Bell peppers (red, yellow, and/or green)
Onions (1-inch chunks separated into pieces
   2 layers thick)
Fennel (1-inch chunks separated into pieces
   2 layers thick)
Apples, cored
Pineapples, peeled and cored
Apricots, pitted
Plums, pitted

ORANGE-ROSEMARY PASTE

1 tablespoon vegetable oil
2 tablespoons minced fresh rosemary
½ cup frozen orange juice concentrate,
     thawed
2 teaspoons light or dark brown sugar

CURRIED APPLE PASTE

1 tablespoon vegetable oil
2 tablespoons curry powder
½ cup frozen apple juice concentrate,
     thawed

PINEAPPLE-CUMIN PASTE

1 tablespoon vegetable oil
4 teaspoons ground cumin
½ cup frozen pineapple juice concentrate,
     thawed

JAMAICAN JERK-STYLE PASTE

1 tablespoon vegetable oil
1 tablespoon dried thyme leaves
1 tablespoon dried oregano
1 teaspoon ground coriander
1 teaspoon ground allspice
2 tablespoons Dijon mustard
2 teaspoons hot red pepper sauce
½ cup frozen limeade concentrate, thawed

ASIAN-STYLE PASTE

2 tablespoons Asian sesame oil
2 teaspoons garlic powder
2 teaspoons ground ginger
1 teaspoon hot red pepper flakes
6 tablespoons soy sauce
½ cup frozen pineapple juice concentrate,
     thawed

MOROCCAN-STYLE PASTE

- 2 tablespoons vegetable oil
- 1½ teaspoons paprika
- 1 teaspoon garlic powder
- 1 teaspoon ground ginger
- 1 teaspoon ground cumin
- ½ teaspoon ground cinnamon
- ½ teaspoon ground cloves
- ½ cup frozen limeade concentrate, thawed

TO MAKE FLAVORING PASTES:
Heat oil and herbs and/or spices in a small (8-inch) skillet or saucepan over medium-high heat until herbs/spices start to sizzle. Add remaining ingredients, bring to a simmer, and simmer until mixture reduces to a thick paste, 3 to 4 minutes.

Mixed Grill with Tandoori Flavorings, page 62

MIXED GRILL
WITH TANDOORI FLAVORINGS

This mixed grill offers something for everyone. You make one basic spice rub and add half to the lamb chops, then mix the other half with yogurt to make a marinade for the chicken. If you like, you can flavor the sausages by rolling them in the lamb chop–spicing bowl after they've been steamed.

SERVES 8

  If you want the chicken, lamb, and sausages to come off the grill at the same time, stagger them, cooking the chicken first, then the lamb, and finally browning the steamed sausages.

¼ cup olive oil
3 tablespoons ground cumin
1 tablespoon curry powder
1½ teaspoons garlic powder
¾ teaspoon ground ginger
¾ teaspoon salt
½ teaspoon cayenne pepper
8 lamb loin chops
½ cup plain yogurt
3 tablespoons red wine vinegar
12 chicken legs, skin removed
2 pounds spicy or mild Italian sausages, cut into 8 pieces

Mix oil, cumin, curry powder, garlic, ginger, salt, and cayenne in a medium bowl. Scrape half the mixture into another medium bowl. Add lamb chops to one bowl and turn to coat well. Stir yogurt and vinegar into other bowl of spices, add chicken legs, and turn to coat well. The meats can marinate at room temperature for up to 2 hours or can be refrigerated overnight; return to room temperature before cooking.

Meanwhile, place sausages and ½ cup water in a large (12-inch) skillet, cover, and bring to a simmer. Steam until sausage loses its raw color throughout, about 8 minutes. Drain and set aside.

About 30 minutes before serving, heat a gas grill, with all burners on high, for 10 to 15 minutes. Use a wire brush to clean grill rack, then use tongs to wipe a vegetable-oil-soaked rag over grill rack to prevent sticking. Close lid and return to temperature.

Place chicken legs on hot grill rack, close lid, and grill-roast for a total of 20 minutes—8 minutes on first side, 8 minutes on second side, and then 4 minutes longer, turning as needed toward the end to ensure doneness.

Add lamb chops and grill-roast for a total of 8 minutes—4 minutes on first side and 4 minutes on second side.

Add sausages and grill-roast for a total of 4 minutes—2 minutes on first side and 2 minutes on second side.

Serve hot or warm.

WHEN SHOULD I SERVE IT?

For a sumptuous last-minute dinner

When entertaining summer or early-fall houseguests

For a summer buffet (cook the chicken up to 2 hours before guests arrive, the Italian sausages and lamb just before serving)

ANY SHORTCUTS?

If you've got good spice rubs in your pantry, use one of them instead of making your own. Check the ingredient list for salt—if it doesn't include it, make sure you salt the lamb and chicken first.

HOW CAN I VARY IT?

Grill pork chops or even steaks instead of the lamb.

Substitute chicken breasts, wings, and/or thighs for the drumsticks. (Reduce the cooking time for boneless, skinless thighs and breasts. Bone-in thighs and wings

will need about the same cooking time as the drumsticks.)

WHAT SHOULD I SERVE WITH IT?
Drinks:

Sparkling Wine Cocktails (page 284) and, for nondrinkers, Sparkling Coolers (page 283)

For casual occasions, Gin (or Your Choice) and Tonic (page 286), with interesting sodas

A spicy, fruity red wine such as Zinfandel, or beer

Appetizers:

One or more of the offerings from Spreads and Crispy Breads and Chips (page 122)

Pastry Triangles with Spinach and Feta (page 136)

Salad:

Mixed Green Salad with Fresh Herbs (page 168), with a really good cheese, after dinner

Sides:

Yellow Rice with Green Peas (page 216)

Couscous with Chickpeas and Carrots (page 215)

Broiled or Grilled Asparagus (page 195)

Sautéed Cherry Tomatoes with Garlic and Basil (page 202)

Desserts:

Sorbet- or Ice Cream–Filled Crisp Cinnamon Cups (page 246)

Instant Strawberry Ice Cream (page 248)

Simple Strawberry Shortcakes (page 272)

HOW FAR AHEAD CAN I MAKE IT?

The chicken and lamb can be coated with the spices and the sausages can be steamed up to a day ahead.

WHAT ABOUT LEFTOVERS?

The meats can be microwaved (or warmed in the oven) until heated through for a family lunch.

GRILLED CHICKEN BREASTS
WITH ORANGE-THYME GLAZE

The orange juice concentrate in the marinade provides just enough natural sugars to brown the chicken quickly. The result: dramatic grill marks, worthy of the best bar and grill. The marinade doubles as a glaze. Cook it until it reduces, then brush it on the chicken just before serving.

SERVES 12

1	can (12 ounces) frozen orange juice concentrate, thawed
¼	cup olive oil
3	tablespoons soy sauce
1	teaspoon dried thyme leaves
1	teaspoon finely grated orange zest
12	boneless, skinless chicken breast halves, trimmed, tenderloins removed (if still attached) and reserved for another use

WHEN SHOULD I SERVE IT?

When you need a warm-weather main course that everyone, including children, will love

For an off-site picnic: the chicken breasts are equally good served at room temperature, so you can grill them ahead.

For a large party: because these can be served at room temperature, you can cook them in batches.

HOW CAN I VARY IT?

You can use this marinade for salmon as well. To keep the fish from sticking, set an oven rack (yes, oven rack!) on the grill, coat it with vegetable cooking spray or oil, and fully preheat the grill. Place salmon fillets flesh side down on the oven rack and grill, lid closed, without turning, until fully cooked, 8 to 9 minutes. Remove the oven rack with the salmon from

the grill, and let rest for 3 to 5 minutes. Run a spatula under the salmon to loosen it from the rack, invert onto a platter, and serve.

HOW FAR AHEAD CAN I MAKE IT?

The chicken can marinate overnight.

WHAT ABOUT LEFTOVERS?

Use leftover chicken to make chicken salad, slice it for sandwiches, or toss it into a green salad.

Mix orange juice concentrate, olive oil, soy sauce, thyme, and zest in a 1-gallon zipper-lock bag. Add chicken breasts and marinate for 1 hour at room temperature.

About 30 minutes before serving, heat a gas grill, with all burners on high, for 10 to 15 minutes. Use a wire brush to clean grill rack, then use tongs to wipe a vegetable-oil-soaked rag over grill rack to prevent sticking. Close lid and return to temperature.

Place chicken breasts skinned side down on hot grill rack; close lid and grill-roast until grill marks appear, 3 to 4 minutes. Turn chicken breasts and continue to cook until grill marks appear on other side and chicken is cooked through, about 3 minutes longer. Transfer to a platter and let rest for 5 minutes.

Meanwhile, pour marinade into a medium saucepan and simmer over low heat until sauce has reduced to a gravy-like consistency. Brush chicken breasts with glaze and serve.

WHAT SHOULD I SERVE WITH IT?
Drinks:
  A Pitcher of Mojitos (page 290), Instant Frozen Margaritas (page 287), Cosmopolitans (page 288), or, for kids and nondrinkers, Bug Juice (page 289)
  Beer and wine (a crisp rosé would fit the bill) or iced tea
Appetizers:
  One or more of the offerings from Spreads and Crispy Breads and Chips (page 122)

Perfect (or Pickled Pink) Deviled Eggs (pages 120–21)
Salads:
  Mixed Green Salad with Fresh Herbs (page 168)
  Chopped Caesar Salad (page 172)
  Baby Greens, Romaine, and Iceberg Lettuce with Blue Cheese, Toasted Pecans, and Dried Cranberries (page 174)
  One of the slaws (pages 180–81)
  Green Bean–Cherry Tomato Salad with Basil-Buttermilk Dressing (page 182)

Sides:
  Roasted New Potato Salad with Olives, Red Onions, and Creamy Vinaigrette (page 185)
  Broiled or Grilled Asparagus (page 195)
Desserts:
  Berry Bread Pudding (page 256)
  Simple Strawberry Shortcakes (page 272)
  One of the cakes made from the recipe for Simple, Tender Yellow Cake (page 257)

SEAR-AHEAD STEAKS OR SALMON

Quick-cooking yet special steaks are on the short list of dishes that work for impromptu entertaining. Here's a chef's tip: lightly sprinkling the steaks with sugar helps them sear quickly and develop a flavorful dark brown crust while they stay raw inside. That means you can sear them on the grill (or stovetop) a couple of hours before guests arrive, then finish them in a warm oven during a leisurely cocktail hour.

The best choices are rib eyes, strip steaks, and filets mignons. Regardless of the cut, choose thick steaks, preferably $1\frac{1}{4}$ to $1\frac{1}{2}$ inches thick. Thinner cuts are more likely to overcook by the time they're seared. Thicker rib eyes and strip steaks usually weigh 12 ounces to a pound, so consider splitting one steak between two people. Smaller than the other two cuts, filets mignons range in size, but 8 to 10 ounces is common.

This same technique works for salmon too.

When buying salmon, ask for thick center-cut fillets—fillets near the tail are thin and very easy to overcook. Like steak, salmon is best somewhere between medium-rare and medium-well. Because the salmon is seared quickly, then gently slow-roasted, it's easy to cook to perfection.

6   filets mignons (8–9 ounces each) or 3–6 strip or rib-eye steaks
        (12–16 ounces each), depending on guests' appetites
    Vegetable oil
    Salt and freshly ground black pepper
    Sugar
    One of the sauces (page 69; optional)

TO GRILL STEAKS AHEAD: Heat a gas grill, with all burners on high, for 10 to 15 minutes. Use a wire brush to clean grill rack, then use tongs to wipe a vegetable-oil-soaked rag over grill grate to prevent sticking. Close lid and return to temperature.

WHEN SHOULD I SERVE IT?

When entertaining on the fly

When entertaining meat lovers — there are few simpler, more generous meals than a good steak dinner

HOW CAN I VARY IT?

Sass it up with a speedy sauce or condiment:

Store-bought tapenade, for steak

Store-bought pesto, for steak or salmon

Pickled Pink Onions, for steak or salmon: Drizzle 2 tablespoons rice wine vinegar over $1/2$ medium red onion, thinly sliced. Season with a pinch of salt and let stand until ready to serve.

Boursin cheese, at room temperature, for steak

Horseradish Cream, for steak or salmon: Mix $1\frac{1}{2}$ tablespoons prepared horseradish and 1 tablespoon sour cream. Sprinkle with a little salt and a few grinds of pepper.

Dollop or place one or more of these condiments, painter's palette–style, alongside the steak or salmon and serve.

Sear the steaks or salmon in a hot pan instead of on the grill (see page 68).

WHAT SHOULD I SERVE WITH IT?

Drinks:

To start, Gin (or Your Choice) and Tonic (page 286) or Mojitos (page 290), Instant Frozen Margaritas (page 287), or beer

A full-bodied red wine or beer

Appetizers:

Oregano-Flavored Feta Spread (page 122), with Baked Pita Triangles (page 124)

Guacamole (page 14) with Fried Corn Tortilla Triangles (page 123)

Potato Crisps with Smoked Salmon and Herbed Cream Cheese (page 128)

First Courses:

Any of the salads (pages 166–92)

Crab-Stuffed Artichokes (page 150; or substitute shrimp for the crab)

Sides:

Creamed Spinach (page 198) or Broiled or Grilled Asparagus (page 195)

Sautéed Cherry Tomatoes with Garlic and Basil (page 202) or Slow-Roasted Plum Tomatoes with Pesto-Flavored Crumbs (page 204)

Roasted Red Potatoes (page 210) or Roasted New Potato Salad with Olives, Red Onions, and Creamy Vinaigrette (page 185)

Desserts:

Instant Strawberry Ice Cream (page 248)

Lemon-Raspberry Triflettes (page 262), with the salmon

Molten Chocolate Cakes with Sugar-Coated Raspberries (page 264), with the steaks

HOW FAR AHEAD CAN I MAKE IT?

You can grill the steaks or salmon up to 2 hours before serving. If you let them rest after grilling, their still-cold interiors will come to room temperature and the steaks will cook more evenly in the oven.

If you plan to go straight from the grill to the oven, be sure to bring the meat or fish to room temperature before grilling so it is not as cold inside. You can speed this process, however, with the microwave. Microwave 2 steaks at a time, uncovered, on the defrost setting for about 2 minutes.

WHAT ABOUT LEFTOVERS?

Serve for breakfast with eggs, make hash, or turn into a meaty main-course salad.

Just before grilling (because sugar melts quickly and would hamper searing) season steaks: rub both sides of each steak with oil and season each side with salt, pepper, and sugar. (For strip steaks and rib eyes, sprinkle on a scant ½ teaspoon sugar per side. For filets mignons, figure about ¼ teaspoon per side.)

Grill until steaks display impressive grill marks, a full 2 minutes per side. Transfer to a wire rack set over a rimmed baking sheet.

TO SLOW-ROAST STEAKS: About 45 minutes before serving, adjust oven rack to lower-middle position and heat oven to 325 degrees.

Cook steaks, still on wire rack and over baking sheet, until rosy inside, or when an instant-read thermometer plunged deep into steak from side registers 135 degrees for rare (about 20 minutes), 140 degrees for medium-rare (25 to 30 minutes), or 145 to 150 degrees for medium (30 to 35 minutes). If steaks are ready but you're not, simply turn off oven and crack the door—that'll buy you another few minutes.

SEAR-AHEAD SALMON FILLETS

Follow instructions for Sear-Ahead Steaks, grilling 6 center-cut salmon fillets (6 to 8 ounces each) for 2 minutes, skin or skinned side up. Then slow-roast until medium-rare (about 135 degrees on an instant-read thermometer), about 20 minutes; for medium-well (about 145 degrees), slow-roast for another 5 minutes or so.

INDOOR SEAR-AHEAD STEAKS OR SALMON

This method gives you delicious pan juices to make a sauce.

Heat oven to 325 degrees.

Set a large heavy roasting pan over two burners and heat over low heat while you season steaks or salmon. Coat both sides of each steak or salmon fillet with oil and sprinkle with salt, pepper, and sugar. Turn exhaust fan on and increase heat to high. When pan is hot (residual oil in well-used nonstick pan will send up wisps of smoke), add steaks or salmon. Sear until a rich brown crust develops, about 2 minutes for steak, 1 minute for salmon. Turn and cook until steaks or salmon develop a crust on other side, about 1 minute longer. Transfer to a wire rack set over a rimmed baking sheet. Set roasting pan aside if you want to make a sauce.

Slow-roast steaks or salmon as directed above.

PORT WINE SAUCE WITH BLUE CHEESE (FOR INDOOR SEAR-AHEAD STEAK)

1 cup port wine

1 tablespoon seedless raspberry jam

2 tablespoons butter

3 ounces blue cheese, crumbled (heaping ½ cup)

Whisk port and jam together in a 2-cup Pyrex measuring cup or microwave-safe bowl. Heat roasting pan, add port and jam mixture and stir until reduced by half, about 2 minutes. Return sauce to measuring cup or bowl and set aside while steaks cook. Just before serving, microwave sauce until hot and steaming, about 1 minute. Whisk in butter. Top each steak with a portion of blue cheese before drizzling with sauce.

SHERRY VINEGAR PAN SAUCE WITH CAPERS AND PARSLEY (FOR INDOOR SEAR-AHEAD STEAK OR SALMON)

¾ cup chicken broth

¼ cup sherry vinegar

1 tablespoon Dijon mustard

3 tablespoons capers, drained

¼ cup chopped fresh parsley (optional)

2 tablespoons butter

Mix chicken broth, vinegar, mustard, and capers in a 2-cup Pyrex measuring cup or microwave-safe bowl. Add to empty hot roasting pan and stir until reduced by half, about 2 minutes. Return sauce to measuring cup or bowl and set aside. Just before serving, microwave sauce until hot and steaming, about 2 minutes. Stir in parsley, if desired, then whisk in butter.

GRAPEFRUIT PAN SAUCE (FOR INDOOR SEAR-AHEAD SALMON)

1 cup grapefruit juice

1 tablespoon Dijon mustard

1 tablespoon minced fresh dill or 1 teaspoon dried dill

2 tablespoons butter

Mix juice and mustard in a 2-cup Pyrex measuring cup or microwave-safe bowl. Add to empty hot roasting pan and stir until reduced by half, about 2 minutes. Return to measuring cup or bowl and set aside. Just before serving, microwave sauce until hot and steaming, about 1 minute. Stir in dill and whisk in butter.

IN THE
DINING ROOM

Birthdays, anniversaries, major
holidays, and romantic dinners for
two: these are times when you want to
be in the dining room. And whether
it's an almost-no-stir risotto, a
stuffed pork loin that doesn't require
making a stuffing, a perfectly cooked
beef tenderloin, or slow-roasted
lobster tails, these recipes are as
simple as they are stunning.

EASY BAKED RISOTTO

Risotto is perfect for an elegant dinner party, but most people don't want to spend nearly an hour stirring it. Unless you drag someone into the kitchen to keep you company, you'll miss a good chunk of your party. But placing a sheet of heavy-duty foil directly over the risotto's surface and double-sealing the pot with the foil and a lid reduce the cooking time and eliminate most of the stirring.

Although you could halve the recipe and decrease the cooking time by 5 to 7 minutes, I wouldn't: the risotto cake recipe (page 75) is exceptional for leftovers.

SERVES 4 TO 6 AS A MAIN COURSE, 8 AS A FIRST COURSE

Flavoring Ingredients (page 75; use a total of 1 pound; optional)

3   tablespoons olive oil, butter, or rendered bacon fat if using bacon

1   small onion, cut into small dice

2   ounces prosciutto, bacon, or pancetta or 4 ounces ham, sliced and cut into small dice (optional)

2   cups Arborio rice

1/2   cup dry white wine

1   quart chicken broth

1   cup grated Parmesan cheese

4   ounces (1 cup) frozen green peas and/or 2 tablespoons chopped fresh parsley

Adjust oven rack to middle position and heat oven to 450 degrees. Prepare flavoring ingredients, if using.

Heat oil in a heavy-bottomed Dutch oven or large ovenproof (12-inch) skillet over medium-high heat. Add onion, prosciutto, if using, and any ingredients to be sautéed and sauté until tender, 4 to 5 minutes. Stir in rice. (Risotto can be made to this point up to 2 hours in advance and covered.)

Add wine and simmer until evaporated. Add chicken broth and 2 cups water. Cover pot with a sheet of heavy-duty foil, pressing down so that it rests on broth, crimp foil around edges of pot, and cover pot with lid for a tighter seal. Set pot in oven and cook for 25 minutes.

Remove from oven and carefully remove lid and foil. Set pot on low heat. If you've chosen ingredients that are to be added at the end of cooking, stir them in now. Cook, stirring, until rice is cooked but still a little chewy at center, liquid is creamy, and flavors have blended, about 5 minutes. Stir in Parmesan and peas and parsley (if using) and serve.

WHEN SHOULD I SERVE IT?

As a first or main course at a dinner party in spring, winter, or fall

As a simple supper with family and friends

ANY SHORTCUTS?

Stick with flavoring ingredients that need little or no preparation — sliced mushrooms, prewashed baby spinach, scallops, or peeled shrimp, for example

HOW CAN I VARY IT?

With this formula, you can create whatever flavor risotto you like.

Suggested Combinations:

Risotto with scallops, spinach, and bacon

Risotto with fennel and scallops

Risotto with shrimp, asparagus, and prosciutto

Risotto with winter squash and prosciutto

Risotto with asparagus and ham

Risotto with cabbage and bacon

Risotto with mushrooms and cabbage

WHAT SHOULD I SERVE WITH IT?
Drinks:

Wine (red or white, depending on the risotto) or sparkling water

Appetizers:

Lacy Cheddar Crisps (page 118)

Potato Crisps with Smoked Salmon and Herbed Cream Cheese (page 128)

Fresh Goat Cheese on Flatbread with Grapes and Rosemary Oil (page 130)

First Courses and Salads:

Big Bowl of Garlicky Mussels or Clams (page 152)

Smoked Salmon and Watercress Salad with Red Onion–Caper Vinaigrette (page 187) in spring and summer

Pear Halves with Blue Cheese and Toasted Nuts (page 166) in fall and winter

If serving the risotto as a first course, consider the following main courses:

Butter-Roasted Lobster Tails (page 90)

Sear-Ahead Salmon (page 66)

Roast Rack of Lamb with Vinegar-Mint Pan Sauce (page 93)

Desserts:

Frozen Tiramisu with Coffee Mascarpone Sauce (page 250)

Roasted Peaches (or Pears, Plums, or Apples) with Caramel Sauce (page 254)

Lemon-Raspberry Triflettes (page 262)

Meringue Cake with Raspberries and Whipped Cream (page 267)

Orange Pudding Cakes with Marmalade Drizzle (page 269)

HOW FAR AHEAD CAN I MAKE IT?

You can do the stovetop cooking and set the rice aside, covered, for up to 2 hours before adding the liquid and baking it.

WHAT ABOUT LEFTOVERS?

Just add a little chicken broth to loosen the rice and heat slowly, stirring occasionally, on the stovetop.

If you have 2 cups leftover risotto, make Risotto Cakes (page 75).

FLAVORING INGREDIENTS

INGREDIENTS THAT ARE SAUTÉED

Choose 8 ounces (heaping 2 cups) of one of the following:

Winter squash, cut into ½-inch dice

Fennel, halved lengthwise, cored, and thinly sliced

Mushrooms, thinly sliced

Cabbage, thinly sliced

INGREDIENTS THAT ARE ADDED DURING THE LAST 5 MINUTES OF COOKING

Asparagus spears, tossed with 1 tablespoon olive oil, sprinkled with salt and pepper, and roasted on a baking sheet in a 450-degree oven for 5 minutes, then cut into 1-inch lengths.

Baby spinach or arugula

Bay scallops

Medium shrimp, peeled

RISOTTO CAKES

You'll need 2 cups leftover risotto. Chop large flavoring ingredients into small chunks. Stir 1 beaten egg into cold risotto. Measure ¾ cup dry bread crumbs into a pie plate. Drop ¼ cup risotto into crumbs, covering risotto mound with crumbs and twirling it to coat completely. Pick up risotto mound and form it into a patty, then drop it back into crumbs to coat again. Transfer to a plate. Repeat to make 8 cakes.

Heat a generous 2 tablespoons oil in a 10-inch skillet over medium heat until hot. Add cakes (8 fit perfectly) and fry until golden brown, about 2 minutes per side. Serve on or alongside a bed of vinaigrette-tossed baby greens sprinkled with crumbled goat or feta cheese.

BUTTERFLIED CORNISH HENS
WITH APRICOT-PISTACHIO DRESSING

SERVES 8

Cornish hens are festive and relatively inexpensive, and they cook quickly. Plan on one hen for every two guests—especially if dinner includes a first course and dessert. To ensure that they roast evenly and quickly and to simplify carving, butterfly the birds before roasting.

You can double the soaking time, but be sure to halve the salt. So the birds will be well seasoned and juicy, they are soaked in a brine.

4	Cornish hens (about 1½ pounds each)
2	cups kosher salt, plus more for seasoning
	Freshly ground black pepper
¼	cup olive oil
4	medium-large onions, cut into medium dice
2	cups dried apricots, cut into medium dice
½	cup apricot jam
¼	cup balsamic vinegar
1	cup pistachio nuts, coarsely chopped
1	cup chopped fresh parsley

To butterfly hens, place each bird breast side down on a work surface, tail end facing you. Using a pair of heavy-duty kitchen shears, cut down middle of entire length of backbone. Turn hen breast side up and use your palm to press hard on breastbone so bird lies flat.

Adjust oven rack to upper-middle position and heat oven to 450 degrees.

Dissolve salt in 5 quarts water in a large nonreactive pot or other container. Add birds, and soak for 1 to 1½ hours.

Drain hens, rinse thoroughly, and pat dry. Season with pepper.

Heat oil in a large (12-inch) skillet. Add onions and cook until softened, about 7 minutes. Stir in apricots, then spread mixture on a large (about 18-by-12-inch) rimmed baking sheet. Lay hens on mixture. Mix jam and vinegar in a small bowl and brush all but a few tablespoons over hens.

Bake hens, brushing 2 or 3 times with remaining jam mixture and accumulated pan juices, until hens are golden brown and juices in thigh run clear, about 45 minutes. Leaving pan in place, turn oven to broil and cook until hens are spotty brown, watching them carefully to make sure that they don't burn, 4 to 5 minutes.

Use tongs to transfer hens to a large serving platter. Return apricot dressing to oven and broil to evaporate some of the excess moisture, about 5 minutes longer.

Stir in pistachios and parsley and mound dressing on serving platter alongside hens. Serve.

WHEN SHOULD I SERVE IT?

For any elegant dinner party

For holidays like Passover, Easter, Christmas, and Thanksgiving

ANY SHORTCUTS?

Skip the Apricot-Pistachio Dressing and serve with a store-bought chutney instead.

Skip the brining step, but be sure to salt and pepper both sides of the hens thoroughly before roasting.

HOW CAN I VARY IT?

Any jam, jelly, preserves, or marmalade, or even honey, can be substituted for the apricot jam.

Substitute other dried fruits for the apricots.

Substitute other toasted chopped nuts for the pistachios — almonds, pecans, walnuts, or skinned hazelnuts.

WHAT SHOULD I SERVE WITH IT?
Drinks:

Before dinner, Sparkling Wine

Cocktails (page 284) or Sparkling Coolers (page 283) or, for fall or winter gatherings, Mulled Cider (page 292)

A rich, full-bodied Chardonnay or a spicy red wine like Zinfandel

Sparkling water

Appetizers:

Fresh Goat Cheese on Flatbread with Grapes and Rosemary Oil (page 130)

Pastry Triangles with Spinach and Feta (page 136)

First Courses and Salads:

Any of the Creamy Vegetable Soups (page 155)

Pureed Wild Mushroom and Potato Soup (page 160)

Mixed Green Salad with Fresh Herbs (page 168), especially in spring

Sides:

Make-Ahead Mashed Potatoes (page 206), Smashed New Potatoes (page 209), or

Roasted Red Potatoes (page 210)

Couscous with Chickpeas and Carrots (page 215)

Orange-Glazed Asparagus (page 196)

Creamed Green Beans with Mustard Sauce and Toasted Almonds (page 200)

Desserts:

Simple Strawberry Shortcakes (page 272)

Orange Pudding Cakes with Marmalade Drizzle (page 269)

Apple Crostata (page 278)

HOW FAR AHEAD CAN I MAKE IT?

The onion-apricot mixture can be made 1 to 2 days ahead.

The birds can be butterflied 1 day ahead.

WHAT ABOUT LEFTOVERS?

Both the birds and the dressing are fine warmed up for lunch or dinner the next day.

TWIN TURKEYS WITH RICH PAN GRAVY

SERVES 10 TO 12, WITH LEFTOVERS

Fantasy: the family is gathered round the dining room table, the golden turkey is ceremoniously presented, and the grand patriarch rises to carve it. Reality: most people don't know how to carve, turkey juices are spilled on the tablecloth, and the side dishes get cold as guests wait for their turkey. The perfect compromise is to roast two small turkeys instead of one big one.

Butterfly and roast the first turkey early in the day and let it rest before carving—the firmer the meat, the easier the carving. Place the sliced meat on a heatproof serving platter and set aside in a cool place or in the refrigerator. Close to serving, gently reheat the turkey.

The second turkey is strictly for show, seconds, and leftovers. Roast it early enough so you have time to make gravy from the drippings of both turkeys before the last-minute rush. Start it breast side down, so the breast stays tender and juicy, then turn it breast side up halfway through the roasting.

You'll need a V-rack for this recipe; for more information, see page 38.

Note: If you live in a warm climate, add ice packs to keep the brining turkeys cool, or dissolve the salt and sugar in a half-gallon of tepid water, then add 2½ gallons ice water.

3   cups kosher salt

2   cups sugar

2   turkeys (10–12 pounds each), neck and giblets removed and discarded
        (or reserved for another use)

2   medium onions, unpeeled, coarsely chopped

2   medium carrots, unpeeled, coarsely chopped

2   medium celery stalks, coarsely chopped

2   tablespoons butter, melted

1   cup dry white wine or dry white vermouth

1   quart chicken broth

¼   cup cornstarch or ½ cup all-purpose flour

The night before roasting, dissolve salt and sugar in 3 gallons cold water in a large clean ice chest or similar-size container in a cold spot (under 40 degrees—the garage or fire escape, for example). Add turkeys, breast side down. Cover and let stand for 12 to 16 hours.

Drain, rinse, and pat turkeys dry. Place turkey #2 in a cool place.

FOR TURKEY #1: Five to 6 hours before serving, adjust oven rack to lower-middle position and heat oven to 425 degrees.

Place turkey, breast side down, on a work surface, cut along both sides of backbone with heavy-duty kitchen shears, and remove. Open up turkey, turn it breast side up, and press hard on it with palm of your hand so it lies flat. Make a bed of half the chopped vegetables on a rimmed baking sheet. Place turkey skin side up on vegetables and brush with butter. Roast until a meat thermometer inserted into thigh registers about 175 degrees, 1 to 1½ hours. Keep an eye on vegetables and pan drippings throughout cooking process—vegetables should be dry enough so they brown but moist enough to keep them from burning; add a little water as needed. Remove pan from oven and transfer turkey to a cutting board. Let rest for 30 minutes and up to 2 hours. Reserve vegetables and pan juices for turkey #2. Carve turkey, transferring slices to an ovenproof platter or a rimmed baking sheet. Cover tightly with foil and set aside in a cool place or the refrigerator while you roast the second turkey.

FOR TURKEY #2: Adjust oven rack to lowest position and reduce oven temperature to 400 degrees. Place cooked vegetables and pan drippings from turkey #1 in a heavy roasting pan, and set a V-rack in pan. Place raw vegetables in turkey cavity and set turkey breast side down on V-rack. Brush turkey back and sides with pan drippings. Roast for 1 hour.

Baste back and sides of turkey with pan drippings. Holding two wads of paper towels to protect yourself, carefully turn turkey breast side up. Baste with pan drippings, and continue to roast until an instant-read thermometer inserted in thickest point of the leg/thigh registers 175 degrees, 1 to 1½ hours longer. Keep an eye on vegetables and pan drippings throughout—as above, vegetables should be dry enough to brown but moist enough to keep them from burning; add a little water as needed.

Transfer turkey to a platter.

Reduce oven temperature to 325 degrees. About 20 minutes before serving, reheat previously carved turkey.

Meanwhile, set roasting pan over two burners on medium-high heat. Add wine and, using a wooden spoon, stir to loosen brown bits on bottom of pan. Strain contents of roasting pan through a large strainer into a large saucepan; discard vegetables. Add chicken broth and bring to a boil. Whisk cornstarch with ½ cup water (or flour with 1 cup water), then gradually whisk into pan juices. Bring to a boil, reduce heat to low, and simmer until gravy thickens. Pour gravy into a serving bowl or boat and serve with turkey.

WHEN SHOULD I SERVE IT?

Thanksgiving, of course! And Christmas too

For any festive fall or winter dinner or buffet

ANY SHORTCUTS?

If you also butterfly the second turkey before roasting, it will cook nearly twice as fast. Or roast just one turkey.

Brining, however, is not optional here. It's just too important — one taste and you'll see.

WHAT SHOULD I SERVE WITH IT?
Drinks:

Before the meal, champagne, sparkling rosé champagne, or one of the Sparkling Wine Cocktails (page 284) and/or Sparkling Coolers (page 283) — especially cranberry or Mulled Cider (page 292), spiked or not

For a pleasant after-dinner touch, Milk Punch (page 291)

Appetizers:

Lacy Cheddar Crisps (page 118)

Roasted Buttery Pecans (page 115)

Fresh Goat Cheese on Flatbread with Grapes and Rosemary Oil (page 130)

First Courses and Salads:

One of the Creamy Vegetable Soups (page 155)

Quick Curried Tomato Soup (page 161)

Baby Greens, Romaine, and Iceberg Lettuce with Blue Cheese, Toasted Pecans, and Dried Cranberries (page 174)

Pear Halves with Blue Cheese and Toasted Nuts (page 166)

Sides:

Make-Ahead Mashed Potatoes (page 206) or Smashed New Potatoes (page 209)

Twice-Baked Sweet Potatoes (page 212)

Classic Bread Stuffing with Sage, Parsley, and Thyme (page 220)

Orange-Glazed Asparagus (page 196) or Broiled Asparagus (page 195)

Creamed Green Beans with Mustard Sauce and Toasted Almonds (page 200)

Roasted Onions in Their Skins (page 205)

Just-Right Cranberry Sauce with Ginger and Orange (page 222)

Desserts:

Perfectly Simple Pumpkin Cheesecake (page 274)

Apple Crostata (page 278)

HOW FAR AHEAD CAN I MAKE IT?

The turkeys can be roasted and left to rest for up to 2 hours before carving. The carved turkey can be covered with plastic wrap and set aside in a cold spot (40 degrees or below) for up to 2 hours before reheating and serving.

WHAT ABOUT LEFTOVERS?

Make (substituting turkey for chicken) Chicken Chili — Red or White (page 13), Pulled Chicken Barbecue Sandwiches (page 19) or Chicken-Mushroom Crepes (page 108).

ROSEMARY-SCENTED ROAST PORK LOIN
Stuffed with Roasted Garlic, Dried Apricots, and Cranberries with Port Wine Sauce

There's hardly a better-looking cut of meat than roast pork loin. Stuffing the loin boosts flavor, and slow-roasting it keeps it moist and juicy.

SERVES UP TO 16, WITH LEFTOVERS LIKELY

If you're serving a smaller loin rather than the whole one, which end of the loin the roast comes from matters. An average whole pork loin is about two feet long and made up of three sections: the rib end, near the shoulder; the center loin; and the loin end, close to the rump. The roast cut from the rib end has a little more fat and is therefore more flavorful.

WHEN SHOULD I SERVE IT?
For festive fall or winter dinner, such as Christmas or New Year's Eve
For large buffets

ANY SHORTCUTS?
You can skip stuffing the loin.

HOW CAN I VARY IT?
Substitute other dried fruit for the apricots.
Substitute raisins for the dried cranberries.

WHAT SHOULD I SERVE WITH IT?
Drinks:
Sparkling Wine Cocktails (page 284) or Sparkling Coolers (page 283) made with cranberry juice
Mulled Cider (page 292)

Appetizers:
Lacy Cheddar Crisps (page 118)
Roasted Buttery Pecans (page 115)
Cheddar Puffs with Scallions and Cayenne (page 131)
First Courses and Salads:
One of the Creamy Vegetable Soups (page 155)
Pear Halves with Blue Cheese and Toasted Nuts (page 166)
Sides:
Make-Ahead Mashed Potatoes (page 206)
Smashed New Potatoes (page 209) or Roasted Red Potatoes (page 210)
Twice-Baked Sweet Potatoes (page 212)
Moist, Savory Corn Muffins (page 226)

Creamed Green Beans with Mustard Sauce (page 200)
Roasted Onions in Their Skins (page 205)
Desserts:
Orange Pudding Cakes with Marmalade Drizzle (page 269)
Perfectly Simple Pumpkin Cheesecake (page 274)
Apple Crostata (page 278)

HOW FAR AHEAD CAN I MAKE IT?
You can stuff the pork a couple hours before roasting.

WHAT ABOUT LEFTOVERS?
Reheat leftover pork in one piece on defrost in the microwave.

3	tablespoons olive oil
16–18	garlic cloves, peeled, plus 2 tablespoons minced garlic
1	whole boneless pork loin (7½–8 pounds), patted dry
	Salt and freshly ground black pepper
3	tablespoons minced fresh rosemary
16–18	dried apricots
⅓	cup dried cranberries
¼	cup plus 2 tablespoons apple jelly
¼	cup port wine
½	cup chicken broth
2	teaspoons cornstarch

Adjust oven rack to upper-middle position and heat oven to 250 degrees.

Heat oil in a small (8-inch) skillet over medium-low heat. Add whole garlic cloves and cook, stirring occasionally, until soft and golden, about 5 minutes. Remove with a slotted spoon and set aside; reserve oil.

Turn pork loin fat side down. Insert point of a sharp knife ½ inch from one end and make a lengthwise incision in pork, stopping ½ inch before other end, cutting almost but not quite through, to form a long pocket.

Brush pocket with some garlic oil and sprinkle generously with salt and pepper, then sprinkle with 1 tablespoon of the rosemary. Stuff pocket with whole garlic cloves and apricots and sprinkle in cranberries. Tie loin together at 1½-inch intervals with butcher's twine.

Brush roast with remaining garlic oil and sprinkle generously with salt and pepper. Set pork loin on a large rimmed baking sheet or jelly-roll pan, placing it on a diagonal and slightly curving it to fit.

Warm ¼ cup apple jelly, minced garlic, and remaining 2 tablespoons rosemary in a small saucepan. Brush mixture all over roast.

Roast until an instant-read thermometer stuck into center registers 125 to 130 degrees; start checking after 1½ hours. Remove roast from oven and increase oven temperature to 400 degrees. Brush loin with pan drippings, return to oven, and continue to roast until golden brown and a thermometer stuck into center registers 155 to 160 degrees, about 20 minutes longer. For even more attractive coloring, turn oven to broil and cook until spotty brown, 3 to 5 minutes longer. Let roast rest for 15 to 20 minutes, then transfer to a carving board.

Stir pan juices to loosen as many browned bits as possible, then strain into a small saucepan. Stir in port, chicken broth, and remaining 2 tablespoons jelly and bring to a simmer. Mix cornstarch with 2 tablespoons cold water. Whisk into sauce and continue to simmer, whisking, until lightly thickened.

Cut pork into slices, and spoon a tablespoon or so of sauce over each serving. Serve immediately.

BEEF TENDERLOIN
with Cracked Black Pepper Coating
and Red Wine–Thyme Pan Sauce

When you want it elegant and easy, why not splurge on a beef tenderloin? It's readily available and priced right at food warehouse clubs like Costco and Sam's.

SERVES 8

To keep the tenderloin from bowing slightly during roasting, clip the silverskin, or shining surface connective tissue, with scissors, since it shrinks during cooking.

A whole tenderloin is thicker at one end than at the other. Cut two or three steaks (filets) from the thick end and save for another meal, so you have a well-proportioned roast that cooks evenly. Or cut off the thin end and slice into strips for a stir-fry.

For a summer party, serve the tenderloin cold, with the parsley salad on page 88.

1	4-pound beef tenderloin roast cut from a 6–7-pound whole beef tenderloin, prepared as directed above, tied with butcher's twine every 1^1/$_2$ inches
	Vegetable oil
	Salt
2	tablespoons coarsely ground black pepper
1	cup chicken broth
^{1}/$_4$	cup dry red wine
2	teaspoons Dijon mustard
1	teaspoon minced fresh thyme or heaping ^{1}/$_4$ teaspoon dried thyme leaves
1^1/$_2$	teaspoons cornstarch

Adjust oven rack to lower-middle position and heat oven to 425 degrees.

Heat a heavy roasting pan large enough to accommodate roast over two burners on medium-high for 5 minutes. While pan is heating, rub roast with oil to coat, and sprinkle generously with salt and pepper.

When pan is very hot, add roast and sear until well browned, about 2^1/$_2$ minutes per side, for a total of 10 minutes. Meanwhile, mix chicken broth, wine, mustard, and thyme in a bowl.

Transfer roast to a platter. Pour fat out of pan and discard (or reserve for Yorkshire puddings, page 224). Return pan to heat and add broth mixture, stirring to scrape up browned bits from bottom. Pour liquid into a small saucepan and set aside.

Set a wire rack in pan and place roast on rack. Roast until an instant-read thermometer registers 130 degrees for medium-rare, or 135 degrees for medium, 40 to 45 minutes. Remove roast from oven and let rest for 15 minutes.

WHEN SHOULD I SERVE IT?

For elegant, festive winter occasions

At a refined summer dinner or buffet

When entertaining the fifty-and-older set — beef tenderloin is both classy and classic

HOW CAN I VARY IT?

For summer entertaining, especially for buffets, skip the pan sauce. Instead, set out little bowls of prepared pesto and tapenade, Boursin cheese, and Pickled Pink Onions (page 127).

WHAT SHOULD I SERVE WITH IT?

Drinks:

To start, champagne or Sparkling Wine Cocktails (page 284)

A full-bodied red wine, such as Cabernet Sauvignon or Bordeaux

Appetizers:

Lacy Cheddar Crisps (page 118)

Potato Crisps with Smoked Salmon and Herbed Cream Cheese (page 128)

Slow-Roasted Cumin-Garlic Shrimp with Lemon-Cilantro Yogurt (page 145)

First Courses and Salads:

Pureed Wild Mushroom and Potato Soup (page 160)

Quick Curried Tomato Soup (page 161)

Baby Greens, Romaine, and Iceberg Lettuce with Blue Cheese, Toasted Pecans, and Dried Cranberries (page 174)

Smoked Salmon and Watercress Salad with Red Onion–Caper Vinaigrette (page 187)

Pear Halves with Blue Cheese and Toasted Nuts (page 166)

Crab-Stuffed Artichokes (page 150; or substitute shrimp for the crab)

Sides:

Any of the potato dishes on pages 206–12

Creamed Spinach (page 198)

Broiled or Grilled Asparagus (page 195)

Roasted Onions in Their Skins (page 205)

Slow-Roasted Plum Tomatoes with Pesto-Flavored Crumbs (page 204)

Sautéed Cherry Tomatoes with Garlic and Basil (page 202)

Bake-Ahead Yorkshire Puddings (page 224)

Desserts:

Lemon-Raspberry Triflettes (page 262)

Molten Chocolate Cakes with Sugar-Coated Raspberries (page 264)

Chocolate Tart (page 276)

HOW FAR AHEAD CAN I MAKE IT?

Unless you are serving the beef at room temperature, no more than about 30 minutes.

WHAT ABOUT LEFTOVERS?

Great in salads, sandwiches, and hash. Leftover meat can also be sliced into thick slabs, seared on both sides, and served like a steak.

Bring reserved liquid to a simmer. Mix cornstarch with 1 table-spoon cold water, whisk into sauce, and cook, whisking, until lightly thickened. Cut tenderloin into ½-inch-thick slices, spoon sauce over, and serve.

PARSLEY SALAD WITH CAPERS AND CORNICHONS

MAKES 1 GENEROUS CUP

Spoon this fresh, piquant salad over room-temperature beef tenderloin for warm-weather gatherings.

1	cup fresh parsley leaves, coarsely chopped
8	cornichons, thinly sliced, plus 2 teaspoons cornichon juice
¼	cup capers, drained
1	medium shallot or 1 scallion, thinly sliced
¾	cup olive oil
	Salt and freshly ground black pepper to taste

Mix all ingredients in a small bowl and serve.

Butter-Roasted Lobster Tails,
page 90

BUTTER-ROASTED LOBSTER TAILS

SERVES 2 AS A
MAIN COURSE, 4
AS AN APPETIZER

Unlike Maine lobster, which is usually sold whole and live, lobster tails are sold frozen. Most come from the warm waters of the Caribbean or the cool waters of South Africa, New Zealand, and Australia. If you have a choice, opt for the cool-water ones, which are slightly sweeter. If you can only find lobster tails from the warm-water regions, try to get those from Brazil and Colombia, which are of better quality than the others. Lobster tails range in size from 2 ounces to well over a pound. Avoid any that are bigger than 9 ounces —at that point, they look better than they taste.

After testing many methods, including those of well-known chefs, I've determined that slow-roasting delivers a pleasantly firm lobster tail and is the easiest, most practical cooking method. Serve the lobster tails with the shell alongside them on the plates so they look festive.

WHEN SHOULD I SERVE IT?
For a simple yet impressive dinner
Drinks:
To start, champagne
A luxurious white, such as a white Burgundy
Appetizers:
Lacy Cheddar Crisps (page 118)
Potato Crisps with Smoked Salmon and Herbed Cream Cheese (page 128)
First Courses and Salads:
Big Bowl of Garlicky Mussels or Clams (page 152)
If you're serving four people, Easy Baked Risotto (page 72)

Smoked Salmon and Watercress Salad with Red Onion–Caper Vinaigrette (page 187)
If serving the lobster tails as a first course, consider the following main courses:
Sear-Ahead Steaks or Salmon (page 66)
Easy Baked Risotto (page 72)
Roast Rack of Lamb with Vinegar-Mint Pan Sauce (page 93)
Sides:
Crisp Potato Cake (page 208) or Roasted Red Potatoes (page 210)
Broiled or Grilled Asparagus (page 195)

Sautéed Cherry Tomatoes with Garlic and Basil (page 202)
Desserts:
Instant Strawberry Ice Cream (page 248)
Turtle Fondue (page 253)

HOW FAR AHEAD CAN I MAKE IT?
The lobster tails can be pulled from their shells a day ahead and refrigerated, tightly covered.

2–4   lobster tails
1–2   tablespoons plus 2–4 tablespoons melted butter, or more if desired
      Lemon wedges
      A few fresh parsley sprigs

Adjust oven rack to middle position and heat oven to 325 degrees.

Use heavy-duty kitchen shears to cut down along both sides of soft undersides of each lobster tail to expose meat. Remove meat, snipping any hard shell—especially near top—that hinders removal. Reserve shells.

Place lobster tails on a small wire rack set over a roasting pan and brush with 1 to 2 tablespoons butter depending on the number of lobster tails. Place lobster shells in a small baking pan. Slow-roast lobster, with shells alongside, until just opaque throughout, about 30 minutes; meat should register 140 degrees on an instant-read thermometer.

Remove lobsters and shells from oven. Spray top of shells with vegetable cooking spray. Pour about 1 tablespoon warm butter (or more if you like) into each of two or four small ramekins. Cut each tail crosswise into ½-inch-thick rounds. Set a ramekin of butter on each plate and arrange sliced lobster tail alongside lobster shell. Add a couple of lemon wedges and garnish with parsley sprigs. Serve immediately.

ROAST RACK OF LAMB
WITH VINEGAR-MINT PAN SAUCE

Rack of lamb is the perfect roast for exquisite little dinners. Since it's one of the priciest cuts, I save this for a special dinner with my husband or when we're having another couple over.

SERVES 2 TO 4

There are usually eight chops on a rack, so if it's the two of us, we feast on four little chops each. If it's a dinner for four, however, each person gets only two chops, so I serve a substantial first course, a potato dish alongside, and a cheese course between dinner and dessert, usually an excellent goat cheese.

Rack of lamb is too small to brown naturally during roasting (it overcooks before it browns), so it's important to sear it first. You can sear it and make the pan sauce early. Then, about thirty minutes before you're ready to serve, pop the lamb into the oven and quickly roast it.

WHEN SHOULD I SERVE IT?

As a special dinner for two, such as Valentine's Day or a birthday

As an elegant dinner for four

HOW CAN I VARY IT?

Make Balsamic Vinegar Pan Sauce by substituting balsamic vinegar for the rice wine vinegar and omitting the jelly and mint leaves.

WHAT SHOULD I SERVE WITH IT?

Drinks:

Champagne or a sparkling rosé

Appetizers:

Lacy Cheddar Crisps (page 118)

Potato Crisps with Smoked Salmon and Herbed Cream Cheese (page 128)

First Courses and Salads:

Big Bowl of Garlicky Mussels or Clams (page 152)

Smoked Salmon and Watercress Salad with Red Onion–Caper Vinaigrette (page 187)

Crab-Stuffed Artichokes (page 150; or substitute shrimp for the crab)

Sides:

Crisp Potato Cake (page 208)

Smashed New Potatoes (page 209) or Roasted Red Potatoes (page 210)

Broiled or Grilled Asparagus (page 195)

Sautéed Cherry Tomatoes with Garlic and Basil (page 202)

Desserts:

Turtle Fondue (page 253)

For a dinner for four, Molten Chocolate Cakes with Sugar-Coated Raspberries (page 264; halve the recipe)

HOW FAR AHEAD CAN I MAKE IT?

The lamb can be seared up to 2 hours before roasting.

The pan sauce, minus the mint and butter, can be made as soon as the lamb has been seared. Pour the sauce into a Pyrex measuring cup or microwave-safe bowl, and set aside until just before serving.

¼   cup chicken broth

¼   cup rice wine vinegar

1   tablespoon mint jelly

1   8-rib rack of lamb, trimmed (about 1½ pounds)
    Salt and freshly ground black pepper

1   teaspoon sugar

2   tablespoons chopped fresh mint

1   tablespoon butter

Adjust oven rack to middle position and heat oven to 450 degrees.

Heat a 10-inch ovenproof skillet over medium heat. Meanwhile, mix broth, vinegar, and jelly in a Pyrex measuring cup or microwave-safe bowl. Lightly sprinkle lamb with salt and pepper, then sprinkle with sugar.

Increase heat under pan to high (turn on exhaust fan). After 1 to 2 minutes, add lamb to skillet, fat side down, and sear, for about 1 minute. Turn lamb over and sear meaty section of bone side. Finally, stand lamb up and sear meaty bottom, about another minute. Transfer lamb to a platter.

Drain fat from pan and set pan over medium-high heat. Add broth mixture and boil until reduced by half, about 3 minutes. Return liquid to cup or bowl.

Place a small wire rack in skillet and set lamb on rack. Place skillet in oven and roast until an instant-read thermometer inserted from one end deep into meaty portion registers about 130 degrees, 20 to 25 minutes. Let lamb rest for about 5 minutes; the internal temperature will rise 5 to 10 degrees and lamb will be medium-rare to medium.

While lamb rests, heat sauce in the microwave until very hot, about 45 seconds. Whisk in mint and butter.

Slice rack into chops and arrange on plates. Spoon over sauce and serve.

BREAKFASTS FOR COMPANY

Morning entertaining has its
advantages. Since coffee is
a whole lot cheaper than
Châteauneuf-du-Pape and a
dozen eggs are less pricey than
a rack of lamb, it's economical.
And most guests expect so
little in the morning that even
a small effort seems like
five-star B-and-B hospitality.

SEASONAL FRUIT PARFAITS

Because you can make these parfaits with whatever fruit is in season, this is a year-round brunch offering. If you're having a sit-down affair, assemble the parfaits in stemmed glasses. If it's a buffet, use ramekins or custard cups. For crowds, I've even served them in disposable 9-ounce beverage cups.

Because oatmeal holds up so well, you can make the parfaits hours in advance without their turning soggy.

SERVES 12

1½ heaping cups pecans, slivered almonds, and/or walnuts
1½ cups old-fashioned oatmeal (not quick or instant)
6 cups fruit (see page 98), plus a little more for garnish
¾ cup honey
3 cups low-fat vanilla yogurt, stirred to loosen

Adjust oven rack to middle position and heat oven to 325 degrees.

Spread nuts in a single layer on a small baking sheet. Scatter oatmeal in a single layer on another small baking sheet. Bake both until fragrant, stirring occasionally, about 10 minutes for nuts and about 15 minutes for oatmeal. Cool.

WHEN SHOULD I SERVE IT?
As part of a brunch buffet, a first course, or a dessert

ANY SHORTCUTS?
Choose fruit that requires little or no preparation — grapes or berries, for example.

HOW CAN I VARY IT?
Choose different yogurt flavors.

WHAT SHOULD I SERVE WITH IT?
My Big Fat Greek Frittata (page 100)
Easy Savory Strata (page 102)
Orange Cream Cheese Strata with Cranberries and Walnuts (page 106)

HOW FAR AHEAD CAN I MAKE IT?
The parfaits can be refrigerated for up to 4 hours.

WHAT ABOUT LEFTOVERS?
Serve any leftover parfaits the next day.

Coarsely chop nuts.

For each parfait, spoon 1 tablespoon oatmeal into a stemmed parfait glass or other dessert dish that holds at least 1 cup. Add ¼ cup fruit, sprinkle with 1 tablespoon nuts, and drizzle with 1½ teaspoons honey, then with 2 tablespoons yogurt. Repeat layering. Garnish with fruit. Cover parfaits and refrigerate for at least 30 minutes so flavors blend.

Serve.

POSSIBLE FRUITS

- 3 pints berries (strawberries, halved or quartered, depending on size; blueberries; blackberries; raspberries; or a mix)
- 12 large or 15 medium oranges, sectioned
- 2¼ pounds red or green grapes (or a mix of the two), stemmed

**My Big Fat Greek Frittata,
page 100**

MY BIG FAT GREEK FRITTATA

When you've got houseguests, a frittata is perfect for breakfast, brunch, or even a lazy lunch. Early risers eat it fresh from the oven; sleepyheads can enjoy it later at room temperature or heated in the microwave for a few seconds.

SERVES 6

12 large eggs

 4 ounces feta cheese, crumbled (1 cup)

¼ cup grated Parmesan cheese

 1 teaspoon dried oregano

    Salt and freshly ground black pepper

 3 tablespoons olive oil

 1 large garlic clove, minced

 1 package (10 ounces) frozen leaf spinach, thawed, squeezed dry, and chopped

 6 ounces ham, cut into small dice

Adjust oven rack to middle position and heat oven to 400 degrees.

WHEN SHOULD I SERVE IT?
  For houseguests
  For an impromptu breakfast or lunch
  For picnics (keep chilled)

WHAT SHOULD I SERVE WITH IT?
Drinks:
  Tomato juice is a natural (if you're not serving tomato side dishes).
Lots of good strong coffee
For brunch, serve Zippy Bloody (or virgin) Marys (page 282) or, in fall or winter, Mulled Cider (page 292), spiked or not
For lunch or a picnic, a dry French rosé

Sides:
  Roasted Red Potatoes (page 210)
  Slow-Roasted Plum Tomatoes with Pesto-Flavored Crumbs (page 204)
  Sautéed Cherry Tomatoes with Garlic and Basil (page 202)
  Grapefruit-Orange Ambrosia (page 234)

In a large bowl, whisk eggs, cheeses, oregano, and salt and pepper to taste.

Heat oil and garlic in a large (12-inch) ovenproof nonstick skillet over medium-high heat until garlic starts to sizzle and turn golden. Add spinach and cook until excess moisture evaporates, about 1 minute. Add ham, shaking skillet to distribute evenly. Add egg mixture. Cook, without stirring, until eggs start to set around edges, about 1 minute.

Transfer pan to oven and bake until frittata is puffed and set, 10 to 12 minutes. Slide or invert onto a large plate, cut into wedges, and serve.

POSSIBLE ADDITIONS

(ADD TO FRITTATA IN PLACE OF SPINACH AND HAM)

Ingredients that need to be sautéed
Sliced bell peppers (see page 127)
Chopped onions
Sliced mushrooms
Sliced zucchini
Crumbled bulk sausage

Ingredients that need to be steam-sautéed
Cubed red boiling potatoes
Cut-up asparagus
Broccoli florets

Heat oil in a large skillet over medium-high heat. Add chosen ingredients and sauté. Once vegetables have softened, add garlic, then egg mixture and cook as directed.

Spread a single layer of chosen ingredient in a large (12-inch) skillet, add ¼ to ⅓ cup water, 1 to 2 tablespoons olive oil, 1 garlic clove, minced, and a generous sprinkling of salt. Cover and steam over high heat until almost cooked. Remove lid and cook until most of water has evaporated and ingredient starts to sauté. Add egg mixture and cook as directed.

Seasonal Fruit Parfaits (page 97)
Moist, Savory Corn Muffins (page 226)
Either of the Mini Muffins (page 228)
Simple Scones (page 230)

HOW FAR AHEAD CAN I MAKE IT?

If you are serving the frittata at room temperature, turn it onto a wire rack to cool; it can stand for up to 2 hours. If serving chilled, cool on a wire rack, then cover and refrigerate for up to 1 day.

WHAT ABOUT LEFTOVERS?

Leftover frittata is fine for a few days, eaten cold or heated briefly in the microwave.

EASY SAVORY STRATA

It's easy to see why strata has become a classic brunch dish. Unlike so many of the other possibilities—scrambled eggs, waffles, pancakes, hot cereals—it can be assembled the night before (though this one doesn't have to be). Rather than racing frantically at the last minute, you calmly slip it into the oven about an hour before serving. And unlike a soufflé that immediately puffs and collapses or scrambled eggs that turn rubbery and cold in seconds, strata stands up well during a long stint on a buffet table.

I tested stratas with every style of bread, from excellent Italian to the soft, squishy variety. Cheap soft white bread works best. Unlike higher-quality breads, which remain aloof and distinct from the custard, it becomes one with it.

- 1 quart half-and-half
- 12 large eggs
- 1 teaspoon salt
  Freshly ground black pepper
- 12–14 slices fluffy white bread
- 1 pound meat or seafood and 1 pound vegetables (see page 105) or 2 pounds vegetables (optional)
- ½ cup thinly sliced scallions (about 3)
- 12 ounces extra-sharp cheddar cheese, grated (about 3 cups)

Whisk half-and-half, eggs, salt, and pepper to taste in a large bowl until smooth.

Spray a 13-by-9-inch baking dish with vegetable cooking spray. Line bottom of baking dish with 6 slices bread. If necessary, cut strips and fit them into any gaps. If using meat and/or vegetables, scatter half of each over bread, then sprinkle with half the scallions and half the cheese. Pour 1 cup egg mixture over bread. Make another layer with remaining bread, cutting strips of bread to fill any spaces as necessary. Top with remaining meat and/or vegetables, scallions, and cheese. Slowly pour remaining egg mixture over bread.

Cover strata with plastic wrap. Lightly weight strata and let stand for at least 15 minutes.

Adjust oven rack to middle position and heat oven to 325 degrees.

Bake strata until custard is just set, about 50 minutes. Leaving baking dish on oven rack, turn on broiler and broil until strata is spotty brown and puffy, about 5 minutes.

Remove from oven and let stand for 8 to 10 minutes. Cut strata into portions and serve.

WHEN SHOULD I SERVE IT?

When you're serving a crowd
For weekend houseguests

ANY SHORTCUTS?

Make the basic strata without any meat or vegetable additions. Or select additions that require minimal preparation (ham, pre-cooked bacon, kielbasa, crab, corn).

WHAT SHOULD I SERVE WITH IT?
Drinks:

Zippy Bloody (or virgin) Marys (page 282), along with some interesting juices — pear or peach nectar, for example
For a more elegant feel, a dry sparkling rosé or Sparkling Coolers (page 283).
A large pot of coffee

Salads:

Boston Lettuce and Baby Spinach Salad (page 176)
Baby Greens, Romaine, and Iceberg Lettuce with Blue Cheese, Toasted Pecans, and Dried Cranberries (page 174)
Mixed Green Salad with Fresh Herbs (page 168)
Chopped Caesar Salad (page 172)
Baby Spinach Salad with Shaved Parmesan and Garlic Vinaigrette (page 170)
Grapefruit-Orange Ambrosia (page 234)
Seasonal Fruit Parfaits (page 97)

Sides:

If making the basic strata or vegetable strata, consider serving a spiral-cut ham.
Slow-Roasted Plum Tomatoes with Pesto-Flavored Crumbs (page 204)

Moist, Savory Corn Muffins (page 226)
Either of the Mini Muffins (page 228)
Simple Scones (page 230)

HOW FAR AHEAD CAN I MAKE IT?

You can prepare the strata the night before and refrigerate it, without weighting it. Return it to room temperature before baking (or add 10 minutes to the cooking time).

WHAT ABOUT LEFTOVERS?

Leftover strata reheats well in the microwave.

POSSIBLE MEAT OR SEAFOOD ADDITIONS

CHOOSE 1 POUND OF ONE OF THE FOLLOWING:

Bacon, cut into 1/2-inch-wide pieces, fried until crisp, and removed from skillet with a slotted spoon

Bulk breakfast or Italian sausage (pork, turkey, or chicken), fried, stirring to break up lumps, until fully cooked, and removed from skillet with a slotted spoon

Ham, cut into small dice

Kielbasa, thinly sliced

Pasteurized backfin crabmeat, picked over for shells and cartilage

POSSIBLE VEGETABLE ADDITIONS

CHOOSE 1 POUND OF ONE OF THE FOLLOWING OR USE 2 POUNDS OF VEGETABLES RATHER THAN 1 POUND MEAT AND VEGETABLES:

Sliced mushrooms, sautéed in a generous tablespoon of olive oil, with a sprinkling of salt, until golden

Sliced red and/or yellow bell peppers, sautéed in a generous tablespoon of olive oil, with a sprinkling of salt, until tender

Sliced onions, sautéed in a generous tablespoon of olive oil, with a sprinkling of salt, until golden

Baby spinach, steamed with 1 tablespoon oil and a sprinkling of salt until wilted, 3 to 4 minutes, then cooked uncovered until liquid evaporates

Medium-thick asparagus, steamed with 1 tablespoon oil, a sprinkling of salt, and 1/3 cup water until just cooked, 3 to 4 minutes, then cooked uncovered until liquid evaporates and cut into 1-inch pieces

Frozen corn, thawed

ORANGE CREAM CHEESE STRATA WITH CRANBERRIES AND WALNUTS

Cream cheese, dried fruit, and nuts flavor this sweet strata. When beating the custard, don't worry about the little cream cheese lumps. Much like the shredded cheddar cheese in the savory version, they flavor the strata better that way than if they were fully incorporated. I like to sweeten the custard minimally and serve the dish with orange marmalade sauce or maple syrup.

SERVES 12 TO 15

If serving a large crowd, make both a savory and a sweet strata.

12	ounces cream cheese
1½	teaspoons finely grated orange zest
9	large eggs
3	cups half-and-half
2	tablespoons sugar
2	teaspoons vanilla extract
12–14	slices fluffy white bread
1	cup dried cranberries
½	cup chopped walnuts
1	cup orange marmalade
¼	cup orange juice

Combine cream cheese and orange zest in a medium bowl and beat with a hand mixer, adding eggs one at a time, to form a lumpy batter. Beat in half-and-half, sugar, and vanilla; batter should still be lumpy.

Spray a 13-by-9-inch baking dish with vegetable cooking spray. Line bottom of baking dish with 6 slices bread. If necessary, cut strips and fit them into any gaps. Pour 1 cup egg mixture over bread, then sprinkle with ½ cup cranberries. Make another layer with remaining bread, cutting strips to fill any spaces as necessary. Slowly pour remaining egg mixture over bread.

Cover with plastic wrap, then lightly weight strata (or lightly press on it with your hand a few times) until bread has almost completely absorbed half-and-half mixture. Let stand for 15 minutes.

Adjust oven rack to middle position and heat oven to 325 degrees.

Sprinkle strata with walnuts and remaining ½ cup cranberries, then lightly press them into bread. Bake until strata is set and puffy, 35 to 40 minutes. Remove from oven and let stand for 8 to 10 minutes.

Meanwhile, warm marmalade and orange juice in a small saucepan.

Cut strata into portions and serve with orange sauce mixture.

WHEN SHOULD I SERVE IT?
When you're serving a crowd
For weekend houseguests

HOW CAN I VARY IT?
Use different nut and dried fruit combinations:
Dried blueberries and slivered almonds; thin blueberry jam with orange juice for sauce
Raisins and pecans; serve with maple syrup

Dried cherries and slivered almonds; thin cherry jam with orange juice for sauce

WHAT SHOULD I SERVE WITH IT?
Drinks:
Lots of strong coffee
Sides:
Spiral-sliced ham
Grapefruit-Orange Ambrosia (page 234)
Seasonal Fruit Parfaits (page 97)
Any seasonal fruit or fruit salad

HOW FAR AHEAD CAN I MAKE IT?
You can prepare the strata the night before and refrigerate it overnight, without weighting it. Return it to room temperature before baking (or add 5 to 10 minutes to the cooking time).

WHAT ABOUT LEFTOVERS?
Leftover strata reheats well in the microwave.

CHICKEN-MUSHROOM CREPES

When my husband, a minister, and I moved to a new community not long ago, we decided to host an open house on two consecutive nights during the first weekend in December. By the time all the RSVPs were in, nearly 250 people had signed on.

SERVES 12

What could I serve to a crowd that size? I wanted something substantial enough to work as a meal yet light enough for those just passing through, something appealing, do-ahead, and inexpensive. Crepes were the answer. Since I needed at least 500, I bought them (see shortcuts) and made the filling myself.

Using instant flour for the batter means you don't have to let it rest to dissolve any lumps before starting to cook the crepes.

CREPES

- 1 cup whole milk
- 4 large eggs
- 1¼ cups instant (quick-mixing) flour, such as Wondra
- ½ teaspoon salt
- 3 tablespoons vegetable oil or olive oil, plus extra for brushing pan

CHICKEN-MUSHROOM FILLING

- 4 cups shredded cooked chicken
- ¼ cup olive oil
- 2 medium-large onions, halved and thinly sliced
  Salt and freshly ground black pepper
- ¾ pound medium mushrooms, thinly sliced
- 1 quart whole milk
- 2 cups chicken broth
- ½ ounce dried mushrooms, rinsed
- 4 tablespoons (½ stick) butter
- ½ cup all-purpose flour
- 1 teaspoon dried thyme leaves
- ¾ cup grated Parmesan cheese
- ½ cup minced fresh parsley

TO MAKE CREPES: Place milk and ⅔ cup water in a 1-quart Pyrex measuring cup or a medium bowl. Whisk in eggs, then flour, salt, and oil.

Heat a small (8-inch) skillet over medium heat. Dip a ¼-cup measuring cup into batter, filling it about half full, and, tilting skillet, pour batter into it, turning skillet so batter completely coats bottom. Cook until crepe bottom is spotty brown, about 30 seconds. Turn and cook until brown on the other side, 10 to 15 seconds. Transfer to a plate and repeat with remaining batter, stacking crepes (there's no need to separate them with parchment or plastic wrap).

TO MAKE FILLING: Place chicken in a large bowl; set aside. Heat 2 tablespoons oil in a large (12-inch) skillet over medium-high heat. Add onions and sauté, seasoning to taste with salt and pepper, until golden brown, 8 to 10 minutes. Add to chicken. Add remaining 2 tablespoons oil to skillet. Add mushrooms and sauté, seasoning to taste with salt and pepper, until golden brown, 8 to 10 minutes. Add to onions and chicken.

Meanwhile, combine milk, chicken broth, and dried mushrooms in a 2-quart Pyrex measuring cup or microwave-safe bowl and microwave (or slowly heat in a large saucepan) until very hot, about 10 minutes. Let stand to blend flavors, about 5 minutes.

Lift mushrooms from milk with a slotted spoon. Mince and return to milk mixture.

Melt butter in a Dutch oven or large pot over medium-high heat. Whisk in flour and thyme, then add hot milk mixture all at once and whisk until smooth. Bring to a simmer, whisking, and continue to simmer until mixture is the texture of thick cream soup. Stir in cheese.

Stir 1½ cups of sauce into chicken mixture and adjust seasonings, adding salt and pepper to taste. If not using immediately, place a sheet of plastic wrap directly over filling and remaining sauce. Refrigerate if not serving within 2 hours.

Heat oven to 325 degrees.

TO ASSEMBLE AND BAKE CREPES: Line a rimmed baking sheet with parchment paper. Working with 1 crepe at a time, spread about ¼ cup

filling across bottom half of crepe, roll into a fairly tight cylinder, and set on baking sheet.

Bake crepes, uncovered, until warm and golden, 15 to 20 minutes. Warm remaining sauce to piping hot, thinning with a little milk or water if necessary. Stir in parsley. Spoon sauce over crepes and serve.

WHEN SHOULD I SERVE IT?

For a brunch, lunch, or light dinner when do-ahead is crucial

For fork-only stand-up buffets

For shower or bridal luncheons or brunches

ANY SHORTCUTS?

Buy the crepes. They're available in many supermarket produce sections and specialty markets.

HOW CAN I VARY IT?

If you'd like a vegetarian option, make Mushroom Crepes. Double the mushrooms, sautéing each batch in 2 tablespoons olive oil, and substitute good vegetable broth for the chicken broth.

WHAT SHOULD I SERVE WITH IT?
Drinks:

Sparkling wine and red wine
Sparkling water

Appetizers:

Lacy Cheddar Crisps (page 118)
Roasted Buttery Pecans (page 115)

Sides:

For late fall, a little spoonful of Just-Right Cranberry Sauce with Ginger and Orange (page 222)

Salads:

Mixed Green Salad with Fresh Herbs (page 168)

Chopped Caesar Salad (page 172)

Baby Greens, Romaine, and Iceberg Lettuce with Blue Cheese, Toasted Pecans, and Dried Cranberries (page 174)

Boston Lettuce and Baby Spinach Salad (page 176)

Carrot Salad with Cumin Vinaigrette (page 178)

Grapefruit-Orange Ambrosia (page 234)

For a sit-down fall luncheon, Pear Halves with Blue Cheese and Toasted Nuts (page 166) as a starter course

Desserts:

Lemon-Raspberry Triflettes (page 262)

Perfectly Simple Pumpkin Cheesecake (page 274)

One of the cakes made from the recipe for Simple, Tender Yellow Cake (page 257)

Chocolate or Lemon Tart (page 276)

HOW FAR AHEAD CAN I MAKE IT?

The batter can be refrigerated, covered, overnight.

The filling can be made up to 2 days ahead and refrigerated in an airtight container.

The unfilled crepes can be double-wrapped in plastic and refrigerated overnight or frozen for up to 1 month.

The filled crepes can be double-wrapped in plastic and refrigerated for up to 2 days.

WHAT ABOUT LEFTOVERS?

Leftover filled crepes freeze well and make a wonderful quick supper. Heat them on a baking sheet in a 300-degree oven until heated through.

ALL THE REST

Mix and match

these dishes

with the main courses

in this book, or serve them

with your own favorites.

APPETIZERS AND
FIRST COURSES

ROASTED BUTTERY PECANS

If a great meal awaits your guests, there's something to be said for serving just a classic bowl of nuts with the predinner drinks. This is my favorite nut recipe. It comes from my grandmother.

MAKES ABOUT
1 QUART

1   pound (about 4 heaping cups) pecan halves

4   tablespoons (½ stick) butter, melted

½   teaspoon salt

1   tablespoon light or dark brown sugar

Adjust oven rack to middle position and heat oven to 325 degrees.

Toss pecans with melted butter and scatter in a 13-by-9-inch baking pan. Toast, stirring once or twice, until fragrant and deep golden brown, about 15 minutes.

Mix salt and sugar in a medium bowl, add hot pecans, and toss to coat evenly. Return pecans to baking pan and continue to toast to melt sugar, about 3 minutes longer. Cool slightly before serving.

WHEN SHOULD I SERVE IT?
Before just about any fall or winter dinner party or buffet, or even brunch

ANY SHORTCUTS?
Halve the recipe and use an 8-inch square pan.

HOW CAN I VARY IT?
For a little heat, add ¼ to ½ teaspoon cayenne pepper along with the salt.

HOW FAR AHEAD CAN I MAKE IT?
For ultimate freshness and flavor, roast the nuts no more than 1 to 2 days ahead.

WHAT ABOUT LEFTOVERS?
Leftover pecans can be stored in an airtight tin for at least 1 month and are perfect for spur-of-the-moment entertaining or for tossing in salads.

CURRIED POPCORN

This year, when our daughters came home from college for Christmas and I asked them what snacks to have on hand, they requested a great big tin of popcorn. Over the vacation, we watched our favorite movies and passed that tin round and round.

If you add the salt to the oil with the unpopped corn, it seasons the corn evenly, without falling to the bottom as it does when you salt popped corn.

MAKES A
HEAPING
2 QUARTS

3   tablespoons vegetable oil
1   tablespoon curry powder
1   teaspoon salt
²/₃   cup popcorn

Place all ingredients in a Dutch oven or other heavy-bottomed pot. Turn heat to medium and cook, stirring occasionally, until corn starts to sizzle. Cover and cook, shaking pot frequently at the beginning, then constantly at the end, until corn is completely popped, 4 to 5 minutes. Serve.

WHEN SHOULD I SERVE IT?
At kid-friendly parties
For casual suppers

HOW FAR AHEAD CAN I MAKE IT?
You can combine the ingredients in the pot up to 3 hours ahead, but don't pop the corn until a few minutes before guests arrive.

WHAT ABOUT LEFTOVERS?
Remember the birds and squirrels.

QUICK MARINATED OLIVES

Traditional marinated olives have to be made at least several days
ahead so the flavors meld. These are nearly instant. Heating red
pepper flakes in the olive oil and then pureeing the garlic in the oil
in the food processor delivers flavorful, marinated olives in seven
minutes, not seven days.

MAKES 2 CUPS

Generous ¼ cup extra-virgin olive oil

½ teaspoon hot red pepper flakes

1 teaspoon herbes de Provence or dried thyme leaves

3 large garlic cloves

2 cups drained kalamata or mixed olives

2 bay leaves for garnish (optional)

Heat oil and red pepper flakes in a small (8-inch) skillet over low
heat until very warm. Add herbes de Provence and remove from heat.

With food processor running, add garlic cloves and process until
minced. With motor running, slowly add oil and process until oil and garlic are well blended, at least 30 seconds. Pour over olives and serve, garnished with bay leaves, if desired.

WHEN SHOULD I SERVE IT?
At almost any dinner, casual or
formal
When you need a light, quick,
do-ahead hors d'oeuvre

HOW CAN I VARY IT?
Use different herbs: dried basil or
oregano or minced fresh rosemary.
Add orange or lemon zest to the
olives.

HOW FAR AHEAD CAN I MAKE IT?
You can make the olives 3 to 4
weeks ahead. In that case, add
whatever flavorings you like — garlic cloves, as well as a strip or two
of orange or lemon zest (removed
with a vegetable peeler), a few
sprigs of fresh thyme and rosemary,
a dozen peppercorns — directly to
the oil instead of mincing the gar-

lic in the food processor. But don't
skip heating the oil with the hot
red pepper flakes first.

WHAT ABOUT LEFTOVERS?
Leftover olives are good for
weeks — as an hors d'oeuvre or pitted and added to salads, sandwiches, pastas, and pizzas.

LACY CHEDDAR CRISPS

These lacy crisps are one of my staple hors d'oeuvres. They're simple but exceptional, with just enough substance to curb but not kill the appetite. They also can be made ahead, and they don't need to be passed. Once they've been set out, they disappear.

Because shredded cheddar cheese available in packages is less moist and oily than freshly grated, it is preferable for this recipe.

MAKES ABOUT 2 DOZEN CRISPS

1½   cups (6 ounces) packaged shredded sharp cheddar cheese

Adjust oven racks to low and middle positions and heat oven to 425 degrees. Line two baking sheets with parchment paper.

Spoon about 1 tablespoon cheese onto one sheet, then spread into a round with your fingertips so that cheese is more or less in a single layer. Repeat with remaining cheese, keeping cheese disks about 1 inch or so apart. (You should get about 12 wafers on a large sheet.)

Bake until crisps stop bubbling, 9 to 10 minutes, switching sheets after 5 minutes if they appear to be cooking unevenly. Transfer to a wire rack to cool.

WHEN SHOULD I SERVE IT?
As a light nibble before just about any dinner
In or with a first-course salad

HOW CAN I VARY IT?
Make Parmesan Crisps by substituting grated Parmesan cheese for the cheddar.

HOW FAR AHEAD CAN I MAKE IT?
For peak freshness, make the crisps no more than 2 days before serving.

WHAT ABOUT LEFTOVERS?
Stored in an airtight tin, the crisps will keep for at least 1 month.

PERFECT DEVILED EGGS

Stuffed eggs are much more attractive when the filling has been piped rather than spooned into them. I make a smooth filling and then garnish the eggs with the finely chopped pickle, herbs, or other ingredients rather than mixing them into the filling, which would clog up the pastry bag.

When boiling a large quantity of eggs, always cook them in a single layer. That way the water heats rapidly and the eggs cook more quickly and evenly.

MAKES 2 DOZEN HORS D'OEUVRES

12 large eggs

6 tablespoons mayonnaise

1 tablespoon Dijon mustard

1 tablespoon sweet pickle relish juice

Salt and freshly ground black pepper

1 tablespoon sweet pickle relish

WHEN SHOULD I SERVE IT?

When you need an hors d'oeuvre with on-hand ingredients

When you need an hors d'oeuvre with broad appeal

When you need a completely do-ahead hors d'oeuvre

For a summer picnic or outdoor party, chilled

HOW CAN I VARY IT?

Use different garnishes: thinly sliced small sweet or dill pickles, diced roasted peppers, olives, a portion of a whole flat-leaf parsley leaf or other minced fresh herbs, snipped chives or sliced scallion greens, minced radishes, diced tomatoes.

When you're feeling extravagant, top them with caviar or salmon roe.

WHAT SHOULD I SERVE WITH IT?

Serve as a starter before:

Buttermilk-Honey Fried Chicken Fingers (page 29)

Oven-Barbecued Pork (page 17)

Grilled Chicken Breasts with Orange-Thyme Glaze (page 64)

Beef Tenderloin with Cracked Black Pepper Coating and Red Wine–Thyme Pan Sauce (page 86)

HOW FAR AHEAD CAN I MAKE IT?

The unfilled eggs and the sandwich bag of filling can be refrigerated overnight.

WHAT ABOUT LEFTOVERS?

They're good for a couple of days.

Place eggs in a single layer in a large saucepan and cover with water. Cover pan and bring to a full boil over medium-high heat. Turn off heat and let eggs stand, covered, for 10 minutes. Drain and run under cold running water until saucepan is cold. Let eggs stand in cold water until cool.

Peel eggs, halve them crosswise, and remove yolks, transferring yolks to a food processor. So that eggs sit level, slice a tiny piece of egg white from each bottom. Arrange eggs on a serving platter.

Process egg yolks until smooth. Add mayonnaise, mustard, pickle juice, and salt and pepper to taste and process again until smooth. Transfer mixture to a small zipper-lock bag. If desired, refrigerate filling and eggs to chill.

Snip ¼ inch off a bottom corner of bag of filling. Pipe filling into each egg half. Garnish each with a tiny pinch of pickle relish and serve.

PICKLED PINK DEVILED EGGS

Omit the mayonnaise, mustard, juice, and pickle relish. For filling: process egg yolks as above until smooth. Add ¼ cup pickled beet juice, 2 tablespoons extra-virgin olive oil, 2 teaspoons rice wine vinegar, ¼ teaspoon salt, and freshly ground black pepper to taste. Process again until smooth. Transfer mixture to a small zipper-lock bag, and proceed as directed above.

For a quick garnish and added flavor, poke a strip of sliced beet into each deviled egg, then place a small sprig of flat-leaf parsley on top.

SPREADS, CRISPY BREADS, AND CHIPS

OLIVE SPREAD WITH LEMON AND THYME

MAKES ABOUT 1 CUP

Serve with Golden Toast Rounds or Fried Corn Tortilla Triangles.

  2   medium garlic cloves
¹⁄₄   cup fresh parsley leaves
¹⁄₂   teaspoon dried thyme leaves
¹⁄₄   teaspoon finely grated lemon zest
  2   teaspoons fresh lemon juice
  2   tablespoons extra-virgin olive oil
1¹⁄₄ cups pimiento-stuffed olives (from a
        10-ounce jar), drained

Process garlic, parsley, thyme, and zest in a food processor until finely minced. Add lemon juice, olive oil, and olives and pulse until olives are evenly chopped but not a paste. Transfer to a serving bowl or a storage container.

OREGANO-FLAVORED FETA SPREAD

MAKES ABOUT 1 CUP

Serve with Golden Toast Rounds or Baked Pita Triangles.

1¹⁄₄ cups crumbled feta cheese (about
        5 ounces)
  4   ounces cream cheese
  1   teaspoon dried oregano
        Freshly ground black pepper

Place 1 cup feta in a food processor and process until fine-textured. Add cream cheese, oregano, and pepper to taste and process until smooth. Scrape into a bowl and stir in remaining feta cheese. Transfer to a serving bowl or a storage container.

WHEN SHOULD I SERVE THEM?
When you want carefree hors d'oeuvres that can be made ahead
For all seasons

HOW FAR AHEAD CAN I MAKE THEM?
All of the spreads can be stored in airtight plastic containers in the refrigerator for 1 week.

SUN-DRIED TOMATO SPREAD WITH FRESH BASIL

MAKES A GENEROUS 1 CUP

Serve with Golden Toast Rounds or Baked Pita Triangles.

½ cup oil-packed sun-dried tomatoes
¼ cup packed fresh basil leaves
1 package (8 ounces) cream cheese

Place sun-dried tomatoes in a food processor and pulse until coarsely chopped. Add basil and pulse until finely chopped. Add cream cheese and process until well mixed. Transfer to a serving bowl or a storage container.

WHITE BEAN SPREAD WITH GARLIC AND ROSEMARY

MAKES A GENEROUS 1 CUP

Serve with any of the crisp breads or chips.

2 tablespoons olive oil, plus extra for drizzling
2 medium garlic cloves
2 teaspoons minced fresh rosemary
1 can (16 ounces) white beans, undrained

Place olive oil, garlic, and rosemary in a 10-inch skillet and heat over medium heat until ingredients start to sizzle. Add beans and their liquid and cook, mashing with a wooden spoon or potato masher, until mixture thickens slightly (it will thicken more as it cools). Transfer to a serving bowl or a storage container.

HUMMUS

MAKES ABOUT 3 CUPS

You'll find tahini in the grocery store's international section. Store leftover tahini in the pantry. If the paste and oil separate, as they usually do, dump into a bowl and whisk until smooth before using.

4 garlic cloves
½ cup extra-virgin olive oil, plus extra for drizzling
2 cans (16 ounces each) chickpeas, drained and rinsed
¼ cup tahini (sesame seed paste)
½ cup fresh lemon juice (from 2–3 lemons), or more to taste
  Salt
  Paprika

With a food processor running, add garlic cloves and mince (or use a blender). Scrape down sides of bowl. With motor running, add oil and process for about 30 seconds. Add chickpeas, tahini, lemon juice, and a generous sprinkling of salt and continue to process until mixture is completely pureed. Adjust seasonings, adding salt and/or lemon juice to taste. Transfer to a serving bowl or a storage container.

To serve hummus, sprinkle with paprika and drizzle with a little olive oil.

FRIED CORN TORTILLA TRIANGLES

MAKES 32 TRIANGLES

You can buy tortilla chips, but with just a little effort you'll get better-flavored and crisper chips by frying them yourself. If there's no time to make fresh salsa, serve these with the jarred kind, which you can improve with a few squirts of fresh lime juice and a little chopped fresh cilantro. I also sometimes fry whole corn tortillas and let everyone break off pieces.

2 cups canola oil or other vegetable oil
8 6-inch corn tortillas, quartered
Salt

Heat oil in a medium-large skillet over medium-high heat to 370 degrees. Drop tortilla triangles into hot oil, 8 at a time, and fry, turning chips once or twice, until they stop sizzling and turn golden brown, about 2 minutes. Remove with tongs or slotted spoon, transfer to a large wire rack set over a baking sheet, and immediately sprinkle with salt.

The tortilla chips can be cooled and stored in an airtight container for up to 2 days.

FRIED WONTON RECTANGLES

MAKES 32 RECTANGLES

These are like the ones served in Chinese restaurants with duck sauce—but better.

2 cups canola oil or vegetable oil
16 wonton wrappers, halved (to make rectangles)

Heat oil in a medium-large skillet over medium heat to 350 degrees. Drop won-

ton rectangles in hot oil, 6 at a time, and fry, turning once or twice, until golden brown, 45 seconds to a minute. Remove with tongs or slotted spoon and transfer to a large wire rack set over a baking sheet to drain.

The cooled wontons can be stored in an airtight container for up to 2 days.

GOLDEN TOAST ROUNDS

MAKES 4 DOZEN ROUNDS

1 long, thin baguette, sliced a generous ¼ inch thick

Adjust oven rack to upper-middle position and heat oven to 425 degrees.

Lay bread on a large wire rack. Put rack on oven rack and bake until golden and crisp, 4 to 5 minutes.

The cooled toasts can be stored in an airtight container for up to 2 weeks.

BAKED PITA TRIANGLES

MAKES 4 DOZEN TRIANGLES

6 pita breads, split and quartered

Remove oven rack and heat oven to 325 degrees. Place pitas directly on rack and return rack to oven in upper-middle position. Bake until golden brown and completely crisp, about 10 minutes.

The cooled pitas can be stored in an airtight container for up to 2 weeks.

CREATING AN APPETIZER BAR

An appetizer bar invites guests to create their own hors d'oeuvres, proving that you can please all of the people all of the time. It's colorful, lively, and interactive. Not only is an appetizer bar a relatively inexpensive way to entertain, it's easy to assemble. The best part? You get credit for an innovative party while your guests do half the work.

Much of the menu is really about presentation. I normally serve the dips in stemmed goblets in the center of a table, so they are easy to reach. I place the breads in baskets lined with cloth napkins at the corners of the table and the toppings in small bowls along the sides.

WHEN SHOULD I SERVE IT?
For an open house
When you want to make a splash
When you're entertaining a diverse group — there's freedom of choice
When entertaining young people
When your guests don't know one another — the bar draws them in and gets them talking
As a prelude to a large buffet

ANY SHORTCUTS?
Buy rather than make the tortilla chips, pita chips, and toast rounds. Also consider fine crackers, bagel chips, and sturdy flatbreads.
Buy spreads instead of making them.

Stick with toppings that need little or no preparation, such as the parsleyed artichoke quarters, cooked shrimp, sliced pepperoni (rather than Italian sausage), and shaved Parmesan.
Limit the number of spreads and toppings.

HOW CAN I VARY IT?
Substitute any topping, spread, or bread that appeals to you.

WHAT SHOULD I SERVE WITH IT?
Red and white wine

HOW FAR AHEAD CAN I MAKE IT?
All of the breads can be made up to 5 days before the party and stored in airtight tins.
All of the spreads can be made up to 5 days ahead and refrigerated in airtight containers.
All of the toppings except the pickled onions can be prepared 1 day ahead and brought back to room temperature to serve.

WHAT ABOUT LEFTOVERS?
Many of the toppings can be used in omelets and salads during the week. The spreads and breads can be pulled out for impromptu entertaining.

BREADS AND CHIPS

Fried Corn Tortilla Triangles (page 123)

Fried Wonton Rectangles (page 124)

Golden Toast Rounds (page 124)

Baked Pita Triangles (page 124)

THE SPREADS

Olive Spread with Lemon and Thyme (page 122)

Oregano-Flavored Feta Spread (page 122)

Sun-Dried Tomato Spread with Fresh Basil (page 123)

White Bean Spread with Garlic and Rosemary (page 123)

THE TOPPINGS

Pickled pink onions:

Drizzle ¼ cup rice wine vinegar over a thinly sliced medium red onion. Season with a pinch of salt. Let stand until ready to serve.

Pulled chicken:

Remove the meat from a roast chicken, homemade (page 38) or store-bought, discarding the skin and bones, and pull or shred the meat into bite-size pieces.

Cooked shrimp:

Remove the tails from 1 pound peeled cooked shrimp. Use a small sharp knife to split the shrimp in half down the back.

Cooked sausage:

Cook links of Italian sausage and cut into thin rounds.

Chopped egg with scallion greens:

Mix 2 finely chopped hard-boiled eggs with the thinly sliced green parts of 2 medium scallions. Stir in 1 tablespoon extra-virgin olive oil and dseason to taste with salt and pepper.

Sautéed yellow and red peppers:

Heat 1 tablespoon olive oil in a 10-inch skillet over medium-high heat. When the oil starts to shimmer, add 1 each yellow and red bell pepper, cored, seeded, and thinly sliced. Sauté, stirring occasionally, until the peppers are soft and lightly browned, about 5 minutes.

(Or substitute roasted peppers, cut into thin strips, for the sautéed ones.)

Wilted spinach:

Heat 1 tablespoon olive oil and a large garlic clove, minced, in a large (12-inch) skillet over medium-high heat until the garlic starts to sizzle. Add 1 bag (9–10 ounces) prewashed spinach and cook until just wilted but still green. Transfer to a large plate and let cool, then transfer to a small serving bowl.

Shaved Parmesan:

Use a potato peeler to shave thin bite-size pieces of cheese from a wedge of Parmesan cheese.

Parsleyed artichoke quarters:

Drain a 14-ounce can of artichoke hearts, pat dry, and quarter (or cut into sixths). Season with 1 tablespoon each minced fresh parsley and extra-virgin olive oil.

POTATO CRISPS WITH SMOKED SALMON AND HERBED CREAM CHEESE

For this recipe I recommend using Terra Chips, which are available nationally. Classic thin chips are often too large or broken. Kettle chips taste great, but you have to pick through to find whole ones.

MAKES ABOUT
3 DOZEN CRISPS

¼   cup packed fresh parsley, plus extra for garnish

3   ounces cream cheese

½   teaspoon finely grated lemon zest

1   teaspoon fresh lemon juice

    Salt and freshly ground black pepper

36 whole bite-size potato chips

3–4 ounces thinly sliced smoked salmon, sliced or pulled into bite-size pieces

Process parsley in a food processor until coarsely chopped. Add cream cheese, lemon zest, juice, a pinch of salt, and a few grinds of pepper. Process until pale green and smooth. Scrape cream cheese into a small zipper-lock bag. Squeeze it down to one bottom corner, and snip ¼ inch off corner.

Top each chip with 1 or 2 pieces salmon, pipe on a dollop of cream cheese, and garnish with a small parsley leaf. Serve.

WHEN SHOULD I SERVE IT?
For festive gatherings — brunch, lunch, or dinner
Any season

ANY SHORTCUTS?
Buy flavored cream cheese. Microwave for a few seconds until it's soft enough to pipe.

HOW CAN I VARY IT?
Top the potato chips with a piece of smoked trout garnished with a little horseradish-flavored sour cream, or rare roast beef topped with Parsley Salad with Capers and Cornichons (page 88)

WHAT SHOULD I SERVE WITH IT?
Serve as a starter before:
Butter-Roasted Lobster Tails (page 90)
Sear-Ahead Steaks or Salmon (page 66)

Beef Tenderloin with Cracked Black Pepper Coating and Red Wine–Thyme Pan Sauce (page 86)
Roast Rack of Lamb with Vinegar-Mint Pan Sauce (page 93)

HOW FAR AHEAD CAN I MAKE IT?
The chips can be assembled about 30 minutes before the party starts.

FRESH GOAT CHEESE ON FLATBREAD WITH GRAPES AND ROSEMARY OIL

MAKES ABOUT
2 DOZEN HORS
D'OEUVRES

With just a little effort, it's possible to make something much more interesting and irresistible than cheese, crackers, and a bunch of grapes. Don't skip the rosemary drizzle. It's a few minutes' effort, but the results will raise eyebrows.

Flatbreads come in all shapes, sizes, and thicknesses. Avoid highly seasoned ones like onion and garlic. You can use any variety, such as lavash or crispini, or any flat, crisp large crackers.

2	teaspoons minced fresh rosemary
3	tablespoons extra-virgin olive oil
	Salt and freshly ground black pepper
10	ounces mild goat cheese
6	ounces flatbread
24	red grapes, halved lengthwise

Mix rosemary and oil with salt and pepper to taste in a small bowl. Cut 24 thin slices of goat cheese with a small knife, dipping it in warm water and wiping dry between each cut.

Break flatbread into 2- to 3-inch irregular pieces and place on a large serving platter. Top each with a goat cheese disk and 2 grape halves. Drizzle with oil, and serve.

WHEN SHOULD I SERVE IT?
For all occasions and all seasons

HOW CAN I VARY IT?
Sprinkle with toasted chopped nuts — pistachios, walnuts, or pecans.
Substitute olives, strips of roasted pepper or sun-dried tomatoes, or fig quarters for the grapes.

WHAT SHOULD I SERVE WITH IT?
Serve as a starter before:
Rosemary-Scented Rost Pork Loin Stuffed with Roasted Garlic, Dried Apricots, and Cranberries with Port Wine Sauce (page 83)
Really Good Lasagna (page 35)

Boneless Coq au Vin (page 42)
Simple Cassoulet (page 44)

HOW FAR AHEAD CAN I MAKE IT?
These can be assembled 2 to 3 hours before serving.

CHEDDAR PUFFS WITH SCALLIONS AND CAYENNE

These savory miniature cream puffs are perfect for one or two dozen guests. (The recipe can be halved for a smaller crowd.) I especially like them because they can be baked ahead and reheated just before serving.

MAKES 40 TO 48 PUFFS

The lighter the batter, the airier the puff, which is why this recipe calls for beating a few extra whites into the eggs. Sharp cheddar cheese and scallions give these puffs enough zing to make guests reach for another.

WHEN SHOULD I SERVE IT?

For buffet parties of a dozen or more

When you need a do-ahead hot hors d'oeuvre

When there are kids in the mix — all but the pickiest will like them

With a traditional or French-style dinner

ANY SHORTCUTS?

Invest in a spring-action ice cream scoop with a 1-tablespoon capacity for dispensing the dough.

For easy cleanup, use parchment paper or Silpat sheets to line the baking pans.

WHAT SHOULD I SERVE WITH IT?
Serve as a starter before:

Boneless Coq au Vin (page 42)

Simple Cassoulet (page 44)

One of the stews (pages 48–53)

Rosemary-Scented Roast Pork Loin Stuffed with Roasted Garlic, Dried Apricots, and Cranberries with Port Wine Sauce (page 83)

Beef Tenderloin with Cracked Black Pepper Coating and Red Wine–Thyme Pan Sauce (page 86)

HOW FAR AHEAD CAN I MAKE IT?

The puffs can be made up to 8 hours ahead. Recrisp in a 300-degree oven for about 10 minutes before serving.

WHAT ABOUT LEFTOVERS?

Although they do start to dry out, leftover puffs are still good reheated in the oven a second time.

8   tablespoons (1 stick) butter
    Big pinch of salt
¼   teaspoon cayenne pepper
1   cup all-purpose flour
2   large eggs
4   large egg whites
1   cup grated extra-sharp cheddar cheese
½   cup thinly sliced scallion greens

Adjust oven racks to lower and upper-middle positions and heat oven to 400 degrees. Line two baking sheets with parchment paper or grease the sheets.

Bring butter, 1 cup water, salt, and cayenne to a simmer in a medium saucepan. When butter has melted, remove from heat. Add flour all at once and beat with a wooden spoon over low heat to form a thick dough. Transfer to a medium bowl. Beat in eggs one at a time, then beat in whites in 2 additions, making sure the first is incorporated before adding the second.

Cool dough to tepid, then stir in cheese and scallions.

Spoon dough in 1-tablespoon portions onto baking sheets, spacing them about 1 inch apart. Bake until crisp and golden, 25 to 30 minutes. Serve warm.

VEGETABLE EGG ROLLS
WITH LIME-GINGER DIPPING SAUCE

Homemade egg rolls may sound like more trouble than they're worth, but these offer the full flavor of a good, complex egg roll with a mere four-ingredient filling. Using coleslaw mix means you don't have to shred the cabbage and carrots. The peanut butter serves not only to flavor the rolls but also to bind the vegetables. With the potent dipping sauce, the rolls do not need to be highly seasoned.

Frying the egg rolls a first time enables you to complete most of the preparation a couple of days ahead.

MAKES 16 EGG ROLLS (32 HORS D'OEUVRES)

EGG ROLLS

1	tablespoon vegetable oil
1	package (16 ounces) coleslaw mix
	Salt
½	cup sliced scallions
2	tablespoons smooth peanut butter
16	egg roll wrappers
2	cups vegetable oil for frying
2	tablespoons minced fresh cilantro for garnish

LIME-GINGER DIPPING SAUCE

2	tablespoons fresh lime juice
2	tablespoons Asian fish sauce
½	teaspoon ground ginger
½	teaspoon hot red pepper flakes
1	tablespoon sugar

TO MAKE EGG ROLLS: Heat 1 tablespoon oil in a large (12-inch) skillet until it starts to shimmer and wisps of smoke are just visible. Add coleslaw mix and sauté, seasoning lightly with salt, until just wilted, 1 to 2 minutes. Pour mixture into a medium bowl. Stir in scallions and peanut butter until evenly distributed.

Place an egg roll wrapper on a work surface. Place 2 tablespoons filling just below center, forming it into a log. Fold both sides of wrapper over filling, then fold bottom of wrapper over filling and roll it up as tightly as you can. Moisten wrapper end with wet fingertips and press it against roll to seal. Repeat with remaining wrappers and filling.

If not serving immediately, heat oil in a Dutch oven or small pot to 300 degrees. Cook egg rolls 6 at a time, turning once, until crisp but still blond, about 2 minutes. Drain on paper towels, cool, and store in a zipper-lock bag. Reserve oil.

TO MAKE SAUCE: Up to 2 hours before serving, mix ingredients with 1 tablespoon water. Transfer to a small serving bowl.

TO FINISH EGG ROLLS: Twenty minutes before serving, heat oven to 200 degrees. Heat oil in a Dutch oven or small pot to 375 degrees.

Cook egg rolls 6 at a time, turning once, until crisp and golden brown, about 2 minutes if rolls have already been fried once, or about 5 minutes if not. Drain on a rack set over a baking sheet and keep fried egg rolls warm in oven while you cook remaining batches (or until ready to serve).

Halve each roll on the diagonal and dip each cut end in cilantro. Stand cut side up on a serving tray and serve with dipping sauce.

WHEN SHOULD I SERVE IT?
Whenever kids are involved
As an hors d'oeuvre at a casual buffet
Before an Asian-themed dinner
At a cocktail party

HOW CAN I VARY IT?
Fill the egg rolls with plain lump crabmeat.
Or fill with shredded roast chicken mixed with sliced scallions, water chestnuts, and peanut butter.

WHAT SHOULD I SERVE WITH IT?
Serve as a starter before:
Stew with Indian Flavorings (page 52)

HOW FAR AHEAD CAN I MAKE IT?
The egg rolls can be fried once, cooled, and stored in a zipper-lock bag in the refrigerator for up to 3 days before serving. Then fry them again just before friends arrive. The cooked egg rolls can also be held for up to 20 minutes in a 200-degree oven.

WHAT ABOUT LEFTOVERS?
Warmed in a 300-degree oven, they're fine for a family supper.

PASTRY TRIANGLES
WITH SPINACH AND FETA

MAKES
30 PASTRIES

These pastries are made with the classic filling of Greek spanakopita—spinach, feta cheese, and garlic—but I use frozen puff pastry rather than the traditional phyllo dough because it's much easier to work with.

Once removed from the packaging, the puff pastry sheets thaw in about 15 minutes. In a pinch, you can even help them along in the microwave.

1   tablespoon olive oil
1   large garlic clove, minced
1   package (10 ounces) frozen chopped spinach, thawed and squeezed dry
1   tablespoon minced fresh dill
1   large scallion, thinly sliced
3/4 cup crumbled feta cheese
    Salt and freshly ground black pepper
1   box (17.3 ounces) frozen Pepperidge Farm Puff Pastry, thawed
30 small fresh dill sprigs for garnish (optional)

Heat oil and garlic in a small (8-inch) skillet. When garlic starts to sizzle and turn golden, remove pan from heat. Stir spinach, dill, scallion, cheese, and salt and pepper to taste in a medium bowl. Stir in garlic mixture.

Adjust oven rack to upper and lower-middle positions and heat oven to 400 degrees.

Unfold 1 pastry sheet on a lightly floured work surface. Rolling with, not across, fold lines, roll sheet to approximately 9 by 15 inches. Trim edges if necessary. Using fold lines as guides, cut pastry lengthwise into thirds, then cut each strip crosswise into fifths to make fifteen 3-inch squares.

Place a scant tablespoon of filling on each pastry square. Use a wet fingertip to moisten two sides of the square, then fold pastry over filling to form a triangle and pinch lightly to seal. (Don't worry if seal is not tight—pastry will bind together during baking.) Place on a large baking sheet. If desired, moisten each pastry top with your fingertips, and gently press on a dill sprig. Repeat with remaining pastry and filling, placing triangles on a second baking sheet.

Bake pastries until golden brown, 18 to 20 minutes, switching positions of sheets at halfway point and turning them from back to front to ensure even baking. Serve.

MUSHROOM–GOAT CHEESE FILLING

½	ounce dried mushrooms
2	large garlic cloves
½	pound white or portobello mushrooms, coarsely chopped
½	teaspoon dried thyme leaves
1	teaspoon olive oil
3	ounces mild goat cheese
	Salt and freshly ground black pepper

Pour ½ cup boiling water over dried mushrooms in a small bowl and let soak until softened, about 5 minutes. Lift mushrooms from water and squeeze dry.

With processor running, add garlic cloves and process to mince. Add soaked mushrooms and process to mince. Add white mushrooms and thyme and process until mushrooms are finely chopped.

Heat olive oil in a 10-inch skillet over medium-high heat. Add mushroom mixture and sauté until nearly all moisture has evaporated, 5 to 7 minutes. Remove from heat and stir in goat cheese until blended. Season with salt and pepper to taste.

WHEN SHOULD I SERVE IT?
Whenever you need a do-ahead hors d'oeuvre
At an open house
As a brunch hors d'oeuvre

ANY SHORTCUTS?
Microwave each pastry sheet on high power to thaw. Check it at 10 seconds. If it's not quite thawed, give it a few seconds more. Since the pastry thaws so quickly, it's better to stop when it's still a little firm.

HOW CAN I VARY IT?
Use Mushroom–Goat Cheese Filling instead of the spinach one.

You can also take the pastry triangles in a sweet direction, filling them with small chunks of bittersweet chocolate or a tablespoonful of your favorite jam or preserves.

WHAT SHOULD I SERVE WITH IT?
Serve as a starter before:
One of the stews (page 48)
Butterflied Cornish Hens with Apricot-Pistachio Dressing (page 76)
Sear-Ahead Steaks or Salmon (page 66)
Beef Tenderloin with Cracked Black Pepper Coating and Red Wine–Thyme Pan Sauce (page 86)

Roast Rack of Lamb with Vinegar-Mint Pan Sauce (page 93)

HOW FAR AHEAD CAN I MAKE IT?
The unbaked triangles can be loosely covered with plastic wrap and refrigerated for up to 4 hours or double-wrapped in plastic wrap and frozen for up to 1 month.

WHAT ABOUT LEFTOVERS?
These reheat beautifully. Enjoy for lunch the next day with a big green salad. Warm them in a 350-degree oven until crisp and warm, about 10 minutes.
Or freeze any extra stuffed pastry triangles for up to 1 month.

QUESADILLAS FOR A CROWD

Quesadillas are easy to make, but the traditional method of heating the filled tortillas one at a time in a skillet is tedious, and they tend to dry out if held in a warm oven. With this technique, you can turn your oven into a giant skillet and produce deliciously crisp tortillas for a group.

SERVES 12

4   10-inch (or six 8-inch or ten 6-inch) flour tortillas
     Oil for brushing tortillas
     Filling of choice (recipes follow)

Adjust oven rack to lowest position and heat oven to 500 degrees.

Lightly brush tortillas with oil and place oiled side down on a foil-lined 18-by-12-inch rimmed baking sheet or jelly-roll pan. Sprinkle cheese from filling of choice (or spread cream cheese) over half of each tortilla, leaving a ½-inch border.

Top each tortilla half with remaining filling ingredients, placing them on tortillas in order listed.

Fold tortillas over filling. Place another baking sheet of similar size over quesadillas to weight them. Bake until bottoms are golden

WHEN SHOULD I SERVE IT?
   Before a southwestern or Mexican-style entrée
   With soup or salad as part of a quick lunch
   At a gathering of both kids and adults

ANY SHORTCUTS?
   Remember that quesadilla fillings can be as simple as grated cheese.

WHAT SHOULD I SERVE WITH IT?
Serve as a starter before:
   Chicken Chili—Red or White (page 13)
   Carnitas (page 20)
   Chicken Soup with Southwestern Flavors (page 9)

HOW FAR AHEAD CAN I MAKE IT?
   The fillings can be prepared several hours ahead and refrigerated. The quesadillas must be baked right before serving.

brown, 6 to 8 minutes (larger ones will need a few extra minutes). Turn quesadillas over and continue to bake, uncovered, until golden brown on second side, about 3 minutes longer.

Transfer to a cutting board, and let cool slightly, about 1 minute. Cut into wedges and serve.

QUESADILLAS WITH GOAT CHEESE, OLIVES, AND RED ONION

- 4 ounces mild goat cheese
- ½ cup pitted kalamata olives, coarsely chopped
- ½ medium red onion, thinly sliced
  Dried thyme leaves for sprinkling

QUESADILLAS WITH SHRIMP, FETA, AND SCALLIONS

- 4 ounces feta cheese, crumbled (about 1 cup)
- ½ pound peeled cooked shrimp, split lengthwise and patted dry
- 4 scallions, thinly sliced
  Dried oregano for sprinkling

QUESADILLAS WITH CRAB, SCALLIONS, AND CREAM CHEESE

- 6 ounces regular or light cream cheese, flavored with ¼ teaspoon finely grated lemon zest, ¼ teaspoon Old Bay or other Maryland-style seasoning, and ¼ teaspoon Tabasco sauce
- 1 cup pasteurized crabmeat, picked over for shells and cartilage
- 4 scallions, thinly sliced

QUESADILLAS WITH ZUCCHINI, GREEN CHILES, AND STRING CHEESE

Serve these with ½ cup sour cream mixed with a couple of teaspoons of fresh lime juice and salt to taste.

- 4 ounces string cheese (or mozzarella), pulled into shreds
- 1 large zucchini (about 8 ounces), cut into ¼-inch-thick rounds, tossed with oil and salt and pepper, and broiled until spotty brown on both sides, about 8 minutes total
- 1 can (4.5 ounces) chopped green chiles, drained

QUESADILLAS WITH BACON AND CHIVE-ONION CREAM CHEESE

Serve these with some chopped fresh tomatoes that have been sprinkled with salt. Feel free to substitute other flavored cream cheeses.

- ¾ cup chive-and-onion-flavored cream cheese (light or regular)
- 8 slices bacon, cooked until crisp, drained, and crumbled

QUESADILLAS WITH SPICY CHEESE AND SCALLIONS

- 4 ounces of packaged shredded Mexican- or taco-flavored cheese
- 4 scallions, thinly sliced

SPICY ASIAN LETTUCE CUPS

These cool, crisp lettuce cups filled with warm, spicy filling are terrific—especially for those who are watching their carbohydrate intake.

MAKES 2 DOZEN CUPS

2   tablespoons vegetable oil

1   medium onion, cut into medium dice

2   garlic cloves, minced

1   can (8 ounces) sliced water chestnuts, drained, rinsed, and chopped medium-fine

1   pound ground turkey, beef, or pork

¼   cup soy sauce

¼   cup ketchup

4   teaspoons rice wine vinegar

4   teaspoons Asian sesame oil

2   teaspoons hot red pepper flakes

2   tablespoons light or dark brown sugar

1   head iceberg lettuce, core removed, leaves separated and torn into approximately 4-inch cups

¼   cup sliced scallions

¼   cup chopped peanuts

WHEN SHOULD I SERVE IT?
At a casual cocktail party or open house
Before an Asian-themed dinner

As a make-ahead hot hors d'oeuvre that doesn't require an oven

HOW FAR AHEAD CAN I MAKE IT?
The filling can be refrigerated in a sealed container for up to 3 days.
The lettuce cups can be prepared up to 1 day ahead and refrigerated in a sealed plastic bag.

Heat oil in a large (12-inch) skillet over medium-high heat. Add onion, garlic, and water chestnuts and sauté until onion softens, 3 to 4 minutes. Add turkey and cook, stirring frequently, until meat loses its raw color and liquid has mostly evaporated, about 5 minutes.

Meanwhile, mix soy sauce, ketchup, vinegar, oil, pepper flakes, and sugar in a small bowl. Add to pan and continue to cook until mixture has thickened to the consistency of thick sloppy joes. Remove from heat.

When ready to serve, reheat turkey mixture if necessary. Lay out lettuce cups on a serving tray. Fill each with 2 tablespoons filling, garnish with scallions and peanuts, and serve.

ANY SHORTCUTS?

Let your guests assemble their own cups, serving a big bowl of lettuce and another big bowl of the filling at the table.

WHAT ABOUT LEFTOVERS?

Any extra filling can be stored in a sealed container for 3 to 4 days and used in sandwiches, salads, or fresh lettuce cups.

COCONUT SHRIMP WITH
SWEET-AND-SOUR ORANGE SAUCE

Bristling with golden, sweet flakes of coconut, these fried shrimp are always a big hit.

MAKES ABOUT
3 DOZEN HORS
D'OEUVRES

Be sure to choose large shrimp (no more than 21 to 25 per pound), or you'll have too much coating. Let the excess batter drip off before dropping the shrimp into the bowl of coconut. If you hold each shrimp by the tail when dragging it through the flour and dipping it in the batter, the process isn't very messy.

Since the batter provides no flavor to the dish but simply serves to glue the coconut onto the shrimp, a store-bought mix is best.

SHRIMP

- 1 cup all-purpose flour
- 1 cup pancake mix, such as Aunt Jemima
- ½ teaspoon salt
- 1 package (14 ounces) sweetened shredded coconut
- 1½ pounds extra-large shrimp (21–25 count), preferably a white or pink variety, peeled but tails left intact
- 6 cups peanut oil or vegetable oil for deep-frying

SAUCE

- ½ cup orange marmalade
- 2 tablespoons Dijon mustard
- 2 tablespoons rice wine vinegar

TO PREPARE SHRIMP: Place flour in a medium bowl. Whisk pancake mix, salt, and 1 cup water in another medium bowl to form a smooth, thin batter. Place coconut in another.

Dredge 1 shrimp in flour, shaking off excess. Holding shrimp by tail, dip it in batter, allowing excess to drip off, then make a well in coconut, drop in batter-coated shrimp, and cover it with coconut, pressing so it adheres. Lay shrimp on a large wire rack. Repeat with remaining shrimp, thinning batter with a little extra water as it thickens.

Freeze coated shrimp for at least 30 minutes before frying. (If preparing ahead, cover tightly once shrimp are frozen hard.)

TO MAKE SAUCE: Mix marmalade, mustard, and vinegar in a small bowl. Set aside.

TO FRY SHRIMP: Heat oven to 200 degrees. Heat oil in an 8-quart pot to 350 degrees. Set a wire rack over a baking sheet.

Fry shrimp in batches, making sure not to crowd pot and turning shrimp halfway through, until golden, 2 to 3 minutes. Transfer to wire rack and keep first batches warm in oven while you fry remaining shrimp. Serve with sauce alongside.

WHEN SHOULD I SERVE IT?
As an appetizer or first course at a casual or fine dinner
At a cocktail party or open house

WHAT SHOULD I SERVE WITH IT?
A selection of other appetizers (pages 115–52)
Or serve as a starter before:
Beef Tenderloin with Cracked Black Pepper Coating and Red Wine–Thyme Pan Sauce (page 86)

HOW FAR AHEAD CAN I MAKE IT?
The battered and coated shrimp can be double-wrapped in plastic and frozen for up to 1 month.

The fried shrimp can be held in a 200-degree oven for 20 minutes before serving.

WHAT ABOUT LEFTOVERS?
Fry only what you'll need — freeze any unfried shrimp for another time.

SLOW-ROASTED CUMIN-GARLIC SHRIMP WITH LEMON-CILANTRO YOGURT

Cooked at low heat in the oven, shrimp are noticeably tenderer and better-looking than boiled shrimp. Instead of tightening into a roly-poly, they have the classic hook shape.

MAKES ABOUT
2 DOZEN HORS
D'OEUVRES

- 4 garlic cloves, minced
- 4 teaspoons ground cumin
- 2 tablespoons olive oil
- ¾ teaspoon salt

  Freshly ground black pepper
- 2 pounds extra-large shrimp (21–25 count), preferably a white or pink variety, peeled but tails left intact
- 1 cup plain yogurt
- 1 teaspoon finely minced lemon zest
- ½ cup minced fresh cilantro or parsley
- 3 tablespoons fresh lemon juice

WHEN SHOULD I SERVE IT?
As an alternative to shrimp cocktail
At a cocktail party or open house

ANY SHORTCUTS?
Look for peeled raw shrimp (if I order ahead, my fish store will peel them for me).
Use ready-peeled garlic.

HOW CAN I VARY IT?
Change the sauce: Mix ½ cup salsa verde, ½ cup sour cream, and ½ cup chopped fresh cilantro.

WHAT SHOULD I SERVE WITH IT?
As part of a cocktail party, serve with a selection of other appetizers (pages 115–52).
Or serve as a starter before:
Bake-Ahead Pizza for a Crowd (page 24)
Chicken Chili — Red or White (page 13)
Mixed Grill with Tandoori Flavorings (page 62)
Sear-Ahead Steaks or Salmon (page 66)

HOW FAR AHEAD CAN I MAKE IT?
The sauce can be made several hours ahead and refrigerated.
If you don't mind serving them at room temperature, the shrimp can be cooked 2 hours before serving.

WHAT ABOUT LEFTOVERS?
Make a composed salad with the leftover shrimp, along with sliced and salted tomatoes and cucumber. Serve with the leftover yogurt sauce as a dressing.

Adjust oven rack to middle position and heat oven to 250 degrees.

Mix garlic, cumin, oil, salt, and pepper to taste in a large bowl. Add shrimp and toss to coat.

Arrange on a rimmed baking sheet, spacing shrimp ½ inch apart. Bake until pink, 18 to 20 minutes.

Meanwhile, mix yogurt, zest, cilantro and salt and pepper to taste; transfer to a small serving bowl.

Toss warm shrimp with lemon juice. Arrange on a platter and serve warm or at room temperature with dipping sauce.

**Easy Butternut Squash Ravioli
with Rosemary Oil, page 148**

EASY BUTTERNUT SQUASH RAVIOLI WITH ROSEMARY OIL

Wonton wrappers are perfect for encasing this well-seasoned filling, and they are much easier than making pasta from scratch.

Since you can cook only a dozen ravioli at a time, it's easier to serve these as a starter than a main course. Cook them in two batches, spooning 3 ravioli onto each of four plates. Take them to the table while the next batch cooks. By the time everyone finds his seat, you'll have the next batch on the table.

MAKES 24 RAVIOLI; SERVES 4 TO 6 AS A MAIN COURSE OR 8 AS AN APPETIZER

RAVIOLI

- 1 pound (½ medium) butternut squash, peeled, seeded, and cut into medium dice
- 1 tablespoon extra-virgin olive oil
-    Salt
- 2 garlic cloves, minced
- ½ teaspoon minced fresh rosemary
- 1 ounce thinly sliced prosciutto, minced
- ¼ cup freshly grated Parmesan cheese
- 48 wonton wrappers

ROSEMARY OIL

- 3 tablespoons extra-virgin olive oil
- 1 tablespoon minced fresh rosemary

   Freshly ground black pepper
   Freshly grated Parmesan cheese

TO MAKE RAVIOLI: Combine squash, ⅓ cup water, olive oil, and a scant ½ teaspoon salt in a Dutch oven or other pot and bring to a boil over high heat. Cover and cook until squash is just tender and water has evaporated, 5 to 6 minutes. Stir in garlic and rosemary and sauté until fragrant, about 1 minute.

Turn mixture into a soup plate or shallow bowl and mash squash with a fork until mostly smooth. Stir in prosciutto and cheese.

Wash out pot and fill with a generous 2 quarts water. Add 1 tablespoon salt and bring to a simmer.

Set out a large wire rack and a small bowl of water. Lay 6 wonton wrappers on a dry work surface. Brush edges with water, then drop 1 tablespoon filling onto each wrapper. Working with 1 at a time, top each wrapper with another wrapper; press to seal completely. Transfer to wire rack. Repeat with remaining wrappers and filling, keeping work surface dry.

TO MAKE ROSEMARY OIL: Heat oil and rosemary in a small (8-inch) skillet over low heat until rosemary starts to sizzle. Remove from heat.

TO COOK RAVIOLI: Drop 12 ravioli into simmering water. Cook until wrappers start to wrinkle and turn from opaque to translucent, 3 to 4 minutes.

With a slotted spoon, remove ravioli and arrange 3 on each plate. Drizzle with 2 teaspoons cooking water and 1 teaspoon rosemary oil. Sprinkle with pepper and Parmesan cheese, and serve. Cook remaining 12 ravioli, and serve them as soon as they are ready.

RICOTTA-FILLED RAVIOLI

Mix 1¼ cups ricotta cheese, ¼ cup grated Parmesan cheese, 2 minced garlic cloves, 3 tablespoons minced fresh parsley, ½ teaspoon dried oregano, 1 large egg, and salt and pepper to taste. Top the ravioli with a simple tomato sauce such as the one on page 27.

WHEN SHOULD I SERVE IT?

For all seasons — butternut-squash ravioli in fall and winter and ricotta-filled ravioli in spring and summer

When you want something quick and elegant

At a dinner with both kids and adults — make half a batch of the ricotta filling for the kids (recipe above)

ANY SHORTCUTS?

Make the no-cook ricotta filling for the ravioli instead.

HOW CAN I VARY IT?

Top with toasted pine nuts, walnuts, or pecans.

WHAT SHOULD I SERVE WITH IT?
Serve as a starter with:

Sear-Ahead Steaks or Salmon (page 66)

Perfect Roast Chicken (page 38)

Rosemary-Scented Roast Pork Loin Stuffed with Roasted Garlic, Dried Apricots, and Cranberries with Port Wine Sauce (page 83)

HOW FAR AHEAD CAN I MAKE IT?

The ravioli can be stored on a wire rack at room temperature, loosely covered with plastic wrap, for a couple of hours.

The ravioli can be frozen until solid on a cookie sheet, then transferred to a freezer bag and frozen for up to 1 month.

WHAT ABOUT LEFTOVERS?

Cook only what you need and freeze the rest. There's no need to thaw — just increase the cooking time by a minute or so.

CRAB-STUFFED ARTICHOKES

I've been making these stuffed artichokes for nearly twenty-five years. Even though they look elegant, they're not stuffy: after guests have enjoyed the crab salad, they eat the artichokes with their fingers.

    Be sure to cook the artichokes until their stems can easily be pierced with a thin-bladed knife. They are one of the few vegetables that are best well done. Since the artichokes cook for such a long time, check the pot once or twice to make sure it doesn't run dry.

SERVES 6

3 large artichokes, stems trimmed and ends of leaves clipped
      with scissors if prickly

1 tablespoon Dijon mustard

¼ cup fresh lemon juice
    Salt and freshly ground black pepper

¾ cup extra-virgin olive oil

1 can (16 ounces) backfin or lump crabmeat, picked over for shells and cartilage

2 tablespoons minced fresh parsley or basil

¼ cup thinly sliced scallion greens

HOW CAN I VARY IT?
    Substitute cooked shrimp, cut into bite-size pieces, for the crab, or use a mix of crab and shrimp.

WHAT SHOULD I SERVE WITH IT?
Serve as a first course before:
    Really Good Lasagna (page 35)
    Sear-Ahead Steaks or Salmon
      (page 66)
    Easy Baked Risotto (page 72)
    Roast Rack of Lamb with Vinegar-
      Mint Pan Sauce (page 93)

HOW FAR AHEAD CAN I MAKE IT?
    The artichokes can be steamed up to 1 day ahead and refrigerated covered.
    The vinaigrette is best made no more than a few hours ahead.

Set artichokes stem side up in about 1 inch of water in a pot. Cover and bring to a boil over high heat. Reduce heat to medium and steam until artichoke stems are tender when pierced with a thin knife, about 30 minutes. Remove and cool slightly, then halve each artichoke with a serrated knife, and spoon out fuzzy choke.

Whisk mustard, lemon juice, and a sprinkling of salt and pepper in a 2-cup Pyrex measuring cup or small bowl. Whisk in oil in a slow stream to make a creamy vinaigrette.

Arrange artichokes cut side up on plates. Toss crab, parsley, and scallions with ½ cup vinaigrette. Spoon remaining vinaigrette into and over artichokes leaves to coat. Fill each cavity with crab and serve.

WHAT ABOUT LEFTOVERS?
Leftover artichokes and salad are fine the next day. Perk them up with a squeeze of lemon juice.

WHEN SHOULD I SERVE IT?
As an impressive first course or light luncheon
When you need something that's do-ahead

ANY SHORTCUTS?
Use avocados rather than artichokes.

BIG BOWL OF GARLICKY MUSSELS OR CLAMS

Many a great dinner that has lasted into the night has begun with this dish. If you're making mussels or clams for a large group, don't try to fit a double quantity into one skillet. Steam them in batches, since they're done in 5 minutes. Discard any shellfish that have broken shells or that don't open during cooking.

SERVES 2 TO 4 AS A FIRST COURSE, MORE AS AN APPETIZER

1½ tablespoons butter

2 garlic cloves, minced

¼ cup dry white wine or dry vermouth

2 pounds mussels, scrubbed and beards removed, or 24 littleneck clams, rinsed thoroughly in a sinkful of cold water

1 tablespoon fresh lemon juice

2 tablespoons minced fresh parsley

Freshly ground black pepper

Heat butter and garlic in a large (12-inch) deep skillet (the wider the skillet, the more evenly the shellfish will cook) over medium-high heat. When garlic starts to sizzle and turn a little golden, add wine and mussels (or clams). Increase heat to high, cover, and steam, shaking pan occasionally for even cooking, until shellfish open, 4 to 5 minutes for mussels, 1 minute or so more for clams.

Using a slotted spoon, transfer shellfish to large soup plates. Add lemon juice to cooking broth, stir in parsley, and season with pepper. Pour broth over shellfish, and serve.

WHEN SHOULD I SERVE IT?
As a hearty first course for two or a light first course for four

WHAT SHOULD I SERVE WITH IT?
Serve as a first course before:
Bake-Ahead Pizza for a Crowd (page 24)
Really Good Lasagna (page 35)
Easy Baked Risotto (page 72)

WHAT ABOUT LEFTOVERS?
Shell the mussels or clams and use them and the accompanying juice the next day in pasta, risotto, or a seafood salad.

FIRST-COURSE SOUPS

CREAMY VEGETABLE SOUP AND MANY VARIATIONS

Creamy vegetable soup is the perfect first course for an elegant dinner or main course at a nice lunch. The following formula ensures a full-flavored soup. The key to flavor is to brown the vegetables perfectly before you add the spices and broth. Each of the vegetables I've suggested has a different sugar and moisture content and will brown at a slightly different rate.

You'll get a creamier, silkier soup if you puree the vegetables in a blender rather than a food processor.

Don't feel locked into the suggested spice blends and garnishes. Many are interchangeable. Try curry in cauliflower soup, for example, saffron in potato, or rosemary in turnip. Whatever you do, flavor the soup with gusto.

SERVES 6 TO 8 AS A FIRST COURSE, 3 TO 4 AS A MAIN COURSE

WHEN SHOULD I SERVE IT?

As a first course for a fall, winter, or early-spring dinner

HOW CAN I VARY IT?

With the master recipe, ten suggested variations, and the freedom to interchange spices and garnishes, there are hundreds of ways to alter this soup.

WHAT SHOULD I SERVE WITH IT?
Serve as a first course before any of the following (avoid a potato side dish):
Rosemary-Scented Roast Pork Loin Stuffed with Roasted Garlic, Dried Apricots, and Cranberries with Port Wine Sauce (page 83)
Sear-Ahead Steaks or Salmon (page 66)

Beef Tenderloin with Cracked Black Pepper Coating and Red Wine–Thyme Pan Sauce (page 86)

HOW FAR AHEAD CAN I MAKE IT?

The soup can be refrigerated for 5 days, and it freezes (and thaws) beautifully.

WHAT ABOUT LEFTOVERS?

Leftover soup is as good as (and perhaps better than) the original.

2	tablespoons olive oil
1½	pounds prepared vegetable of choice (recipes follow)
1	large onion, cut into large dice
1	tablespoon butter
	Large pinch of sugar
3	large garlic cloves, thickly sliced
	Dried herbs and/or spices (see recipes)
3	cups chicken broth
	Fresh herbs, if using (see recipes)
1–1½	cups half-and-half or whole milk
	Salt and freshly ground black pepper
	Optional garnish (see recipes)

Heat oil in a large (12-inch) deep skillet over medium-high heat until shimmering. Add vegetable of choice, then onion, and sauté, stirring very little at first and more frequently toward the end, until vegetables start to turn golden brown, 7 to 8 minutes. Reduce heat to low and add butter, sugar, and garlic. Continue to cook, stirring occasionally, until all vegetables are a rich caramel color, about 10 minutes longer.

Add dried herbs and/or spices and cook until fragrant, 30 seconds to 1 minute. Add broth and bring to a simmer over medium-high heat. Reduce heat to low and simmer, partially covered, until vegetables are tender, about 10 minutes.

Transfer to a blender, add fresh herbs, if using, and puree in batches. Make sure to vent blender by removing pop-out center or lifting one edge, drape a kitchen towel over top to keep soup from spewing, and blend, holding lid in place, until very smooth, 30 seconds to 1 minute.

Return to skillet (or pour into a pot if pan will not hold the milk). Add enough milk to thin soup to desired consistency, season with salt and pepper to taste, and heat through. Ladle into bowls, add garnish, if using, and serve.

CREAMY CARROT SOUP WITH CURRY

1½	pounds carrots, peeled and cut into about 1-inch chunks (4–5 cups)
2	tablespoons curry powder
	Chopped roasted pistachio nuts for garnish (optional)

CREAMY SWEET POTATO SOUP WITH GINGER AND NUTMEG

1½   pounds sweet potatoes, peeled and
      cut into about 1-inch cubes
      (4–5 cups)
1½   teaspoons ground ginger
½   teaspoon ground nutmeg
⅛   teaspoon cayenne pepper
      Chopped honey-roasted peanuts for
      garnish (optional)

CREAMY BROCCOLI SOUP WITH MUSTARD, BASIL, AND OREGANO

1½   pounds broccoli, stems peeled and cut
      into 1-inch chunks, florets broken
      into medium-size pieces (7–8 cups)
1½   teaspoons dry mustard
½   teaspoon dried basil
¼   teaspoon dried oregano
⅛   teaspoon cayenne pepper
      Toasted pine nuts for garnish (optional)

TO TOAST PINE NUTS: Heat a small (8-inch) skillet over medium-low heat. Add pine nuts and toast, stirring and shaking pan frequently, until fragrant and golden brown.

CREAMY BEET SOUP WITH CARAWAY AND DILL

1½   pounds beets, peeled and cut into about
      1-inch cubes (about 4 cups)
1   scant teaspoon crushed toasted caraway
      seeds
⅛   teaspoon cayenne pepper
2   tablespoons loosely packed chopped
      fresh dill leaves

Chopped hard-boiled egg for garnish
(optional)

TO TOAST AND CRUSH CARAWAY SEEDS: Heat ½ teaspoon caraway seeds in a small (8-inch) skillet over medium-low heat until they start to pop gently and smell fragrant. Cool slightly, then turn out onto a work surface, and crush with a rolling pin.

CREAMY WINTER SQUASH SOUP WITH CINNAMON, GINGER, AND CLOVES

1½   pounds butternut squash, peeled,
      seeded, and cut into about 1-inch
      cubes (about 5 cups)
1½   teaspoons ground cinnamon
1   teaspoon ground ginger
¼   teaspoon ground cloves
⅛   teaspoon cayenne pepper
      Store-bought apple chips for garnish
      (optional)

CREAMY PARSNIP SOUP WITH GINGER AND CARDAMOM

1½   pounds parsnips, peeled and cut into
      about 1-inch cubes (4–5 cups)
1   teaspoon ground ginger
¼   teaspoon ground cardamom
¼   teaspoon ground allspice
⅛   teaspoon cayenne pepper
1   tablespoon coarsely chopped skinned
      hazelnuts, sautéed (optional; see
      page 158)
1   tablespoon dried cranberries, sautéed,
      for garnish (optional)

TO SAUTÉ HAZELNUTS AND CRAN-BERRIES: Heat 1 teaspoon butter in a small (8-inch) skillet. Add hazelnuts and dried cranberries and cook until golden and fragrant, 1 to 2 minutes.

CREAMY TURNIP (OR RUTABAGA) SOUP WITH PAPRIKA AND THYME

1½   pounds turnips or rutabagas, peeled and cut into about 1-inch cubes (about 5 cups)

2   teaspoons paprika

1   teaspoon dried thyme leaves

⅛   teaspoon cayenne pepper
Shallot crisps for garnish (optional)

TO MAKE SHALLOT CRISPS: Heat 2 tablespoons butter and 1 tablespoon olive oil in a small (8-inch) skillet over medium heat. Add 2 large shallots, peeled and thinly sliced, and fry, stirring frequently, until golden, 8 to 10 minutes. Drain on paper towels and cool.

CREAMY ROSEMARY-SCENTED POTATO SOUP

1½   pounds Idaho (baking) potatoes, peeled and cut into about 1-inch cubes (4–5 cups)

1½   teaspoons minced fresh rosemary (add where dried herbs are called for; rosemary needs to cook longer than other fresh herbs)

⅛   teaspoon cayenne pepper
Cooked minced bacon for garnish (optional)

CREAMY CORN SOUP WITH CUMIN AND CAYENNE

Because the corn kernels don't puree, this soup must be strained through a colander after pureeing. Then thin with milk. The yield will be slightly less, serving six.

1½   pounds frozen corn, thawed and drained (about 4 cups)

2   teaspoons ground cumin

⅛   teaspoon cayenne pepper

¼   cup loosely packed fresh cilantro leaves
Chopped fresh tomato and corn chips, such as Fritos, for garnish (optional)

CREAMY CAULIFLOWER SOUP WITH SAFFRON AND GINGER

1½   pounds cauliflower (about 1 small head), trimmed and cut into large florets (about 6 heaping cups)

1   teaspoon ground ginger

½   teaspoon ground turmeric

⅛   teaspoon saffron threads

⅛   teaspoon cayenne pepper

6–8   sea scallops for garnish (optional)

TO SEAR SEA SCALLOPS: Just before serving, heat a small (8-inch) heavy-bottomed skillet over medium-high heat. Lightly coat sea scallops with oil and season with salt and pepper. Add scallops to hot skillet and sear until caramel brown, about 3 minutes on first side and 2 to 3 minutes on second side. Garnish soup with scallops, 2 per bowl if serving as a main course.

PUREED WILD MUSHROOM AND POTATO SOUP

The potatoes give body and smoothness, and the mushrooms take the flavor lead.

SERVES 6 TO 8 AS A FIRST COURSE, 3 TO 4 AS A MAIN COURSE

    2 tablespoons butter
    1 medium onion, chopped
  3/4 ounce dried mushrooms, rinsed
1 1/2 pounds red potatoes, unpeeled
    6 cups chicken broth
  1/2 teaspoon dried thyme leaves
       Salt and freshly ground black pepper
       Sour cream for garnish

Heat butter in a Dutch oven or large saucepan over medium-high heat. Add onion and sauté until tender and golden brown, about 5 minutes. Add mushrooms, potatoes, broth, and thyme and bring to a simmer. Cover, reduce heat to low, and simmer until potatoes are tender, about 10 minutes.

Working in 2 batches, puree soup in a blender until silky smooth. Return to pot and heat to a simmer. Season with salt and pepper to taste. Ladle into bowls and garnish each bowl with a dollop of sour cream.

WHEN SHOULD I SERVE IT?
As a first course for a fall, winter, or early-spring dinner
For fall and spring picnics (keep hot in thermoses or containers in thermal bags)

HOW CAN I VARY IT?
In addition to the sour cream, top the soup with bacon bits, thinly sliced scallions, or minced fresh chives.

WHAT SHOULD I SERVE WITH IT?
Serve as a first course before any of the following (avoid a potato side dish):
Rosemary-Scented Roast Pork Loin Stuffed with Roasted Garlic, Dried Apricots, and Cranberries with Port Wine Sauce (page 83)
Sear-Ahead Steaks or Salmon (page 66)

Beef Tenderloin with Cracked Black Pepper Coating and Red Wine–Thyme Pan Sauce (page 86)

HOW FAR AHEAD CAN I MAKE IT?
The soup can be refrigerated for at least 5 days.

WHAT ABOUT LEFTOVERS?
The leftover soup is as good as the original.

QUICK CURRIED TOMATO SOUP

Many people don't realize how sensational homemade tomato soup can be. Don't omit the baking soda; it neutralizes the tomatoes' acidity and keeps the milk from curdling.

SERVES 6 AS A FIRST COURSE, 4 AS A MAIN COURSE

3 tablespoons vegetable oil
1 medium-large onion, chopped
1 tablespoon curry powder
1 can (28 ounces) crushed tomatoes
½ teaspoon baking soda
1 cup low-fat milk
½ cup heavy cream
   Salt and freshly ground black pepper

Heat oil in a large saucepan or Dutch oven over medium heat. Add onion and sauté until tender, about 5 minutes. Add curry powder and cook until fragrant, less than 1 minute. Add tomatoes and baking soda and bring to a simmer. Reduce heat to low and simmer, partially covered, to blend flavors, about 5 minutes.

Stir in milk and cream. Pour soup into a blender and puree until creamy smooth. Return to pan and reheat to a simmer, seasoning with salt and pepper to taste. Serve.

WHEN SHOULD I SERVE IT?
As a first course for a fine dinner
As a lunch or first course for both children and adults
As a vegetarian dish

HOW CAN I VARY IT?
Substitute dried basil and oregano or dried thyme leaves for the curry.

WHAT SHOULD I SERVE WITH IT?
Serve as a first course before:
Twin Turkeys with Rich Pan Gravy (page 78)
Beef Tenderloin with Cracked Black Pepper Coating and Red Wine–Thyme Pan Sauce (page 86)
Sear-Ahead Steaks or Salmon (page 66)

HOW FAR AHEAD CAN I MAKE IT?
The soup can be refrigerated for at least 5 days.

WHAT ABOUT LEFTOVERS?
You can even serve it for a special occasion the second time around.

YEAR-ROUND CLASSIC GAZPACHO

What if you want to make gazpacho but don't have fresh tomatoes? The canned diced variety makes an excellent substitute for fresh. Another advantage to using canned tomatoes: they are unaffected by refrigeration, unlike fresh tomatoes, whose taste is dulled and texture compromised by cold. This soup will retain all its flavor when you chill it.

SERVES 6 AS A FIRST COURSE, 3 AS A MAIN COURSE

2   cans (14.5 ounces each) diced tomatoes, preferably Hunt's "petite diced"

2   tablespoons extra-virgin olive oil

1   small seedless cucumber, peeled and cut into small dice (about 2 cups)

1   small yellow bell pepper, cored, seeded, and cut into small dice (about ¾ cup)

1   small onion, cut into small dice (about ½ cup)

2   medium garlic cloves, minced

1   small jalapeño, seeded and minced (optional)

2   tablespoons sherry vinegar

2   tablespoons chopped fresh parsley, basil, or cilantro

Salt and freshly ground black pepper to taste

WHEN SHOULD I SERVE IT?
As a first course for a warm-weather dinner
As a main course for a warm-weather lunch
As a cold soup for a picnic
As part of a summer vegetarian dinner

HOW CAN I VARY IT?
Top it with Garlic Croutons (page 172).

Turn it into a more substantial dish by topping it with grilled shrimp.
Make one of the variations (page 164).

WHAT SHOULD I SERVE WITH IT?
Serve as a first course before:
Mixed Grill with Tandoori Flavorings (page 62)
Sear-Ahead Steaks or Salmon (page 66)

Niçoise-Style Tuna Salad with White Beans and Olives (page 190)

HOW FAR AHEAD CAN I MAKE IT?
The gazpacho can be refrigerated for several hours before serving.

WHAT ABOUT LEFTOVERS?
It's fine the following day.

Combine ½ cup tomatoes, ½ cup water, and olive oil in a food processor or blender and process until pureed. Transfer to a medium bowl and stir in remaining ingredients. Cover and refrigerate until ready to serve. To chill soup quickly, transfer to a 13-by-9-inch or other shallow pan.

PINEAPPLE GAZPACHO

Make as directed, but substitute 2 heaping cups small-diced fresh pineapple and 2 cups pineapple juice for tomatoes and water. Use a red bell pepper instead of the yellow one. Substitute 3 tablespoons fresh lime juice for vinegar.

WATERMELON GAZPACHO

Make as directed, but substitute 2 heaping cups small-diced seeded watermelon and 2 cups orange juice for tomatoes and water. Substitute 3 tablespoons fresh lime juice for vinegar.

MANGO GAZPACHO

Make as directed, but substitute 2 heaping cups small-diced fresh mangoes and 2 cups orange juice for tomatoes and water. Use a red bell pepper instead of the yellow one. Substitute 3 tablespoons fresh lime juice for vinegar.

SALADS

PEAR HALVES WITH BLUE CHEESE AND TOASTED NUTS

SERVES 8

The trick to this salad is having pears that are perfectly ripe. Pears that are rock-hard when you buy them will need about 5 days to soften. If they ripen before you plan to use them, transfer them to the refrigerator or to a cool garage to slow down the process.

Serve this salad as a starter or as a cheese course after dinner. I've paired pears with a variety of blue cheeses, but my favorite is creamy Gorgonzola dolce.

1/2   cup chopped toasted walnuts, pecans, or hazelnuts
4   large ripe pears
4   ounces blue cheese

To toast nuts, spread on a small baking sheet and toast in a 325-degree oven, stirring occasionally, until fragrant, about 10 minutes. To peel hazelnuts, dump hot toasted nuts onto a tea towel and rub vigorously to remove as much skin as possible.

WHEN SHOULD I SERVE IT?
As a first course or cheese course for a festive fall or winter dinner

WHAT SHOULD I SERVE WITH IT?
Serve before or after:
Twin Turkeys with Rich Pan Gravy (page 78)

Rosemary-Scented Roast Pork Loin Stuffed with Roasted Garlic, Dried Apricots, and Cranberries with Port Wine Sauce (page 83)
Sear-Ahead Steaks or Salmon (page 66)

Roast Beef Tenderloin with Cracked Black Pepper Coating and Red Wine–Thyme Pan Sauce (page 86)
Roast Rack of Lamb with Vinegar-Mint Pan Sauce (page 93)
Chicken-Mushroom Crepes (page 108)

About 15 minutes before serving, halve pears. Cut a thin slice off bottom of each half so pears will sit stable on the plates. Use a melon baller (or small ice cream scoop) to core each pear half. Place on salad plates.

Scoop 8 cheese balls, each about 1 packed generous tablespoon, and stuff pears with cheese. Sprinkle with nuts and serve.

ANY SHORTCUTS?

Although the nuts add textural and flavor contrast, they're not essential.

Or simply buy a container of deluxe roasted mixed nuts, pick out the hazelnuts, and add them to the salad.

HOW CAN I VARY IT?

If serving children too, you can stuff their pears with chunks of cheddar or other mild cheese — or skip the cheese.

Substitute fresh goat cheese for the blue cheese.

Scatter a few dried cranberries over the plates.

HOW FAR AHEAD CAN I MAKE IT?

The blue cheese can be scooped, covered with plastic wrap, and set aside for several hours, or refrigerated for longer.

Because the pears discolor quickly, don't halve and core them until the last minute.

MIXED GREEN SALAD WITH FRESH HERBS

A simple bowl of greens requires more than a drizzling of olive oil and vinegar. A vinaigrette takes less than five minutes to make, and if you don't have time to put it together before guests arrive, don't worry. You'll mesmerize onlookers as you dip your whisk into the Dijon jar and then beat the oil and vinegar into a thick emulsified dressing. It will taste so much better than anything from a plastic bottle in the refrigerator door.

A vinaigrette can be made in any bowl or container, but I've found that it emulsifies more quickly and easily in the smaller volume of a Pyrex measuring cup.

SERVES 8 TO 12

1	small head *each* red leaf lettuce, Boston lettuce, and radicchio
1	romaine heart
½	cup thinly sliced scallion greens
½	cup coarsely chopped mixed fresh herbs (parsley, dill, basil, tarragon, and/or cilantro)

VINAIGRETTE

2	tablespoons rice wine vinegar
2	tablespoons fresh lemon juice
1	tablespoon Dijon mustard
	Salt and freshly ground black pepper
¾	cup extra-virgin olive oil

WHEN SHOULD I SERVE IT?
As a light, refreshing first course or a buffet salad, or after the main course, with a nice cheese

HOW CAN I VARY IT?
Choose other lettuces, making sure there's a mix of mild and assertive greens.

Add a minced garlic clove or two to the vinaigrette, whisking it in with the vinegar and lemon juice.
Add capers, citrus zest, or blue cheese to the dressing.

Rinse, dry, and tear lettuces into large bite-size pieces (you should have about 4 quarts). Put in a large salad or other bowl and add scallions and herbs.

TO MAKE VINAIGRETTE: Whisk vinegar, lemon juice, mustard, and a generous sprinkling of salt and pepper in a 2-cup Pyrex measuring cup or small bowl. Slowly whisk in oil, first in droplets, then in a slow, steady stream, until vinaigrette is smooth and thick.

Pour vinaigrette over salad, toss to coat, and serve.

WHAT SHOULD I SERVE WITH IT?
This versatile salad is good with almost any dish.

HOW FAR AHEAD CAN I MAKE IT?
The vinaigrette can be made up to 2 days in advance and refrigerat-

ed. Bring to room temperature, and whisk briskly if it has separated.
The lettuces can be covered with damp paper towels and stored in the refrigerator overnight.

WHAT ABOUT LEFTOVERS?
Use extra vinaigrette to dress another salad or drizzle it over steamed broccoli, asparagus, beets, cauliflower, or green beans.

BABY SPINACH SALAD WITH SHAVED PARMESAN AND GARLIC VINAIGRETTE

Baby spinach studded with shaved Parmesan is dressed with a potent vinaigrette made with a quick homemade garlic oil.

SERVES 12

Be sure to process the garlic and oil thoroughly—long enough so that the two become one. And since mincing garlic is such a chore, make sure you save the garlic for another use once the oil has been strained. For a bolder garlic flavor, stir a little of the minced garlic into the dressing.

- 3 garlic cloves
- ³/₄ cup extra-virgin olive oil
- ¹/₄ cup fresh lemon juice
- 1 tablespoon Dijon mustard
- ¹/₂ teaspoon salt
  Freshly ground black pepper
- 2 bags (9 ounces each) prewashed baby spinach (about 2 quarts each)
- 1 3-ounce wedge Parmesan cheese, preferably Parmigiano-Reggiano, shaved with a vegetable peeler (about 1 cup shavings)

With motor running, drop garlic cloves into a food processor or blender and process to mince. With motor running, add oil in a steady stream and process for about 30 seconds longer. Strain oil and set aside; reserve garlic for another use.

WHEN SHOULD I SERVE IT?
As a light, refreshing first course or a buffet salad, or after the entrée, accompanied by a good cheese

ANY SHORTCUTS?
Although I prefer big slivers of Parmigiano-Reggiano, you can substitute coarsely grated good Parmesan.

Substitute store-bought garlic oil.

Add lemon juice, mustard, salt, and a few grinds of pepper to processor or blender (without washing it) and process until smooth. With motor running, slowly add garlic oil to make a thick, smooth dressing.

Mix spinach and cheese in a large bowl. Pour dressing over salad, toss, and serve.

HOW CAN I VARY IT?
Substitute arugula for the baby spinach.

Add a little chopped bacon (cooked until crisp) or a package of sliced fresh mushrooms.

WHAT SHOULD I SERVE WITH IT?
Almost any dish

HOW FAR AHEAD CAN I MAKE IT?
The dressing is best made at least 1 hour before serving.

CHOPPED CAESAR SALAD

When I want to serve the ultimate crowd-pleasing salad, I choose Caesar and make it in an enormous wooden bowl that my younger daughter gave me one Mother's Day. For large gatherings, I mix it in something bigger, such as an ice chest. No matter how much I make, there's barely a crouton left at the end of the night.

SERVES 12

GARLIC CROUTONS

8	garlic cloves
⅓	cup olive oil
4	cups ¾-inch bread cubes — cut from a good baguette
	Salt

SALAD

¼	cup fresh lemon juice (from 2 lemons)
⅓	cup mayonnaise
	Generous ½ teaspoon Worcestershire sauce
6	romaine hearts, halved lengthwise, cored, and sliced lengthwise and crosswise 3 or 4 times
⅔	cup olive oil
	Salt and freshly ground black pepper
½	cup freshly grated Parmesan cheese, preferably Parmigiano-Reggiano, plus more for sprinkling

TO MAKE CROUTONS: Heat a large (12-inch) skillet over low heat. Meanwhile, with motor running, drop garlic into a food processor or blender and process to mince. Scrape down sides of bowl. With motor running, slowly add olive oil. Continue to process for about 30 seconds. Strain oil through a fine-mesh strainer. Reserve half the garlic for salad, the remainder for another use.

Increase heat under skillet to medium. Place bread cubes in a medium bowl, drizzle with half the garlic oil and a big pinch of salt, and toss to coat. Add remaining garlic oil and toss again. Add bread cubes to hot skillet and toast, turning cubes and shaking pan often, until golden brown, 5 to 7 minutes. Return croutons to bowl and set aside.

TO MAKE SALAD: Whisk lemon juice, mayonnaise, Worcestershire, and reserved garlic in a small bowl.

Place lettuce in a large bowl. Drizzle with remaining olive oil, sprinkle with salt and pepper to taste, and toss to coat. Drizzle lemon mixture over lettuce; toss again. Sprinkle in ½ cup Parmesan and toss to coat. Sprinkle croutons over the salad and toss.

Serve, sprinkling each portion with a little more Parmesan cheese.

WHEN SHOULD I SERVE IT?

When you need a salad that pleases nearly everybody

All seasons

As a first-course salad for a sit-down dinner or as a buffet side salad

ANY SHORTCUTS?

Since the salad calls for 8 garlic cloves, using ready-peeled garlic helps.

Parmigiano-Reggiano makes a superior salad, but you can substitute coarsely grated Parmesan.

Don't cheat on the croutons — the boxed versions are vastly inferior to homemade.

HOW CAN I VARY IT?

Turn it into a main course by adding grilled chicken or shrimp.

WHAT SHOULD I SERVE WITH IT?

Bake-Ahead Pizza for a Crowd (page 24)

Really Good Lasagna (page 35)

Creamy Baked Macaroni and Cheese (page 32)

Buttermilk-Honey Fried Chicken Fingers (page 29)

Grown-Up Sloppy Joes (page 22)

Sear-Ahead Steaks or Salmon (page 66)

HOW FAR AHEAD CAN I MAKE IT?

The garlic oil can be made 2 days ahead and refrigerated. Bring to room temperature and strain the garlic from the oil just before making the croutons.

The cheese can be grated and stored in a covered container, and the lettuce chopped and placed in a cool place or refrigerated, covered with a damp towel, 3 to 4 hours ahead.

The croutons can be sautéed up to 1 hour ahead.

The lemon-mayonnaise mixture can be made 2 hours ahead.

BABY GREENS, ROMAINE, AND ICEBERG LETTUCE with Blue Cheese, Toasted Pecans, and Dried Cranberries

Mixed baby greens offer color and variety, but for texture and color contrast, I like to anchor the salad with iceberg and romaine hearts.

SERVES 12

1   bag (5 ounces) baby greens

½   large head iceberg lettuce, cut into bite-size pieces

1   large romaine heart, cut into bite-size pieces

¾   cup pecans toasted in a 325-degree oven, coarsely chopped

¾   cup dried cranberries

1   cup crumbled blue cheese (about 4 ounces)

½   cup extra-virgin olive oil

    Salt and freshly ground black pepper

2   tablespoons balsamic vinegar

Place greens in a large bowl. Add pecans, dried cranberries, and blue cheese. Drizzle olive oil over salad and sprinkle generously with salt and pepper; toss to coat. Taste for seasonings and adjust if necessary. Add balsamic vinegar and toss to coat again. Serve.

WHEN SHOULD I SERVE IT?
As a crowd-pleasing first course or buffet salad
For a fine dinner

ANY SHORTCUTS?
Use packaged washed lettuces.
Use store-bought toasted nuts, such as pistachios.

HOW CAN I VARY IT?
Substitute other nuts for the pecans — walnuts, pistachios, slivered almonds, or pine nuts.

WHAT SHOULD I SERVE WITH IT?
Creamy Baked Macaroni and Cheese (page 32)
Boneless Coq au Vin (page 42)
Simple Cassoulet (page 44)
One of the stews (pages 48–53)
Twin Turkeys with Rich Pan Gravy (page 78)
Chicken-Mushroom Crepes (page 108)
Beef Tenderloin with Cracked Black Pepper Coating and Red Wine–Thyme Pan Sauce (page 86)

HOW FAR AHEAD CAN I MAKE IT?
The toasted pecans can be stored in an airtight container for at least 1 month.
The lettuces can be prepared and refrigerated, covered, for 3 to 4 hours.

BOSTON LETTUCE
AND BABY SPINACH SALAD

SERVES 12

There's no need to make a separate dressing that could mask the bright, natural flavors of this salad. All that's needed is a drizzling of olive oil and vinegar to pull it together.

Be generous with the oil and stingy with the vinegar. Eyeballing about 2 teaspoons for each portion, drizzle extra-virgin olive oil over the salad ingredients, lightly sprinkle generously with salt and pepper, and then toss. (I like spring-action tongs for tossing.) If, after a thorough tossing, the ingredients aren't lightly coated with oil, drizzle in a little more, toss again, and then taste. At this point the ingredients should be lightly coated but not dripping with oil and taste properly seasoned. Add vinegar, which should be subtle and in balance with the oil. If the vinegar bottle doesn't have a spout or plastic top that controls the flow, hold your index finger over the top as you add the vinegar so that it sprinkles rather than pours. Toss and taste again. If the salad is not acidic enough, add another couple drops of vinegar.

1	medium red onion, thinly sliced
¼	cup rice wine vinegar
1	container or bag (5 ounces) prewashed baby spinach
1	large head Boston lettuce, torn into bite-size pieces (about 10 cups)
1	cup Glazed Toasted Almonds (recipe follows)
4	Valencia oranges, sectioned
½	cup extra-virgin olive oil
	Salt and freshly ground black pepper

Mix onion and vinegar in a small bowl. Let stand for 5 to 10 minutes while you prepare salad.

Place spinach and lettuce in a large salad bowl. Add almonds and oranges. Lift onion from vinegar (reserve vinegar) and add to salad. Drizzle salad with olive oil and sprinkle with salt and pepper. Toss until ingredients are well coated. Drizzle reserved vinegar over salad, toss again, and serve.

GLAZED TOASTED ALMONDS

MAKES 1 CUP

1	cup slivered almonds
1/3	cup sugar, dissolved in 2 tablespoons water

Toast almonds in a 10-inch skillet over medium-low heat, stirring occasionally at first, then more frequently toward the end, until golden and fragrant, 5 to 6 minutes. Pour dissolved sugar over almonds and cook until liquid evaporates, almonds are glazed, and sugar coating just starts to turn golden, about 3 minutes. Pour into a pie plate to cool.

WHEN SHOULD I SERVE IT?
As a first course or buffet salad
For a fine dinner
During spring and summer

ANY SHORTCUTS?
Instead of making the almonds, you can buy glazed nuts, or use honey-roasted peanuts or cashews.
Although mandarin oranges in a jar lack the flavor of fresh oranges, you can substitute them for the Valencias; they are available in the refrigerated section of many produce departments. Use 1 jar (24 ounces), drained. Avoid canned mandarins, which taste tinny.

HOW CAN I VARY IT?
Add thin-sliced fennel or even Parmesan cheese, shaved with a vegetable peeler, and omit the nuts.
For a fall and winter salad, substitute a more substantial lettuce (arugula or mixed baby greens, for example).
In place of the oranges, use hulled and halved or quartered strawberries (or other whole fresh berries), halved red grapes, or apricots, plums, peaches, or mangoes, pitted and cut into bite-size pieces.
Use scallions in place of the red onion — they don't have to be soaked in the vinegar.

WHAT SHOULD I SERVE WITH IT?
Quick White Chicken Chili with Hominy (page 15)
Mixed Grill with Tandoori Flavorings (page 62)
Grilled Chicken Breasts with Orange-Thyme Glaze (page 64)
Chicken-Mushroom Crepes (page 108)

HOW FAR AHEAD CAN I MAKE IT?
The nuts can be stored in an airtight tin for 1 month.
The oranges can be sectioned and the Boston lettuce prepared, covered, and refrigerated 3 to 4 hours ahead.
Don't soak the onion for more than 30 minutes, or it will wilt.

CARROT SALAD
WITH CUMIN VINAIGRETTE

SERVES 6

Most of us don't think of serving a carrot salad as a first course, but when it's tossed in vinaigrette and flavored with a little cumin, it will introduce guests to a side of the vegetable they never knew.

If you're tempted to simplify the recipe by making it with factory-shredded carrots, don't. It's those carrots, in fact, that give packaged salad mixes a cheap salad bar odor. Peel and grate your own. For a small quantity, use a box grater. For shredding more than a pound, it's worth pulling out the food processor.

WHEN SHOULD I SERVE IT?

When you're entertaining on the fly

For all seasons

For a small dinner or a large buffet

As a side salad for casual entertaining

As a first-course salad at an elegant dinner — especially if you add the dried cranberries and present the salad in radicchio leaf cups

ANY SHORTCUTS?

Although the salad will not be as complex, you can omit the vinaigrette and toss the carrots with the olive oil, salt and pepper, and cumin. Add the lemon juice and toss again.

HOW CAN I VARY IT?

Garnish the salad with toasted nuts — pistachios are a particularly good choice.

Rather than cumin, flavor the carrots with a pinch or two of dried basil, oregano, or tarragon or a generous sprinkling of fresh herbs.

WHAT SHOULD I SERVE WITH IT?

Mixed Grill with Tandoori Flavorings (page 62)

Sear-Ahead Steaks or Salmon (page 66)

Butterflied Cornish Hens with Apricot-Pistachio Dressing (page 76)

Rosemary-Scented Roast Pork Loin Stuffed with Roasted Garlic, Dried Apricots, and Cranberries with Port Wine Sauce (page 83)

Easy Baked Risotto (page 72)

Roast Rack of Lamb with Vinegar-Mint Pan Sauce (page 93)

HOW FAR AHEAD CAN I MAKE IT?

The vinaigrette can be covered and refrigerated for 3 to 4 days.

The carrots can be grated 3 to 4 hours ahead, but toss them with the vinaigrette no more than 1 hour before serving.

WHAT ABOUT LEFTOVERS?

Much like coleslaw, leftover carrot salad is fine for lunch or dinner the next day. You may need to perk it up with a squeeze of fresh lemon juice.

1 medium garlic clove, minced

½ teaspoon ground cumin

1 heaping teaspoon Dijon mustard

2 tablespoons fresh lemon juice or rice wine vinegar

Salt and freshly ground black pepper

6 tablespoons extra-virgin olive oil

1 pound carrots, peeled and coarsely grated

¼ cup raisins, dried currants, dried cranberries, or chopped dried apricots
(optional)

6 small red cabbage or radicchio leaves

Place garlic in a medium bowl. Whisk in cumin, mustard, lemon juice, a generous pinch of salt, and a few grinds of pepper. Slowly whisk in olive oil to make a thick vinaigrette. Add carrots and optional dried fruit.

Set cabbage or radicchio leaves on salad plates, fill with salad, and serve.

FOUR SLAWS

Unlike chopped lettuce, which browns and wilts, cabbage is hearty and built for survival. Store-bought coleslaw mix is snip-and-dump quick, and because it's factory-dried, there's no puddle of water to dilute the dressing as there is with freshly chopped cabbage. All you need to do is add fresh vegetables such as shredded carrots, bell pepper strips, chopped onion or scallions, and minced fresh herbs.

Using one basic formula, you can make four very different slaws—classic American, Asian, and two from south of the border, one sweet, one savory. The dressing recipes are easily increased or reduced.

1   bag (8 ounces) coleslaw mix
1   medium carrot, coarsely grated
½   medium red or yellow bell pepper (or ¼ of each), cut into thin strips
4   medium scallions, thinly sliced
¼   cup minced fresh cilantro (omit when making the American-style slaw)
    Dressing of choice (facing page)
    Salt and freshly ground black pepper

Combine coleslaw mix, carrot, bell pepper, scallions, and cilantro in a large bowl. Add dressing and a generous sprinkling of salt and pepper. Toss, and let stand for a few minutes for flavors to blend. Serve.

WHEN SHOULD I SERVE IT?
For all seasons
As a side salad at a buffet

HOW FAR AHEAD CAN I MAKE IT?
The slaw is best when dressed no more than 2 hours ahead. If it is made any further in advance, you may need to adjust the seasonings, especially the vinegar, adding a drop or two more.

CREAMY AMERICAN DRESSING

MAKES A SCANT ¾ CUP

- ½ teaspoon celery seeds
- ½ cup plus 1 tablespoon mayonnaise
- 2 tablespoons rice wine vinegar

Mix celery seeds, mayonnaise, and vinegar in a small bowl.

ASIAN DRESSING

MAKES ABOUT ⅔ CUP

Add ½ cup chopped honey-roasted peanuts to this slaw, if you like.

- ¼ cup rice wine vinegar
- ¼ cup soy sauce
- 2 tablespoons sugar
- 1 teaspoon ground ginger
- ½ teaspoon hot red pepper flakes

Whisk ingredients together with 2 tablespoons water in a small bowl until sugar dissolves.

ORANGE-CUMIN DRESSING

MAKES ¾ CUP

- ¼ cup frozen orange juice concentrate, thawed
- ¼ cup rice wine vinegar
- 1 teaspoon ground cumin
- ¼ cup olive oil

Whisk orange juice concentrate, vinegar, and cumin together in a 2-cup Pyrex measuring cup or small bowl. Slowly whisk in olive oil.

SALSA VERDE DRESSING

MAKES ABOUT 1 CUP

- 6 tablespoons jarred salsa verde
- ¼ cup fresh lime juice (from 2 limes)
- ¼ cup rice wine vinegar
- ¼ cup olive oil

Whisk salsa, lime juice, and vinegar together in a 2-cup Pyrex measuring cup or small bowl. Slowly whisk in olive oil.

GREEN BEAN–CHERRY TOMATO SALAD WITH BASIL-BUTTERMILK DRESSING

SERVES 12

I prefer to steam green beans in just enough salted water that they're perfectly done and seasoned by the time the water has almost evaporated, instead of boiling them in lots of water. Cooking them this way, however, does require your presence. As long as you're in the kitchen, you'll hear the sizzle of the last water droplets turning to steam; if you decide to visit the garden or fold some laundry in the basement, you may end up scorching the beans.

To cool them, dump them onto a paper towel–lined cookie sheet. That way, you won't wash away their flavor, as you would if you chilled them in cold running water. But be sure to undercook them slightly, since they'll continue to cook as they cool.

3 pounds green beans or 1½ pounds *each* yellow wax and green beans

1 teaspoon salt

1½ pints cherry tomatoes, halved lengthwise

DRESSING

⅓ cup mayonnaise

⅓ cup sour cream

⅓ cup buttermilk

¼ cup snipped fresh basil leaves

1 large garlic clove, minced

2 tablespoons rice wine vinegar

Salt and freshly ground black pepper to taste

WHEN SHOULD I SERVE IT?
As a side salad for spring and summer buffets and dinners
When you need a sturdy salad that holds up well

WHAT SHOULD I SERVE WITH IT?
Buttermilk-Honey Fried Chicken Fingers (page 29)
Mixed Grill with Tandoori Flavorings (page 62)

Grilled Chicken Breasts with Orange-Thyme Glaze (page 64)
Sear-Ahead Steaks or Salmon (page 66)

Place beans, ⅔ cup water, and salt in a large (12-inch) skillet. Cover, turn heat to high, and bring water to a boil. Once beans start to steam, set timer and cook until beans are crisp-tender, about 5 minutes. (Do not let skillet run dry.) Drain beans, then dump them onto a paper towel–lined cookie sheet to cool quickly.

Transfer cooled beans to a large bowl; add tomatoes.

TO MAKE DRESSING: Mix ingredients together in a small bowl. Pour dressing over beans and tomatoes, toss to coat, and serve.

HOW FAR AHEAD CAN I MAKE IT?
The beans, tomatoes, and dressing can all be prepared several hours ahead; toss together just before serving.

WHAT ABOUT LEFTOVERS?
The dressing's acidity will eventually dull the color of green beans, but the salad tastes fine the next

day. Drizzle with a few drops of vinegar to wake it up again.

FRESH CORN SALAD WITH CABBAGE AND BELL PEPPERS

You don't even have to cook the corn to make this salad. Simply cut it off the cob and toss it with a bag of coleslaw mix. Add red bell pepper, scallions, cilantro, and some black olives, if you like, for color and textural contrast. The dressing is simply a drizzling of olive oil and lime juice.

SERVES 16 TO 20

6   cups fresh corn (from about 7 large ears corn)
1   bag (12 ounces) coleslaw mix
1   red bell pepper, cored, seeded, and cut into medium dice
1   cup sliced scallions
1   can (16 ounces) black olives, drained and sliced (optional)
6   tablespoons chopped fresh cilantro
3/4 cup extra-virgin olive oil
    Juice of 2 large limes (about 1/4 cup)
1 1/2 teaspoons Old Bay or other Maryland-style spice blend
    Salt and freshly ground black pepper to taste

Mix all ingredients in a large bowl. If there's time, let salad stand for a few minutes to allow flavors to blend, then serve.

WHEN SHOULD I SERVE IT?
As a side salad for summer and early-fall buffets and dinners
When you need a sturdy salad that holds up well

ANY SHORTCUTS?
Although the salad will have a completely different flavor and texture, you can use thawed frozen corn.

HOW CAN I VARY IT?
Flavor it with basil instead of cilantro.

WHAT SHOULD I SERVE WITH IT?
Buttermilk-Honey Fried Chicken Fingers (page 29)
Oven-Barbecued Pork for Sandwiches or Carnitas (page 17)
Grown-Up Sloppy Joes (page 22)
Grilled Chicken Breasts with Orange-Thyme Glaze (page 64)

Sear-Ahead Steaks or Salmon (page 66)

HOW FAR AHEAD CAN I MAKE IT?
The salad and dressing can be prepared several hours ahead; toss together just before serving.

WHAT ABOUT LEFTOVERS?
The salad is excellent the next day. Squeeze in a little lime juice to freshen it.

ROASTED NEW POTATO SALAD WITH OLIVES, RED ONIONS, AND CREAMY VINAIGRETTE

This salad exploits a quick-cooking technique. Instead of roasting the potatoes in a preheated oven, start them in a cold oven so they can begin roasting while the oven heats. With the heating element on full blast for nearly the entire cooking time, the potatoes will take only half the usual time to brown — making it possible to have warm potato salad on the table in about half an hour.

SERVES 12

3½ pounds golf-ball-size red potatoes, rinsed, dried, and halved

¼ cup olive oil

2 teaspoons herbes de Provence or dried thyme leaves

   Salt and freshly ground black pepper

3 tablespoons rice wine vinegar

1½ tablespoons mayonnaise

1 medium garlic clove, minced

6 tablespoons extra-virgin olive oil

1 cup coarsely chopped pitted kalamata olives

½ medium red onion, cut into thin slivers

¼ cup chopped fresh parsley

WHEN SHOULD I SERVE IT?

For picnics, cookouts, and buffet suppers

At room temperature, for warm-weather entertaining

Warm, for rustic winter dinners

HOW CAN I VARY IT?

Substitute capers to taste for the olives.

WHAT SHOULD I SERVE WITH IT?

Buttermilk-Honey Fried Chicken Fingers (page 29)

Grilled Chicken Breasts with Orange-Thyme Glaze (page 64)

Sear-Ahead Steaks or Salmon (page 66)

Any grilled meats, especially sausages, or chicken or fish

HOW FAR AHEAD CAN I MAKE IT?

The salad can be made several hours before serving.

WHAT ABOUT LEFTOVERS?

It's good for at least 2 days.

Toss potatoes with olive oil, herbs, and a generous sprinkling of salt and pepper. Place them cut side down in a single layer on a rimmed baking sheet. Set pan in cold oven on the lowest oven rack and set oven to 425 degrees. Roast, without stirring, until potatoes are tender and golden brown, about 20 minutes.

Meanwhile, whisk vinegar, mayonnaise, garlic, a big pinch of salt, and a couple grinds of pepper in a 2-cup Pyrex measuring cup or a small bowl. Slowly whisk in oil, first in droplets, then in a slow, steady stream, to make a thick dressing.

Transfer potatoes to a large bowl. Toss with olives, onion, and parsley. Pour dressing over warm salad, and toss to coat. Serve warm or at room temperature.

SMOKED SALMON AND WATERCRESS SALAD WITH RED ONION–CAPER VINAIGRETTE

Here's a simple salmon salad that can be an excellent first course or part of a brunch buffet. Adding the sliced onion to the dressing instead of directly to the salad wilts it slightly so it loses its bitter bite.

SERVES 8

3 tablespoons fresh lemon juice

1 tablespoon rice wine vinegar

1 tablespoon Dijon mustard

Salt and freshly ground black pepper

¼ cup drained capers

½ medium red onion, thinly sliced

½ cup extra-virgin olive oil

8 cups trimmed watercress

6 ounces (about 8 thin slices) smoked salmon, torn or cut into bite-size pieces

WHEN SHOULD I SERVE IT?
When you need an impressive salad fast

As a first course for spring and summer dinners — Christmas too

HOW CAN I VARY IT?
Substitute mesclun, baby spinach, or arugula for the watercress.

Add a little chopped hard-boiled egg along with the salmon when tossing the salad.

WHAT SHOULD I SERVE WITH IT?
As a starter before:
Grilled Chicken Breasts with Orange-Thyme Glaze (page 64)
Butter-Roasted Lobster Tails (page 90)
Butterflied Cornish Hens with Apricot-Pistachio Dressing (page 76)
Beef Tenderloin with Cracked Black Pepper Coating and Red Wine–Thyme Pan Sauce (page 86)

Easy Baked Risotto (page 72)
Roast Rack of Lamb with Vinegar-Mint Pan Sauce (page 93)
Chicken-Mushroom Crepes (page 108)

HOW FAR AHEAD CAN I MAKE IT?
The dressing can be made 1 hour before serving.

WHAT ABOUT LEFTOVERS?
This doesn't keep well; make only what you think you'll use.

Mix lemon juice, vinegar, mustard, a big pinch of salt, and pepper to taste in a 2-cup Pyrex measuring cup or small bowl. Add capers and onion and toss to coat. Slowly add oil, pushing onion aside with a small whisk or fork and beating to form a thick dressing.

Mix watercress and half the salmon in a large bowl.

To serve, pour dressing over watercress and salmon and toss to coat. Arrange on salad plates, garnish with remaining smoked salmon, and serve.

Niçoise-Style Tuna Salad
with White Beans and Olives,
page 190

NIÇOISE-STYLE TUNA SALAD WITH WHITE BEANS AND OLIVES

I make this tuna salad often. I've nearly always got the majority of the ingredients on hand. You probably do too.

SERVES 4

4	large eggs
½	pound green beans, trimmed and halved
	Salt
2	cans (6 ounces each) solid white albacore tuna, drained
1	can (16 ounces) white beans, drained and rinsed
¼	cup sliced pitted black olives (California or kalamata)
¼	medium red onion, cut into thin slivers
1	teaspoon dried oregano
6	tablespoons extra-virgin olive oil
½	teaspoon finely grated lemon zest
3	tablespoons fresh lemon juice
	Freshly ground black pepper

Place eggs in a large saucepan and cover with water. Cover pan and bring to a full boil over medium-high heat. Turn off heat and let eggs stand, covered, for 10 minutes. Drain and run under cold running water until saucepan is cold. Let eggs stand in cold water until cool, then peel and quarter.

WHEN SHOULD I SERVE IT?
When you need a substantial starter before a light main course, such as soup
When you need an impressive lunch quickly

For gatherings of any size — the recipe multiplies well
As part of a cold buffet supper

ANY SHORTCUTS?
Skip the green beans and serve the tuna salad on a bed of lettuce instead.

Omit the eggs or buy them from the salad bar.

HOW CAN I VARY IT?
Substitute scallions for the red onion.

Combine green beans, ⅓ cup water, and a large pinch of salt in a 10-inch skillet, cover, and bring to a boil over high heat. Steam until crisp-tender, about 5 minutes. (Don't let skillet run dry.) Drain and cool on a paper towel–lined baking sheet.

Mix tuna, white beans, olives, onion, oregano, oil, lemon zest, and juice in a medium bowl. Adjust seasonings, adding salt and pepper to taste.

Arrange green beans, tuna salad, and eggs on four plates. Serve.

WHAT SHOULD I SERVE WITH IT?
Soups:
  Quick Curried Tomato Soup (page
    161)
  Year-Round Classic Gazpacho
    (page 162)

HOW FAR AHEAD CAN I MAKE IT?
A few hours ahead is fine.

WHAT ABOUT LEFTOVERS?
  What a treat to find leftover tuna salad in the fridge. Brighten the flavors with an extra squirt of fresh lemon juice.

SALMON CUCUMBER SALAD WITH SOUR CREAM–DILL DRESSING

Cucumbers and salmon are classic partners. Don't skip the salting and draining of the cucumbers, which both intensifies their flavor and makes the salad less watery. I learned the technique from my friend Betty Beccari.

SERVES 4

2   large cucumbers, peeled, halved lengthwise, seeds scraped out,
       and thinly sliced
     Salt
¼   medium red onion, thinly sliced
6   tablespoons sour cream
1   tablespoon red wine vinegar
½   teaspoon dried dill
     Freshly ground black pepper
4   4- to 5-ounce salmon fillets
     Olive oil

WHEN SHOULD I SERVE IT?
  As a spring or summer lunch
  As a light summer dinner
  As a substantial first course before a light main course — risotto, for example
  When you want a do-ahead meal

ANY SHORTCUTS?
  Steam or poach the salmon instead of grilling it. (Or skip the salmon and serve the cucumber as a summer side dish.)

HOW CAN I VARY IT?
  Substitute chopped fresh parsley or basil for the dill.

WHAT SHOULD I SERVE WITH IT?
Soups:
  Pureed Wild Mushroom and Potato Soup (page 160)
  Quick Curried Tomato Soup (page 161)
  Creamy Beet Soup with Caraway and Dill (page 157)
Sides:
  Easy Baked Risotto (page 72)
  Easy Butternut Squash Ravioli with Rosemary Oil (page 148)

HOW FAR AHEAD CAN I MAKE IT?
  The cucumber salad can be refrigerated for up to 3 hours. The salmon can be grilled up to 2 hours ahead. Cover loosely when cool.

WHAT ABOUT LEFTOVERS?
  Both the salad and the salmon make an excellent lunch or supper the next day.

Toss cucumbers with 1 teaspoon salt in a colander. Let stand, set over a bowl, until several tablespoons of juice have drained, 30 to 45 minutes. Pat cucumbers dry and transfer to a medium bowl. Add onion, sour cream, vinegar, dill, and pepper to taste and toss to coat.

About 30 minutes before serving, heat a gas grill, with all burners on high, for 10 to 15 minutes. Use a wire brush to clean grill rack, then use tongs to wipe a vegetable-oil-soaked rag over grill rack to prevent sticking. Close lid and return to temperature.

Brush salmon on both sides with oil and season with salt and pepper. Grill until just opaque, about 3 minutes per side. Serve hot or just warm. Place fillets on plates and spoon cucumber salad over and alongside salmon and serve.

SIDE DISHES

BROILED OR GRILLED ASPARAGUS

Make sure to preheat the grill fully and don't overcrowd it. Stay close by: it doesn't take long for the spears to cook.

SERVES 8

3 pounds medium to medium-thick asparagus, tough ends snapped off
Extra-virgin olive oil
Salt and freshly ground black pepper

Adjust oven rack to highest position and preheat broiler. Or preheat a gas grill, with all burners on high, for 10 to 15 minutes. Before grilling, use a wire brush to clean grill rack, then use tongs to wipe a vegetable-oil-soaked rag over grill rack to prevent sticking. Close lid and return to temperature.

Drizzle asparagus with enough olive oil to coat and season generously with salt and pepper. Place in a single layer on a rimmed baking sheet and place under broiler. Or place spears on grill, arranging them perpendicular to rack. Cook until bright green and just tender, about 4 minutes for medium asparagus; turn thicker spears once after 4 minutes and cook about 2 minutes longer.

WHEN SHOULD I SERVE IT?
For small or large parties

HOW CAN I VARY IT?
As it finishes cooking, toss with minced garlic, finely grated orange or lemon zest, or chopped fresh herbs, such as parsley, cilantro, dill, or basil.

WHAT SHOULD I SERVE WITH IT?
Grilled Chicken Breasts with Orange-Thyme Glaze (page 64)
Sear-Ahead Steaks or Salmon (page 66)
Beef Tenderloin with Cracked Black Pepper Coating and Red Wine–Thyme Pan Sauce (page 86)
Roast Rack of Lamb with Vinegar-Mint Pan Sauce (page 93)

HOW FAR AHEAD CAN I MAKE IT?
It can be grilled or broiled a couple of hours ahead. Cool, then cover loosely with plastic wrap.

WHAT ABOUT LEFTOVERS?
Drizzle with vinaigrette, sprinkle with chopped hard-boiled egg, and serve as a salad.

ORANGE-GLAZED ASPARAGUS

There isn't another green vegetable that's as easy to prepare as asparagus. Just snap each spear—it always breaks at the point between tender and tough—and discard the tough part. In this recipe, the asparagus is steamed in a small amount of orange juice and oil. The orange juice naturally reduces to a glaze.

SERVES 8

3 bunches (about 3 pounds) medium asparagus, tough ends snapped off
½ teaspoon salt
2 tablespoons extra-virgin olive oil
½ cup orange juice
   Grated zest of 1 large orange (optional)

Toss asparagus with salt and place in a large (12-inch) skillet. Add oil and juice to skillet, cover, and set over high heat. Once wisps of steam begin to escape around lid, cook for about 3 to 5 minutes longer, or until asparagus is just tender.

Transfer asparagus to a serving dish. Add zest, if using, to skillet, and continue to cook until pan juices reduce to a glaze, 2 to 3 minutes longer. Pour over asparagus and serve.

WHEN SHOULD I SERVE IT?
   At both small and large parties, as an accompaniment to any roasted or sautéed meat, poultry, or fish

HOW CAN I VARY IT?
   Substitute water for the orange juice.

WHAT SHOULD I SERVE WITH IT?
   Grilled Chicken Breasts with Orange-Thyme Glaze (page 64)
   Sear-Ahead Steaks or Salmon (page 66)
   Roast Rack of Lamb with Vinegar-Mint Pan Sauce (page 93)

HOW FAR AHEAD CAN I MAKE IT?
   The asparagus can be prepared and the ingredients put in the skillet 2 hours ahead.

WHAT ABOUT LEFTOVERS?
   The asparagus can be warmed in the microwave and served for lunch or supper the next day or so.

CREAMED SPINACH

Anyone who tries to serve sautéed spinach for a large dinner party does it only once. You pull out your biggest pot for that mountain of greens, and it's never big enough. By the time all the liquid evaporates, the spinach is drab and overcooked. Here's a much better dish for those occasions. It can be completely prepared ahead of time, and it's quick.

SERVES 8

$1\frac{1}{2}$ cups whole milk

4 boxes (10 ounces each) frozen chopped spinach, thawed and squeezed dry; reserve $\frac{1}{2}$ cup liquid

3 large garlic cloves, minced

2 tablespoons butter

3 tablespoons all-purpose flour

$\frac{1}{2}$ cup grated Parmesan cheese

$\frac{1}{2}$ teaspoon ground nutmeg

Salt and freshly ground black pepper

WHEN SHOULD I SERVE IT?
As an accompaniment to any roast at a dinner party or buffet
When you need a make-ahead vegetable
At both small and large parties — the recipe can be halved or multiplied

ANY SHORTCUTS?
Use pregrated Parmesan cheese.
Buy ready-peeled garlic cloves.

WHAT SHOULD I SERVE WITH IT?
Perfect Roast Chicken (page 38)
Sear-Ahead Steaks or Salmon (page 66)

Beef Tenderloin with Cracked Black Pepper Coating and Red Wine–Thyme Pan Sauce (page 86)
Roast Rack of Lamb with Vinegar-Mint Pan Sauce (page 93)

Combine milk, reserved spinach liquid, and garlic in a 1-quart Pyrex measuring cup or small microwave-safe bowl covered with a saucer and microwave (or heat slowly in a medium saucepan) until very hot and steamy. Let stand for 5 to 10 minutes to soften garlic.

Melt butter in a Dutch oven over medium-high heat. Whisk in flour. Add hot milk mixture all at once, then whisk until smooth. Stir in spinach and cook until sauce is thick and bubbly and spinach is tender but still green, about 5 minutes.

Stir in cheese and season with nutmeg and a generous sprinkling of salt and pepper. Serve hot.

HOW FAR AHEAD CAN I MAKE IT?
The spinach can be cooked 1 to 2 days ahead: Turn the cooked spinach onto a large rimmed baking sheet to cool quickly, then transfer

to a covered container and refrigerate. When ready to serve, warm over very low heat until heated through.

WHAT ABOUT LEFTOVERS?
Leftover creamed spinach can be thinned with chicken broth to make cream of spinach soup.

CREAMED GREEN BEANS WITH MUSTARD SAUCE AND TOASTED ALMONDS

With so many other dishes on the Thanksgiving menu demanding last-minute attention, many cooks turn to the clichéd green bean casserole made with canned green beans, cream of mushroom soup, and fried onions. With just a bit of effort, however, it's possible to make a casserole with fresh beans that is far more appealing.

SERVES 8 TO 10

½   cup slivered almonds, toasted
4   tablespoons (½ stick) butter
1   package (16 ounces) frozen pearl onions
2   pounds green beans, trimmed and snapped into 2-inch pieces
    Salt
1½ cups whole milk
½   cup chicken broth
¼   cup Dijon mustard
3   tablespoons all-purpose flour
    Freshly ground black pepper

Spread almonds on a small baking sheet and toast in a 325-degree oven, stirring occasionally, until fragrant, about 10 minutes.

Melt 2 tablespoons butter in a large (12-inch) deep skillet over medium-high heat. Add still-frozen pearl onions and sauté, shaking pan occasionally until golden brown, 5 to 7 minutes. Dump onto a large rimmed baking sheet.

Add green beans, ¾ cup water, and a scant teaspoon salt to same skillet. Turn heat to high, cover, and cook until wisps of steam begin to escape around lid. Continue to cook until beans are tender but still bright green, about 7 minutes longer. Drain beans, transfer to baking sheet with onions, and spread out to cool. Set skillet aside.

SLOW-ROASTED PLUM TOMATOES WITH PESTO-FLAVORED CRUMBS

Salting tomatoes rids them of their excess juice, and slowly roasting them concentrates their flavor, making even those that are out of season taste good. Italian plums work especially well.

SERVES 12

12	large plum tomatoes, halved
1½	teaspoons salt
½	cup plain dry bread crumbs
2	tablespoons store-bought pesto
1	tablespoon extra-virgin olive oil, plus extra for drizzling

Place tomato halves cut side up on a large wire rack set over a rimmed baking sheet and sprinkle with salt. Turn tomatoes over and let stand for 30 minutes to drain some of their liquid.

Adjust oven rack to upper-middle position and heat oven to 325 degrees. Grease a 13-by-9-inch baking pan.

Mix bread crumbs, pesto, and oil in a small bowl. Sprinkle a portion of crumbs on cut side of each tomato half, and place them in baking pan. Bake until soft but not falling apart, about 30 minutes.

Without moving baking pan, turn on broiler and cook until crumbs are crisp and golden brown, about 5 minutes. Drizzle with oil and serve.

WHEN SHOULD I SERVE IT?
With any sautéed, grilled, or roasted meat
As a brunch dish — with eggs
As a side dish for a large group

WHAT SHOULD I SERVE WITH IT?
Creamy Baked Macaroni and Cheese (page 32)
Beef Tenderloin with Cracked Black Pepper Coating and Red Wine–Thyme Pan Sauce (page 86)
Roast Rack of Lamb with Vinegar-Mint Pan Sauce (page 93)
Easy Savory Strata (page 102)

HOW FAR AHEAD CAN I MAKE IT?
The crumb topping can be made 1 day ahead.

WHAT ABOUT LEFTOVERS?
Chop them and make a pasta sauce with them, add them to soup, or use them in an omelet or frittata.

ROASTED ONIONS IN THEIR SKINS

Not only are roasted onions handsome, they're simple. The onions steam in their skins, and the cut surfaces brown.

SERVES 8

4   medium yellow onions, unpeeled, halved
2   tablespoons olive oil
    Salt and freshly ground black pepper

Adjust oven rack to lowest position and heat oven to 425 degrees.

Toss onions with oil and a generous sprinkling of salt and pepper. Place cut side down on a rimmed baking sheet. Roast until onions are tender and cut surfaces are a rich golden brown, 30 to 35 minutes.

Adjust seasonings, adding salt and/or pepper if needed, and serve in their skins.

WHEN SHOULD I SERVE IT?

With any fall or winter dinner—the recipe is easily halved or doubled

For a completely do-ahead vegetable

ANY SHORTCUTS?

To reduce the cooking time, select smaller onions and serve 1 to 2 halves per person; be sure to spread them out on the baking sheet. The less crowded they are, the more quickly they brown.

HOW CAN I VARY IT?

Toss the onions with dried herbs such as thyme leaves or herbes de Provence before roasting.

Sprinkle them with minced fresh thyme or rosemary as soon as they come out of the oven. Or sprinkle with chopped fresh parsley just before serving.

The roasted onions are excellent drizzled with a little balsamic vinegar.

WHAT SHOULD I SERVE WITH IT?

Rosemary-Scented Roast Pork Loin Stuffed with Roasted Garlic, Dried Apricots, and Cranberries with Port Wine Sauce (page 83)

Beef Tenderloin with Cracked Black Pepper Coating and Red Wine–Thyme Pan Sauce (page 86)

Roast Rack of Lamb with Vinegar-Mint Pan Sauce (page 93)

HOW FAR AHEAD CAN I MAKE IT?

The onions can be roasted 3 to 4 hours ahead. Serve at room temperature or warm in a 300-degree oven for about 10 minutes.

WHAT ABOUT LEFTOVERS?

Warm leftover roasted onions as suggested above or cut them into medium dice and use in place of sautéed onions in any dish.

MAKE-AHEAD MASHED POTATOES

As much as I love mashed potatoes, I don't like trying to prepare them at the last minute. After a few tests, I discovered that mashed potatoes can be made up to a couple of days in advance, as long as you don't add the butter until the end.

SERVES 8 TO 10

3 pounds medium Idaho (baking) potatoes, scrubbed
1½ cups half-and-half, heated, plus extra if necessary
Salt
6 tablespoons (¾ stick) butter, softened

Place potatoes in a large pot with water to cover. Cover and bring to a boil over high heat. Reduce heat to medium-low and simmer until potatoes are tender when pierced with a thin-bladed knife, about 20 minutes.

Run unpeeled potatoes through a food mill or a ricer into a medium bowl. Or, holding hot potatoes with a pot holder, peel them, then place them in a standing mixer fitted with the paddle attachment and beat until smooth; or place in a large bowl and beat with a hand mixer. Add half-

WHEN SHOULD I SERVE IT?
With just about any meat, poultry, or fish dish
When you need a do-ahead accompaniment

WHAT SHOULD I SERVE WITH IT?
Perfect Roast Chicken (page 38)
Boneless Coq au Vin (page 42)
One of the stews (pages 48–53)

Butter-Roasted Lobster Tails (page 90)
Butterflied Cornish Hens with Apricot-Pistachio Dressing (page 76)
Twin Turkeys with Rich Pan Gravy (page 78)
Rosemary-Scented Roast Pork Loin Stuffed with Roasted Garlic,

Dried Apricots, and Cranberries with Port Wine Sauce (page 83)
Beef Tenderloin with Cracked Black Pepper Coating and Red Wine–Thyme Pan Sauce (page 86)
Sear-Ahead Steaks or Salmon (page 66)
Roast Rack of Lamb with Vinegar-Mint Pan Sauce (page 93)

and-half and a generous sprinkling of salt to potatoes. Stir, or continue to beat, adding more half-and-half, if necessary, until smooth, light, and fluffy.

If not serving immediately, transfer potatoes to a heatproof bowl set over a pan of simmering water. Or, if making potatoes ahead, cool, cover, and refrigerate. Then, 30 minutes before serving, microwave potatoes until warm and pour into heatproof bowl set over a pan of simmering water (or simply warm potatoes in heatproof bowl set over a pan of simmering water).

Stir butter into potatoes until melted. Serve, or cover with plastic wrap and keep warm over simmering water until ready to serve.

GARLIC MASHED POTATOES

Sauté 8 to 10 whole garlic cloves in 2 tablespoons olive oil in a small (8-inch) skillet over medium-low heat until golden brown and soft and creamy inside, about 5 minutes. Remove with a slotted spoon and mash to a paste with a fork. Stir into potatoes either when you mash them or along with the butter.

HOW CAN I VARY IT?
Make Garlic Mashed Potatoes (see above).

HOW FAR AHEAD CAN I MAKE IT?
The mashed potatoes, without the butter, can be cooled and refrigerated in a covered container for up to 2 days. Once the butter has been added, the potatoes can sit in a heatproof bowl over a pan of simmering water for up to 30 minutes.

WHAT ABOUT LEFTOVERS?
Mashed potatoes reheat well in the microwave. Beat in a little more butter to freshen them up or a little more milk to moisten them, if necessary, or throw in a handful of chopped fresh herbs, such as parsley, chives, or basil.

CRISP POTATO CAKE

Elegant and quick, this potato cake is on my short list of weeknight side dishes.

SERVES 4

1½   tablespoons butter
2   medium Idaho (baking) potatoes, peeled
¼   teaspoon salt
    Freshly ground black pepper

Melt 1 tablespoon butter in a 10-inch skillet over low heat. Meanwhile, grate potatoes on large holes of a box grater into a bowl. Squeeze as much excess liquid from potatoes as possible.

Increase heat under pan to medium-high and heat for a minute or two. Put potatoes in pan, pressing with your fingertips or a metal spatula to form a flat cake. Cook until bottom is crisp and golden, 4 to 5 minutes. Place a small plate over pan and invert cake onto plate. Add remaining ½ tablespoon butter to pan, and slide cake back into pan as soon as butter melts. Continue to cook until golden brown on second side, 4 to 5 minutes.

Transfer to a cutting board, sprinkle with salt and pepper to taste, and cut into wedges. Serve.

WHEN SHOULD I SERVE IT?
For dinner parties
When you need a potato dish fast

ANY SHORTCUTS?
Grate the potatoes, unpeeled, in the food processor.

HOW CAN I VARY IT?
To serve two, halve the recipe, and cook the potato cake in an 8-inch skillet. The cooking time will be slightly less.

For six to eight people, use 3 potatoes, increase the butter to 2½ tablespoons, and cook in a large (12-inch) skillet. Increase the cooking time slightly.

WHAT SHOULD I SERVE WITH IT?
Butter-Roasted Lobster Tails (page 90)
Sear-Ahead Steaks or Salmon (page 66)
Roast Rack of Lamb with Vinegar-Mint Pan Sauce (page 93)
My Big Fat Greek Frittata (page 100)

HOW FAR AHEAD CAN I MAKE IT?
The cooked potato cake can be left in the skillet over very low heat for up to 30 minutes; turn it over occasionally to keep both sides crisp.

SMASHED NEW POTATOES

These appealingly rustic potatoes are simpler than classic mashed potatoes and more interesting than plain boiled.

SERVES 6

2 pounds small red potatoes
6 tablespoons (³/₄ stick) butter
   Salt and freshly ground black pepper

Cover potatoes with water in a Dutch oven or other large pot and bring to a boil, lid ajar, then reduce heat and simmer until a skewer inserted into potatoes can be removed with no resistance, 15 to 20 minutes.

Reserve ¹/₂ cup potato cooking liquid.

Smash potatoes with a large fork. Add butter, reserved potato water, and a generous sprinkling of salt and pepper. Continue to stir and mash until potatoes are part lumpy, part smooth. Adjust seasonings, adding more salt and pepper if necessary. Serve or keep warm, covered with plastic wrap, over a pot of simmering water until ready to serve.

WHEN SHOULD I SERVE IT?
When you don't have time to make mashed potatoes

HOW CAN I VARY IT?
Add a handful of chopped fresh herbs, such as parsley or basil, or snipped fresh chives.

WHAT SHOULD I SERVE WITH IT?
Perfect Roast Chicken (page 38)
Boneless Coq au Vin (page 42)

One of the stews (pages 48–53)
Butter-Roasted Lobster Tails (page 90)
Rosemary-Scented Roast Pork Loin Stuffed with Roasted Garlic, Dried Apricots, and Cranberries with Port Wine Sauce (page 83)
Sear-Ahead Steaks or Salmon (page 66)
Roast Rack of Lamb with Vinegar-Mint Pan Sauce (page 93)

HOW FAR AHEAD CAN I MAKE IT?
The mashed potatoes can be kept warm in a heatproof bowl set over a pan of barely simmering water for up to 30 minutes.

WHAT ABOUT LEFTOVERS?
Leftover potatoes are good warmed in the microwave.

ROASTED RED POTATOES

Roasting potatoes on the bottom rack of the oven as it heats makes them brown beautifully, and they also roast nearly twice as quickly.

SERVES 8 TO 12

3 pounds small red new potatoes, rinsed, dried, and halved
¼ cup olive oil
1 teaspoon salt
   Freshly ground black pepper

Toss potatoes with oil, salt, and pepper to taste. Arrange cut side down on a large rimmed baking sheet. Set pan on lowest rack in cold oven, turn oven on to 425 degrees, and roast until potatoes are tender and golden brown, about 20 minutes.

Transfer to a serving dish and serve hot, warm, or at room temperature.

WHEN SHOULD I SERVE IT?

When you want a carefree side dish

For a big dinner or a buffet — the potatoes hold well and are equally good served hot, warm, or at room temperature

HOW CAN I VARY IT?

Toss potatoes with dried herbs before roasting: dried thyme leaves and herbes de Provence are two of my favorites.

Add fresh herbs — chopped parsley, basil, or chives, or sliced scallion greens — at the end.

WHAT SHOULD I SERVE WITH IT?

Perfect Roast Chicken (page 38)

Butterflied Cornish Hens with Apricot-Pistachio Dressing (page 76)

Rosemary-Scented Roast Pork Loin Stuffed with Roasted Garlic, Dried Apricots, and Cranberries with Port Wine Sauce (page 83)

Beef Tenderloin with Cracked Black Pepper Coating and Red Wine–Thyme Pan Sauce (page 86)

Roast Rack of Lamb with Vinegar-Mint Pan Sauce (page 93)

My Big Fat Greek Frittata (page 100)

HOW FAR AHEAD CAN I MAKE IT?

Roasted new potatoes are so simple that you can, and should, make them close to serving time, 30 minutes ahead at most. If they are done before you're ready, simply turn off the oven and crack the door.

WHAT ABOUT LEFTOVERS?

Pop leftover potatoes in the microwave to take the chill off them, then place cut side down in a skillet to recrisp over medium heat for breakfast. Or cube them and make home fries or hash browns.

POTATO GRATIN
WITH GARLIC AND THYME

Bold and garlicky, these potatoes complement most stews and braises. I like using chicken broth instead of the usual cream.

SERVES 12

6	garlic cloves
½	cup extra-virgin olive oil
1½	teaspoons dried thyme leaves
4	pounds Idaho (baking) potatoes
	Salt and freshly ground black pepper
3	cups chicken broth

Adjust oven rack to lowest position and heat oven to 325 degrees.

With a food processor running, add garlic and process to mince. With motor running, add oil and continue to process for about 30 seconds. Transfer mixture to a small bowl, stir in thyme, and set aside.

When ready to assemble gratin, peel potatoes. Slice using slicing blade of processor or thinly slice with a sharp knife.

Brush a little garlic oil mixture over bottom of a 13-by-9-inch (or similar size) baking dish. Make 4 layers in the following order: potatoes, a generous brushing of garlic oil, and a light sprinkling of salt and pepper. Pour chicken broth around edges of pan to avoid washing off garlic and herbs. Bake until most of broth has been absorbed, about 45 minutes.

Turn on broiler, move pan to middle rack, and broil until potatoes are spotty brown, about 5 minutes. Let rest for 10 minutes, and serve.

WHEN SHOULD I SERVE IT?
Whenever you need a do-ahead potato dish

WHAT SHOULD I SERVE WITH IT?
Boneless Coq au Vin (page 42)
One of the stews (pages 48–53)

Rosemary-Scented Roast Pork Loin Stuffed with Roasted Garlic, Dried Apricots, and Cranberries with Port Wine Sauce (page 83)
Beef Tenderloin with Cracked Black Pepper Coating and Red Wine–Thyme Pan Sauce (page 86)

HOW FAR AHEAD CAN I MAKE IT?
You can bake the gratin 2 hours ahead and reheat it.

WHAT ABOUT LEFTOVERS?
Potato gratin is almost as good the second time around.

TWICE-BAKED SWEET POTATOES

A variation on twice-baked potatoes, these are an eye-catching takeoff on a sweet potato casserole. The sweet potato flesh is pureed with butter and milk, returned to the hollowed-out shells, and topped with mini marshmallows before a final baking.

    You can puree the potatoes in a blender or a food processor; use the blender for an especially silky texture.

SERVES 8

4   medium sweet potatoes (about 2 pounds), scrubbed and halved lengthwise

¹⁄₃   cup buttermilk

¹⁄₃   cup milk, or as needed

4   tablespoons (¹⁄₂ stick) butter

¹⁄₄   teaspoon salt

    Freshly ground black pepper

¹⁄₂   cup miniature marshmallows for garnish

Adjust oven rack to lowest position and heat oven to 400 degrees.

Place potatoes cut side down on a foil- or parchment-lined baking sheet. Bake until fork-tender, about 30 minutes. Let cool slightly.

Holding a potato half with a pot holder, scoop potato flesh into a blender or food processor, leaving a ¹⁄₄-inch shell. Repeat with remaining potatoes; set shells aside.

With motor running, gradually add both milks to potatoes. Add

butter, then process, adding a little more milk if necessary, until potatoes are silky smooth. Add salt and pepper to taste.

Spoon puree back into potato shells. Sprinkle marshmallows over potatoes. Place on baking sheet and bake until potatoes are hot and marshmallows are golden brown, 10 to 12 minutes. Serve hot.

WHEN SHOULD I SERVE IT?

For classic fall and winter celebrations like Thanksgiving, Christmas, and New Year's Day

For any fall or winter dinner party or buffet — the recipe is easily multiplied

When do-ahead is important

For a roast pork or poultry dinner

ANY SHORTCUTS?

Serve the sweet potato puree on its own rather than stuffing it back into the shells.

HOW CAN I VARY IT?

If you don't want to top the potatoes with marshmallows, consider pecans, walnuts, or shredded coconut.

Flavor the potatoes with ground nutmeg, finely grated orange or lemon zest, dried thyme leaves, minced fresh rosemary, or, for a little heat, cayenne pepper.

WHAT SHOULD I SERVE WITH IT?

Butterflied Cornish Hens with Apricot-Pistachio Dressing (page 76)

Twin Turkeys with Rich Pan Gravy (page 78)

Rosemary-Scented Roast Pork Loin Stuffed with Roasted Garlic, Dried Apricots, and Cranberries with Port Wine Sauce (page 83)

HOW FAR AHEAD CAN I MAKE IT?

The stuffed potatoes, without the marshmallows, can be covered and refrigerated for up to 2 days.

WHAT ABOUT LEFTOVERS?

The puree can be refrigerated for 2 days. Warm in the microwave or in a covered saucepan over very low heat, thinning it with extra milk if necessary.

COUSCOUS WITH CHICKPEAS AND CARROTS

Quick and foolproof, couscous is another of those side dishes that's equally good for a simple supper or a large feast.

SERVES 6 TO 8

1   tablespoon vegetable oil or olive oil
½   medium onion, cut into small dice
1   large garlic clove, minced
2   medium carrots, peeled and coarsely grated (about 1 cup)
1   box (10 ounces) plain couscous
1   can (16 ounces) chickpeas, drained and rinsed
2   cups chicken broth
    Salt and freshly ground black pepper

Heat oil in a large saucepan over medium-high heat. Add onion and garlic and sauté until softened, 2 to 3 minutes. Add carrots, couscous, and chickpeas and stir to combine. Stir in broth and bring to a simmer. Cover, turn off heat, and let stand until broth is absorbed, 4 to 5 minutes.

Adjust seasonings, adding salt if necessary and pepper to taste. Fluff with a fork and serve.

WHEN SHOULD I SERVE IT?
As a sturdy, simple, but attractive side dish
For a small dinner party or a large buffet

ANY SHORTCUTS?
Don't be tempted to use packaged shredded carrots; they have an off flavor that will permeate the dish.

HOW CAN I VARY IT?
When fluffing the couscous, add

a handful of raisins, dried currants, dried cranberries, or diced dried apricots.
Add toasted pine nuts, slivered almonds, or pistachios.
Stir in a couple of tablespoons of chopped fresh parsley or cilantro.

WHAT SHOULD I SERVE WITH IT?
Shish Kebabs (page 56)
Mixed Grill with Tandoori Flavorings (page 62)

Butterflied Cornish Hens with Apricot-Pistachio Dressing (page 76)

HOW FAR AHEAD CAN I MAKE IT?
You can make the couscous up to the point of adding the broth 2 hours ahead and set aside, covered, at room temperature.

WHAT ABOUT LEFTOVERS?
Leftover couscous heats up beautifully in the microwave.

YELLOW RICE WITH GREEN PEAS

Because it's so versatile, this rice pilaf is suitable for a wide variety of occasions. You can sauté the onion ahead, stir in the rice and turmeric, and set the pan aside; then, about half an hour before serving, just add chicken broth and simmer until done. The turmeric colors the rice a festive yellow. The green peas, like parsley, add color—but unlike parsley, they also count as a vegetable if you don't want to cook another one.

SERVES 6 TO 8

2   tablespoons olive oil
1   medium onion
2   cups long-grain white rice
2   teaspoons ground turmeric
1   quart chicken broth
1   cup frozen green peas, thawed
    Salt and freshly ground black pepper

Heat oil in a Dutch oven or other heavy pot over medium-high heat. Add onion and sauté until softened, 3 to 4 minutes. Add rice and turmeric and stir to coat rice. Add broth and bring to a simmer, then reduce heat to low, cover, and simmer until broth is absorbed and rice is just tender, about 20 minutes.

Stir in peas. Adjust seasonings, adding salt if necessary and pepper to taste. Serve.

LEMON RICE

Omit turmeric and peas and substitute ½ cup fresh lemon juice for ½ cup broth. Stir in 2 teaspoons grated lemon zest and 2 tablespoons chopped fresh parsley when rice is cooked.

COCONUT RICE

Omit turmeric and peas and substitute 2 cups unsweetened coconut milk for 2 cups broth. Stir in 2 thinly sliced scallions when rice is cooked.

SAFFRON RICE

Omit turmeric and peas and add 4 generous pinches of saffron threads along with broth.

PARMESAN RICE

Omit turmeric and peas and stir in ¾ cup grated Parmesan cheese and several grinds of black pepper when rice is cooked.

WHEN SHOULD I SERVE IT?
As a colorful side dish
For any season
When you want to keep it simple

HOW CAN I VARY IT?
Omit the turmeric and peas and flavor the rice however you like.

WHAT SHOULD I SERVE WITH IT?
Perfect Roast Chicken (page 38)
Boneless Coq au Vin (page 42)
Shish Kebabs (page 56)
Mixed Grill with Tandoori
   Flavorings (page 62)

Grilled Chicken Breasts with
   Orange-Thyme Glaze (page 64)
Butterflied Cornish Hens with
   Apricot-Pistachio Dressing
   (page 76)

HOW FAR AHEAD CAN I MAKE IT?
You can sauté the onion and add the rice and turmeric 3 to 4 hours before serving. Set aside, covered, at room temperature.

WHAT ABOUT LEFTOVERS?
Leftover rice heats up well in the microwave (moisten with a little water if it needs softening). Or add to a pot of soup.

QUICK SOUTHERN-STYLE BAKED BEANS

Why bother spending a day making baked beans from scratch when you can doctor up canned ones so they taste just as good? This recipe can be easily multiplied or divided. Figure on a large (28-ounce) can of beans for every six guests and make sure the baking pan is wide and shallow so the liquid from the beans will evaporate as quickly as possible. Some canned beans contain more liquid than others, so they may take longer to reduce. My favorite brand of beans is Bush's, which has a higher ratio of beans to liquid.

SERVES 18

For sweeter baked beans, try KC Masterpiece Barbecue Sauce. Kraft Original Barbecue Sauce will produce beans with a bit more tang.

8	slices bacon, halved
1	medium onion, cut into small dice
1/2	medium green bell pepper, cut into small dice
3	large cans (28 ounces each) pork and beans
3/4	cup store-bought barbecue sauce
1/2	cup packed light or dark brown sugar
1/4	cup distilled white vinegar or cider vinegar
2	teaspoons dried mustard or 2 tablespoons Dijon mustard

Adjust oven rack to lower-middle position and heat oven to 325 degrees. Grease a 13-by-9-inch (or similar size) baking pan.

Fry bacon in a large (12-inch) deep skillet until it is partially cooked and has released about ¼ cup drippings. Remove bacon from pan and drain on paper towels. Add onion and bell pepper to drippings in pan and sauté until tender, about 5 minutes. Add beans and remaining ingredients and bring to a simmer. (If skillet is not large enough, add beans and heat to a simmer, then transfer to a large bowl and stir in remaining ingredients.)

Pour beans into greased baking pan. Top with bacon and bake until beans are bubbly and sauce is the consistency of pancake syrup, about 2 hours. Let stand to thicken slightly before serving.

WHEN SHOULD I SERVE IT?

For casual American-style gatherings, such as reunions and potlucks

For small dinners (reduce the recipe) as well as big buffets

When do-ahead is important

HOW CAN I VARY IT?

For a more traditional New England–style dish, omit the green pepper and substitute molasses for the brown sugar.

WHAT SHOULD I SERVE WITH IT?

Buttermilk-Honey Fried Chicken Fingers (page 29)

Oven-Barbecued Pork for Sandwiches (page 17)

Grown-Up Sloppy Joes (page 22)

It's the essential accompaniment to barbecued chicken and ribs.

HOW FAR AHEAD CAN I MAKE IT?

The beans can be prepared 3 hours before baking, and they can be baked 2 hours before serving.

Once baked, the beans can be held in a 200-degree oven for an hour or more. They're good served hot, warm, or at room temperature.

WHAT ABOUT LEFTOVERS?

Leftover baked beans are almost as good as the first time around. Warm in the microwave or on the stovetop over low heat.

CLASSIC BREAD STUFFING WITH SAGE, PARSLEY, AND THYME

For an easy yet memorable stuffing, one key is the right bread. To make a light stuffing with a crisp exterior and moist interior, choose crusty Italian- or French-style loaves. Take the time to air-dry the bread cubes. Adding a couple of eggs with the broth helps the bread cubes cling together. Finally, stuffing benefits from a two-step cooking process: bake it covered until it becomes hot and steamy, then uncover it and bake until it develops an appealingly crusted top.

SERVES 10 TO 12

Baking the stuffing separately allows it to cook through without overcooking the bird.

1	pound crusty Italian or French bread, cut into ½-inch cubes (10–12 cups)
4	tablespoons (½ stick) butter
2	medium onions, cut into medium dice (about 2 cups)
2	medium celery stalks, cut into medium dice (about 1 cup)
¼	cup minced fresh parsley
1	teaspoon dried rubbed sage
1	teaspoon dried thyme leaves
¾	teaspoon salt
½	teaspoon freshly ground black pepper
2	cups chicken broth
2	large eggs, lightly beaten

Spread bread cubes in a single layer on two large baking sheets or jelly-roll pans and let dry for a couple of hours at room temperature. (Bread can be left to dry overnight.)

Adjust oven racks to lower- and upper-middle positions and heat oven to 400 degrees.

Bake bread until toasty and dry, 12 to 15 minutes. Remove from oven and set aside. Reduce oven temperature to 350 degrees.

Meanwhile, melt butter in a large (12-inch) skillet over medium-high heat. Add onions and celery and sauté until soft, 8 to 10 minutes.

Transfer sautéed vegetables to a large bowl, add bread and remaining ingredients, and mix well. Turn into a greased 3-quart baking dish. Cover with foil and bake until steamy hot, about 30 minutes.

Remove foil and continue to bake until top is crusty, about 10 minutes longer. Serve.

CLASSIC BREAD STUFFING WITH SAUSAGE OR BACON

Omit butter. Fry 1 pound bulk breakfast or Italian sausage in a large (12-inch) skillet until it loses its raw color or fry 1 pound bacon, cut into 1-inch pieces, until crisp. Remove with a slotted spoon and set aside. Then sauté onions and celery as directed, in 4 tablespoons drippings (rather than butter). Add the sausage or bacon with remaining stuffing ingredients.

WHEN SHOULD I SERVE IT?

For the fall and winter holidays, such as Thanksgiving, Christmas, and New Year's Day

For any fall or winter dinner party or buffet — the recipe is easily multiplied

For a roast pork or poultry dinner

ANY SHORTCUTS?

Fresh or toasted plain bread cubes are usually available around the holidays.

HOW CAN I VARY IT?

Use a combination of 8 cups dried, toasted cubed corn bread and 4 cups dried, toasted cubed French or Italian bread.

Add ¾ cup dried fruit — prunes, cranberries, cherries, apricots or pitted oil-cured olives

Add ¾ cup toasted pecans, walnuts, hazelnuts, or pine nuts. Toast in a 325-degree oven for 5 to 10 minutes; rub hazelnuts with a kitchen towel while still hot to remove most skins.

WHAT SHOULD I SERVE WITH IT?

Butterflied Cornish Hens with Apricot-Pistachio Dressing (page 76)

Rosemary-Scented Roast Pork Loin Stuffed with Roasted Garlic, Dried Apricots, and Cranberries with Port Wine Sauce (page 83)

Twin Turkeys with Rich Pan Gravy (page 78)

HOW FAR AHEAD CAN I MAKE IT?

The bread can be dried and toasted up to 1 week ahead.

The onions and celery can be sautéed, cooled, covered, and refrigerated for up to 2 days.

The broth, herbs, and eggs can be mixed 2 hours ahead and refrigerated; mix the stuffing ingredients shortly before baking.

WHAT ABOUT LEFTOVERS?

Warm in the microwave or in a 300-degree oven and serve with the leftover turkey.

JUST-RIGHT CRANBERRY SAUCE WITH GINGER AND ORANGE

This cranberry sauce is soft yet substantial, with some of the tart berries remaining whole and others collapsing into the sweet sauce. This one keeps its shape instead of invading everything else on the plate.

MAKES ABOUT 2 CUPS

1   bag (12 ounces) fresh or frozen cranberries, rinsed, stems and any bruised berries discarded
1   cup sugar
    Grated zest and juice of 1 large orange (¹⁄₂ cup juice)
³⁄₄   teaspoon ground ginger

Bring cranberries, sugar, orange juice (reserve zest), and ginger to a boil over medium-high heat in a medium saucepan. Reduce heat and simmer until some of the berries start to pop, about 1 minute. Cover, turn off heat, and let stand for 10 minutes.

Stir zest into sauce. Cool to room temperature, then refrigerate. Serve cold.

WHEN SHOULD I SERVE IT?

As an accompaniment to fall and winter dinners — especially for pork, game, and poultry

For buffets — it's easy to make a lot

When you want an accompaniment that can be made ahead

ANY SHORTCUTS?

Although it will have a less distinct orange flavor, you can omit the zest and use bottled or cartoned orange juice.

HOW CAN I VARY IT?

Add a cinnamon stick or 6 whole cloves along with the ginger.

Add dried fruits such as raisins or currants at the beginning of cooking.

Stir in toasted chopped nuts once the sauce has cooled.

WHAT SHOULD I SERVE WITH IT?

Twin Turkeys with Rich Pan Gravy (page 78)

Chicken-Mushroom Crepes (page 108)

Rosemary-Scented Roast Pork Loin Stuffed with Roasted Garlic, Dried Apricots, and Cranberries with Port Wine Sauce (page 83)

HOW FAR AHEAD CAN I MAKE IT?

The cranberry sauce can be refrigerated in an airtight container for up to 1 month.

WHAT ABOUT LEFTOVERS?

Serve with leftover pork and poultry roasts or sandwiches.

BREADS

BAKE-AHEAD YORKSHIRE PUDDINGS (OR POPOVERS)

For easy-to-serve Yorkshire pudding, bake it in individual molds. But don't buy special popover pans—just use muffin tins. To save time, set the batter-filled muffin tins in a cold oven and bake the puddings while the oven heats (this technique also produces crisper puddings).

Using instant flour results in large, shapely puddings (or popovers) that won't stick to the pan. Located in the baking aisle, Wondra is a nationally available brand. If making classic Yorkshire puddings, use beef drippings. To make popovers, opt for the butter.

MAKES 12 PUDDINGS; SERVES 8 TO 12

- 1½ cups instant (quick-mixing) flour, such as Wondra
- 1 teaspoon salt
- 1½ cups nonfat milk
- 4 large eggs
- 2 tablespoons butter, melted, or beef drippings

Mix flour and salt in a medium bowl. Mix milk, eggs, and butter (or beef drippings) in a 1-quart Pyrex measuring cup or a small bowl. Pour egg mixture into flour mixture; stir until smooth. Return mixture to measuring cup for easy pouring.

Spray a 12-cup muffin tin (with ½-cup-capacity cups) with vegetable cooking spray. Fill each cup three-quarters full.

Adjust oven rack to middle position and set muffin tin on rack. Set oven to 425 degrees. Bake, without opening oven door, until puddings are crisp and golden brown, 35 minutes.

Remove from oven and transfer to a wire rack, then serve hot.

WHEN SHOULD I SERVE IT?
With a good roast or stew
To perk up a soup supper or salad lunch
To make a simple breakfast or brunch special

WHAT SHOULD I SERVE WITH IT?
Boneless Coq au Vin (page 42)
One of the stews (pages 48–53)

Beef Tenderloin with Cracked Black Pepper Coating and Red Wine–Thyme Pan Sauce (page 86)

HOW FAR AHEAD CAN I MAKE IT?
The popovers can be made several hours ahead and crisped in a 300-degree oven for 5 to 7 minutes.

WHAT ABOUT LEFTOVERS?
You can recrisp them in a warm oven, but they'll lack that creamy interior. Still, they'll be very good with butter (and jam).

MOIST, SAVORY CORN MUFFINS

Many corn muffins become dry and crumbly after they've cooled. Not these. When warm, they're irresistible; at room temperature, they're delicious; and even after a day or two in a plastic bag on the countertop, they're amazingly moist.

For big muffins, you need a thick batter that will rise up but not overflow the muffin cups. Follow the instructions carefully: the batter's texture is right if it is stiff enough to be spooned into the muffin cups with a spring-action ice cream scoop.

MAKES 1 DOZEN MUFFINS

1	can (14.75 ounces) creamed corn
2	cups yellow cornmeal
1	cup buttermilk
2	large eggs
8	tablespoons (1 stick) unsalted butter, melted
1	cup all-purpose flour
1	tablespoon sugar
1½	teaspoons salt
2	teaspoons baking powder
½	teaspoon baking soda

Adjust oven rack to middle position and heat oven to 450 degrees. Set a 12-cup muffin tin (with ½-cup-capacity cups) in oven to heat while you make batter.

Put creamed corn in a covered 1-quart Pyrex measuring cup or small microwave-safe bowl and microwave until it comes to a full boil (or heat in a medium saucepan over medium heat). Stir in 1 cup cornmeal to make a very thick, pasty mush. (If mush is not stiff, microwave or heat for another 30 seconds or so.) Whisk in buttermilk, then eggs, and finally butter.

Mix remaining 1 cup cornmeal with flour, sugar, salt, baking powder, and baking soda in a medium bowl. Pour wet ingredients into dry and stir until just combined.

Remove muffin tin from oven and spray lightly with vegetable cooking spray. Divide batter evenly among cups (a spring-action ice cream scoop works well). Bake until muffins are golden brown, more noticeably on sides and bottom, about 15 minutes.

Turn muffins out onto a wire rack and let cool for 5 minutes. Serve warm.

WHEN SHOULD I SERVE IT?
With a soup course or meal
With a casual American-style supper

HOW CAN I VARY IT?
Add 1 cup shredded sharp cheddar cheese and/or 1 minced jalapeño to the batter.
Turn it into corn bread by baking in a 13-by-9-inch baking pan for 20 minutes, or until golden. Or make cornsticks by heating a cornstick mold as you would the muffin tin and bake for 15 minutes, or until golden (makes 16 cornsticks).

WHAT SHOULD I SERVE WITH IT?
Creamy Baked Macaroni and Cheese (page 32)
Chicken Chili — Red or White (page 13)
One of the chicken soups (pages 4–7, 9)
Sausage and White Bean Soup (page 10)

HOW FAR AHEAD CAN I MAKE IT?
The muffins can be cooled, wrapped in plastic, and stored for a day.

WHAT ABOUT LEFTOVERS?
The muffins can be frozen in an airtight bag for 1 month. Warm briefly in the microwave or heat in a 300-degree oven for about 10 minutes.

BANANA–CINNAMON CHIP MINI MUFFINS

Miniature muffins are easy for guests to eat at a crowded breakfast or brunch, but following a standard muffin recipe for the mini version doesn't always work. After a few experiments, I discovered that high heat (a blistering 450 degrees) is the best way to get mini muffins that are both golden brown and moist. Make the two popular flavors here — Banana–Cinnamon Chip and Double Chocolate– Mocha — or use this recipe as a model to create your own muffins (see How Can I Vary It?).

MAKES 2 DOZEN MUFFINS

$1/2$	cup mashed banana (from 2 small very ripe bananas)
$3/4$	cup plain low-fat yogurt
1	teaspoon vanilla extract
$1^1/2$	cups all-purpose flour
$1^1/2$	teaspoons baking powder
$1/4$	teaspoon baking soda
$1/4$	teaspoon salt
5	tablespoons unsalted butter, softened
$1/2$	cup sugar
1	large egg
$3/4$	cup Hershey's cinnamon chips, plus (optional) extra for studding batter

Adjust oven rack to middle position and heat oven to 425 degrees. Spray two 12-cup miniature muffin tins with vegetable cooking spray.

Mix banana, yogurt, and vanilla in a small bowl. Mix flour, baking powder, baking soda, and salt in a medium bowl.

Beat butter and sugar in a large bowl with an electric mixer at medium-high speed until light and fluffy. Add egg and beat until smooth. Reduce speed to low and beat in one third of the dry ingredients, then half the yogurt mixture. Add another one third of the dry ingredients, then remaining yogurt, and remaining dry ingredients, beating until batter is just smooth. Increase speed to medium-high and beat until batter is light and fluffy, about 30 seconds. Stir in chips.

Completely fill each muffin cup with batter. Stud tops of muffins with extra chips, if you like. Bake until golden brown, 12 to 14 minutes.

Set pans on a wire rack to cool slightly. Remove muffins from tins and invert on rack to cool. Serve warm or at room temperature.

DOUBLE CHOCOLATE–MOCHA MINI MUFFINS

Omit banana and substitute mini chocolate chips for cinnamon chips. Whisk 6 tablespoons unsweetened cocoa powder and 2 teaspoons instant coffee into 6 tablespoons boiling water in a 2-cup Pyrex measuring cup or small bowl until smooth (dissolving cocoa in liquid makes the flavor bloom). Stir in yogurt and vanilla, then proceed as directed.

WHEN SHOULD I SERVE IT?

For a buffet-style breakfast or brunch

For any intergenerational morning gathering

For a morning coffee or afternoon tea

HOW CAN I VARY IT?

Omit the bananas and cinnamon chips from the Banana–Cinnamon Chip Mini Muffins and you have a base batter to make muffins of your choice.

Stir in ³/₄ cup of your favorite dried fruit — blueberries, cranberries, or coarsely chopped cherries — to the batter.

Substitute chocolate chips for the cinnamon chips in the banana muffin recipe.

Add ¹/₂ teaspoon finely grated lemon or orange zest when beating the butter and sugar.

The recipe will make 6 standard ¹/₂-cup muffins; it can be doubled to make a dozen. Reduce the oven temperature to 375 degrees and increase the baking time to 20 to 25 minutes.

WHAT SHOULD I SERVE WITH IT?

Easy Savory Strata (page 102)

Orange Cream Cheese Strata with Cranberries and Walnuts (page 106)

Grapefruit-Orange Ambrosia (page 234)

HOW FAR AHEAD CAN I MAKE IT?

The muffins are best hot out of the oven, but they can be baked, cooled, double-wrapped, and frozen for up to 1 month. Thaw and then warm in a 300-degree oven.

SIMPLE SCONES

Unlike biscuits, which are best served fresh from the oven, these sweeter, denser quick breads are equally good hot, warm, or at room temperature. And they reheat beautifully.

SERVES 8

     For light, flaky scones, it's important that the butter be frozen. Make sure to work quickly so that it doesn't soften before the scones hit the oven. And mix the dough as little as possible so that they bake up tender.

½	cup sour cream
1	large egg
2	cups all-purpose flour
6	tablespoons plus 2 teaspoons sugar
1	teaspoon baking powder
½	teaspoon salt
¼	teaspoon baking soda
½	cup raisins
8	tablespoons (1 stick) unsalted butter, frozen

    Adjust oven rack to lower-middle position and heat oven to 400 degrees. Grease a cookie sheet or line it with parchment paper.

    Whisk sour cream and egg in a small bowl until smooth.

    Mix flour, 6 tablespoons sugar, baking powder, salt, baking soda, and raisins in a medium bowl. Grate butter into flour mixture, using large holes of a box grater; toss to combine. Stir in sour cream mixture until large clumps of dough form. Use your hands to press dough against sides and bottom of bowl to form a ball. (There may not seem like enough liquid at first, but as you press, the dough will come together.)

    Place dough on a lightly floured work surface and pat into a 7½-inch circle about ¾ inch thick. Use a sharp knife to cut into 8 triangles. Place about 1 inch apart on cookie sheet.

    Bake until golden, 15 to 17 minutes. Cool for at least 5 minutes. Serve hot, warm, or at room temperature.

CRANBERRY-ORANGE SCONES

Add a generous 1 teaspoon finely grated orange zest to dry ingredients and substitute dried cranberries for raisins.

LEMON-BLUEBERRY SCONES

Add a generous 1 teaspoon finely grated lemon zest to dry ingredients and substitute dried blueberries for raisins.

CHERRY-ALMOND SCONES

Add ½ teaspoon almond extract to sour cream mixture and substitute dried cherries for raisins.

WHEN SHOULD I SERVE IT?
For a houseful of breakfast guests
For a do-ahead breakfast or brunch
For a morning coffee or afternoon tea

ANY SHORTCUTS?
If doubling or tripling the recipe, it's worth pulling out the food processor to grate the butter.

HOW CAN I VARY IT?
See the three variations above, or use them as guides for your own combinations.

WHAT SHOULD I SERVE WITH IT?
My Big Fat Greek Frittata (page 100)
Easy Savory Strata (page 102)
Or serve with scrambled eggs for breakfast with:
Grapefruit-Orange Ambrosia (page 234)

HOW FAR AHEAD CAN I MAKE IT?
The dry ingredients with the grated butter can be mixed and stored in a bag or an airtight container in the freezer for up to 1 week.
The dough can be made and cut up to 4 hours ahead; cover and refrigerate on a baking sheet until ready to bake.
The scones can be baked 1 day ahead; cool, and store wrapped in foil. To reheat, remove from the foil, place on a baking sheet, and warm in a 300-degree oven for about 5 minutes.

REALLY SIMPLE DESSERTS

GRAPEFRUIT-ORANGE AMBROSIA

I usually serve this bracing fruit salad as a light dessert or even a palate cleanser. It can also be served with breakfast or brunch. It's a variation on the southern classic, with grapefruit added to the usual oranges.

SERVES 6

3 grapefruits (preferably a mix of pink and white), peeled
3 oranges, peeled
½ cup sweetened flaked coconut
¼ cup sugar

Section grapefruits and oranges, working over a medium bowl to catch juices and dropping segments into bowl.

Stir in coconut and sugar. Let stand until sugar dissolves, about 5 minutes.

Serve in bowls or goblets.

WHEN SHOULD I SERVE IT?
Year-round as a breakfast or brunch fruit salad or first course
As a light dessert
As a light offering on a dessert buffet

HOW CAN I VARY IT?
Make it with all oranges.

WHAT SHOULD I SERVE WITH IT?
My Big Fat Greek Frittata (page 100)
Easy Savory Strata (page 102)
Chicken-Mushroom Crepes (page 108)

HOW FAR AHEAD CAN I MAKE IT?
Although you can prepare the citrus up to 1 day ahead, ambrosia is at its best assembled no more than 2 hours ahead; cover and refrigerate.

WHAT ABOUT LEFTOVERS?
Leftover ambrosia is good.

Using a 1½-ounce (3-tablespoon) spring-action ice cream scoop, scoop 6 dough balls on each of the cookie sheets. Bake until golden brown, 16 to 18 minutes, switching positions of sheets and turning them around after 12 minutes. Use a metal spatula to transfer cookies to a wire rack to cool. Repeat with remaining dough.

WHEN SHOULD I SERVE IT?

For casual year-round parties

For a crowd — the recipe's easy to multiply and bake in batches

For a party with adults and kids

For potlucks, picnics, and tail-gate parties

When you want as little serving responsibility as possible for dessert

HOW CAN I VARY IT?

Substitute 1 cup toasted walnuts or pecans, coarsely chopped, or 1 cup toasted slivered almonds for the chocolate.

Substitute 1 cup chopped dried apricots or 1 cup raisins for the cranberries.

WHAT SHOULD I SERVE WITH IT?

Buttermilk-Honey Fried Chicken Fingers (page 29)

Oven-Barbecued Pulled Pork Sandwiches (page 20)

Grown-Up Sloppy Joes (page 22)

One of the chicken soups (pages 6–7, 9)

Sausage and White Bean Soup (page 10)

HOW FAR AHEAD CAN I MAKE IT?

The oatmeal dough balls can be placed on a cookie sheet and frozen until solid, then transferred to a freezer bag and frozen for up to 2 months. Thaw as many as needed slightly until soft on the outside and bake.

Although the cookies can be baked a day ahead, I prefer them freshly baked.

WHAT ABOUT LEFTOVERS?

Although they will become crisper and less chewy, the cookies can be stored in an airtight tin for up to 1 week.

TORTILLA SUNDAES
WITH MINTED MANGO SALSA

This simple sundae consists of three varieties of sorbet (or a mix of sorbets and ice cream) scooped onto a crisp cinnamon-sugared fried tortilla "plate" and topped with a colorful chunky fruit salsa. It's light, festive, and very easy to make and assemble. Make sure to fry the tortillas until they stop sizzling, or they'll be chewy instead of crisp, and when stored, they'll quickly go stale.

SERVES 8

¼	cup sugar
1	tablespoon ground cinnamon
2	cups flavorless oil, such as vegetable or canola
8	6-inch corn tortillas

SALSA

1	small mango, peeled, seeded, and cut into small dice (about 1 cup)
½	Granny Smith apple, unpeeled, cored, and cut into small dice
4	large strawberries, hulled and cut into small dice
1½	tablespoons chopped fresh mint
1	tablespoon fresh lime juice
1½	teaspoons minced fresh ginger
2	tablespoons orange marmalade

3	pints assorted sorbets and/or ice creams (raspberry, peach, or vanilla, for example)

Mix sugar with cinnamon in a small bowl.

Heat oil in a medium-large skillet over medium-high heat to 350 degrees. One at a time, drop tortillas into hot oil and fry, turning once, until they stop sizzling and turn golden brown, about 2 minutes. Remove with tongs and set on a large wire rack set over a baking sheet. Immediately sprinkle liberally on both sides with cinnamon sugar.

TO MAKE SALSA: Mix all ingredients in a medium bowl.

TO ASSEMBLE: Spoon 3 small scoops of sorbet onto each tortilla, top with salsa, and serve immediately.

WHEN SHOULD I SERVE IT?

As a simple dessert that's fun

For sit-down dinners, especially after spicy ethnic meals when you want something light and refreshing

During the warmer months

ANY SHORTCUTS?

Although it won't be as colorful, you can skip the fruit salsa and top with frozen sweetened strawberries, or sliced bananas and chocolate sauce, or caramel sauce.

HOW CAN I VARY IT?

For a garnish, cut 2 additional tortillas into ½-inch-wide strips. Fry them, in 2 batches, until golden brown, and sprinkle with the cinnamon sugar. Stick a few strips in each dessert.

Keeping color in mind, use other fruits in the sauce — peaches and watermelon, for example (but do keep the crisp Granny Smith apple for color and textural contrast).

Mint perfectly complements the fruit, but if you're adventurous, other herbs could work — basil, for example, or even cilantro.

WHAT SHOULD I SERVE WITH IT?

Bake-Ahead Pizza for a Crowd (page 24)

Chicken Chili — Red or White (page 13)

Shish Kebabs (page 56)

Mixed Grill with Tandoori Flavorings (page 62)

Chicken Soup with Southwestern Flavors (page 9)

HOW FAR AHEAD CAN I MAKE IT?

The fried tortillas can be stored overnight in foil or a large tin.

The salsa can be made up to 4 hours ahead.

WHAT ABOUT LEFTOVERS?

The tortillas will stay fresh for 1 week or more as long as they're stored in a tin. Enjoy with a cup of afternoon tea.

HOT FUDGE BROWNIE SUNDAES

Brownies baked in disposable pans are moister than those baked in metal or Pyrex pans. Because these flimsy pans don't retain heat, the sides and bottom don't overcook and harden. The fudge sauce is gloriously thick.

MAKES 18
BROWNIES AND
3 1/2 CUPS SAUCE;
SERVES 18

BROWNIES

1 1/3	cups all-purpose flour
1	teaspoon salt
1	teaspoon baking powder
8	ounces bittersweet or semisweet chocolate, cut or broken into small chunks
4	ounces unsweetened chocolate, cut or broken into small chunks
1 1/4	cups (2 1/2 sticks) unsalted butter
2 1/2	cups sugar
4	teaspoons vanilla extract
6	large eggs, lightly beaten

HOT FUDGE SAUCE

2	cans (14 ounces each) sweetened condensed milk
4	ounces unsweetened chocolate, cut into small chunks
1/2	cup milk
1	teaspoon instant coffee powder
1	tablespoon vanilla extract
1/2	gallon vanilla ice cream

TO MAKE BROWNIES: Adjust oven rack to lower-middle position and heat oven to 325 degrees.

Line a disposable or regular 13-by-9-inch baking pan with heavy-duty foil, leaving an overhang on two long sides to facilitate removal of brownies. Spray pan with vegetable cooking spray.

Mix flour, salt, and baking powder in a small bowl; set aside.

Melt chocolates and butter in a large heatproof bowl set over a pan of simmering water. Remove from heat and stir in sugar and vanilla.

Add eggs and stir until mixture turns from grainy-looking to smooth and glossy. Stir in dry ingredients until just incorporated.

Pour batter into prepared pan and bake until a toothpick inserted in center comes out with wet crumbs, about 40 minutes. Cool brownies in pan for 5 minutes, then use foil to transfer them to a wire rack to cool completely.

TO MAKE SAUCE: Heat condensed milk, chocolate, milk, and coffee powder in a medium saucepan over medium heat, stirring frequently at first and then constantly, until sauce is creamy smooth. Remove from heat and stir in vanilla.

Cut brownies into 18 squares and arrange on plates. Top each with a scoop of ice cream and a few tablespoons of warm chocolate sauce. Serve immediately.

WHEN SHOULD I SERVE IT?
For cookouts and family reunions At all seasons

ANY SHORTCUTS?
Buy the brownies and make just the sauce.

HOW CAN I VARY IT?
Add 1½ cups chopped toasted walnuts or pecans to the batter. (I leave out the nuts when I'm serving a large group, since some people don't like them.)

WHAT SHOULD I SERVE WITH IT?
Bake-Ahead Pizza for a Crowd (page 24)
Chicken Chili — Red or White (page 13)
Buttermilk-Honey Fried Chicken Fingers (page 29)
Oven-Barbecued Pulled Pork Sandwiches (page 20)
Grown-Up Sloppy Joes (page 22)

HOW FAR AHEAD CAN I MAKE IT?
The uncut brownie slab can be wrapped in plastic, then foil, and refrigerated for up to 5 days or frozen for up to 1 month.
The sauce can be made up to 1 week ahead and refrigerated. Reheat over low heat, stirring in a little more milk, if necessary.

WHAT ABOUT LEFTOVERS?
The cut brownies keep well, tightly wrapped, for 3 days.

SORBET- OR ICE CREAM–FILLED CRISP CINNAMON CUPS

SERVES 8

Brushed with a little butter, sprinkled with cinnamon sugar, and laid over individual pie plates, egg roll wrappers bake into crisp, edible bowls for sorbet, ice cream, pudding, or fruit. Make sure the wrappers don't touch one another as they bake, or they'll be leathery.

You'll need eight individual-size foil pie pans for this recipe; they are available in most supermarkets, sometimes labeled tart pans.

    8   egg roll wrappers
    3   tablespoons unsalted butter, melted
  ¼   cup sugar
1½   teaspoons ground cinnamon
    2   pints sorbet or ice cream (preferably two different flavors)

Adjust oven rack to upper and lower-middle positions and heat oven to 350 degrees. Lay eight disposable individual pie pans upside down on two large cookie sheets.

Lay egg roll wrappers on a work surface and brush lightly with butter. Turn over and brush with remaining butter. Mix sugar and cinnamon and sprinkle over top. Drape egg roll wrappers sugared side up over pie pans to make free-form cups.

WHEN SHOULD I SERVE IT?
  When you want to serve ice cream with a flair
  For small or large dinners

HOW CAN I VARY IT?
  Use raspberry and chocolate sorbets and sprinkle with fresh raspberries.
  Use strawberry ice cream and top with fresh sugared berries.

Use pistachio ice cream and sprinkle with additional chopped pistachios.

Bake cups until crisp and golden, switching positions of sheets and turning to ensure even browning, about 12 minutes. Turn out onto a wire rack and let cool.

When ready to serve, fill cups with sorbet or ice cream. Serve immediately.

WHAT SHOULD I SERVE WITH IT?
Shish Kebabs (page 56)
Mixed Grill with Tandoori Flavorings (page 62)
Sear-Ahead Steaks or Salmon (page 66)

HOW FAR AHEAD CAN I MAKE IT?
The cinnamon cups store beautifully in an airtight container for 3 days.

WHAT ABOUT LEFTOVERS?
Leftover cups will keep for 1 week.

INSTANT STRAWBERRY ICE CREAM

"Why," you might ask, "would I make instant homemade ice cream when I can buy good strawberry ice cream?" Taste this, and you'll understand why. The ratio of fruit to cream is extraordinarily generous. And although the texture is not as smooth as that of commercial ice cream, the berry flavor is amazingly fresh.

It takes only five minutes (or less) to prepare the ice cream and an hour for it to harden (there's always an hour before dessert after guests have arrived). And you don't need an ice cream freezer.

MAKES 1 QUART; SERVES 8

1   container (24 ounces) frozen sweetened strawberries, chopped into large (frozen) chunks
½   cup plus 1 tablespoon sugar
1½   cups heavy cream
      Whole or sliced fresh strawberries for garnish (optional)

Place frozen berries in a blender. Whisk sugar into cream. With blender running, slowly add cream-sugar mixture, stopping to stir 3 or 4 times, until ice cream is smooth with small bits of strawberries.

Transfer to a shallow metal pan and freeze to a scoopable texture, about 1 hour. Garnish with fresh strawberries, if using, and serve.

WHEN SHOULD I SERVE IT?
   When you have almost no time to make dessert
   At a meal with both adults and kids
   When you want to keep it light
   For large or small groups — the recipe easily halves and multiplies if made in batches

HOW FAR AHEAD CAN I MAKE IT?
   The ice cream can be frozen in an airtight container for up to 1 month.

WHAT ABOUT LEFTOVERS?
   Scoop into the blender, add milk or even cream, and you'll have a great strawberry milkshake.

FROZEN TIRAMISU WITH COFFEE MASCARPONE SAUCE

Love tiramisu but don't have time to make it? This ice cream version rivals the real thing and can be prepared in under half an hour, no pastry skills required. Not bad for a dessert that serves up to fourteen people.

SERVES 12 TO 14

If you think you can't find mascarpone cheese at the grocery store, look carefully—you may be surprised. The sauce can also be made with cream cheese.

This is the moment to bring out those espresso cups collecting dust in the china cabinet. Fill with the coffee mascarpone sauce, sprinkle with grated chocolate, and set one on each dessert plate. Let your guests pour the sauce over their frozen tiramisu.

- ½ cup strong coffee (instant is fine)
- 3 tablespoons (dark or light) rum
- 2 packages (3 ounces each, about 48 total) ladyfingers, split
- 4 ounces bittersweet chocolate, coarsely grated
- ½ gallon coffee ice cream, softened on microwave's defrost setting for 1 minute
- 1 container (8 ounces) mascarpone cheese or 1 package (8 ounces) cream cheese
- 3 tablespoons coffee-flavored liqueur
- 1 tablespoon sugar
- ⅓ cup half-and-half, plus more if necessary

Mix coffee and rum in a small bowl. Line a 9-by-8-inch loaf pan with plastic wrap. Line bottom of pan with ladyfingers, first using a pastry brush to brush them generously with coffee mixture, then placing them rounded side down. Line sides of pan with more soaked ladyfingers, rounded side out, standing them up in pan.

Reserve ½ cup grated chocolate for garnish, and stir remaining chocolate into softened ice cream. Turn ice cream into loaf pan, and use a rubber spatula to spread it evenly. Cover with a layer of coffee-soaked ladyfingers, rounded side up. Cover and freeze for at least 2 hours.

Whisk mascarpone, liqueur, sugar, and half-and-half together in a medium bowl to form a thick, pourable sauce. (You'll need to add a little more half-and-half if you used cream cheese.)

To serve, unmold tiramisu onto a cutting board (set pan in warm water for a few seconds if necessary to loosen it) and peel off plastic wrap. Cut into slices and arrange on plates. Drizzle with sauce, sprinkle with reserved grated chocolate, and serve immediately.

WHEN SHOULD I SERVE IT?
When you want a dessert that's both elegant and fun
When you've got a crowd
For a do-ahead dessert — when you're ready, just slice the tiramisu and pour over the sauce

WHAT SHOULD I SERVE WITH IT?
Bake-Ahead Pizza for a Crowd (page 24)

HOW FAR AHEAD CAN I MAKE IT?
The tiramisu must be made at least 2 hours ahead, and it can be double-wrapped and frozen for up to 1 week.

TURTLE FONDUE
(WITH OR WITHOUT THE POT)

This dessert is designed for two, or four at the most. If you have a fondue pot, use it, but the chocolate-caramel mixture retains heat well, so a heavy pot works too. Just heat the fondue until hot and bring the pot to the table; if it starts to cool off, simply return it to the stove. With a small group, it's easy.

SERVES 2 TO 4

Toast the nuts in a 325-degree oven, stirring occasionally, until fragrant, about 10 minutes.

8   ounces caramels

2   ounces semisweet chocolate, cut into small pieces

¼   cup finely chopped toasted (see above) pecans or walnuts (optional)

¼   cup milk

Fresh fruit, such as apples, pears, bananas, strawberries, grapes, or figs; larger fruit cut into bite-size chunks

Combine caramels, chocolate, nuts (if using), and milk in a small heavy saucepan (or a fondue pot) and heat over low heat, stirring frequently, until smooth and warm. Serve with skewers (or fondue forks) for dipping fruit.

WHEN SHOULD I SERVE IT?

For a small dinner party

All year round, using seasonal fruits

When you've got very little time to prepare (the most difficult part of the recipe is unwrapping the caramels)

HOW CAN I VARY IT?

Besides fruit, you can dip cake chunks, cookies, macaroons, marsh-mallows, and dried fruit.

Omit the nuts.

WHAT SHOULD I SERVE WITH IT?

Butter-Roasted Lobster Tails (page 90)

Sear-Ahead Steaks or Salmon (page 66)

Roast Rack of Lamb with Vinegar-Mint Pan Sauce (page 93)

HOW FAR AHEAD CAN I MAKE IT?

You can toast the nuts, if using, 3 days ahead.

You can make the fondue several hours ahead and set it aside, covered, at room temperature; reheat before serving.

WHAT ABOUT LEFTOVERS?

The leftover fondue can be refrigerated for 3 days. Add milk if necessary to thin it when reheating.

ROASTED PEACHES (OR PEARS, PLUMS, OR APPLES) WITH CARAMEL SAUCE

Slow-roasting intensifies the flavor and improves the texture of even underripe pears, peaches, and plums.

SERVES 6

Toast the almonds in a 325-degree oven, stirring occasionally, until golden and fragrant, about 10 minutes. Then increase the oven temperature to roast the fruit.

3 tablespoons unsalted butter

1 cup packed light or dark brown sugar

3 peaches, pears, or apples or 6 plums, halved and seeded or cored

6 tablespoons sour cream

¼ cup almonds, toasted (see above)

Adjust oven rack to middle position and heat oven to 400 degrees.

In oven, melt butter in a baking pan large enough to hold fruit in a single layer. Sprinkle brown sugar over butter, then place fruit cut side down on top. Bake until fruit is tender, 30 to 40 minutes.

Turn fruit over, baste with pan sauce, and continue to bake until golden and glossy, about 10 minutes longer. Let cool to warm.

Transfer fruit to serving bowls. Top each with a dollop of sour cream, drizzle with caramel pan sauce, sprinkle with nuts, and serve.

WHEN SHOULD I SERVE IT?
As a relatively light but satisfying end to a meal
Summer through late fall
For a small group or a crowd

ANY SHORTCUTS?
Buy roasted shelled pistachios instead of toasting the almonds.

HOW CAN I VARY IT?
Serve over ice cream rather than topping with sour cream.
Use other nuts — walnuts with pears, pecans with apples, pistachios with peaches.

WHAT SHOULD I SERVE WITH IT?
Really Good Lasagna (page 35)
Boneless Coq au Vin (page 42)
Simple Cassoulet (page 44)

HOW FAR AHEAD CAN I MAKE IT?
The fruit can be roasted up to 3 hours ahead and rewarmed before serving.

WHAT ABOUT LEFTOVERS?
Leftover fruit can be refrigerated for 1 week. Warm and serve as dessert, on its own or over ice cream. Or serve over hot cereal.

BERRY BREAD PUDDING

This unbaked, fresh-tasting summer pudding is ideal for the Fourth of July. The bread, cream, and berry juices meld, becoming soft and mousselike. You can halve the recipe and assemble in an 8- or 9-inch pan.

SERVES 12

2	pounds (about 2 quarts) strawberries, hulled and quartered
³⁄₄	pound (1¹⁄₂ pints) blueberries
³⁄₄	pound (1¹⁄₂ pints) raspberries
1¹⁄₄	cups sugar
1	quart heavy cream
¹⁄₄	cup orange-flavored liqueur, such as Grand Marnier or Triple Sec
12	slices firm white sandwich bread, cut into 1-inch squares

Mix berries with 1 cup sugar in a large bowl. Set aside for 30 minutes to allow juices to form.

Whip cream to soft peaks with an electric mixer in a large bowl, gradually adding remaining ¹⁄₄ cup sugar, then liqueur.

Layer the dessert in a 13-by-9-inch (or similar-size) dish: first half the bread, then half the berries and half the whipped cream; repeat. Cover and refrigerate for at least 4 hours, preferably overnight.

Spoon the pudding into goblets or bowls and serve.

WHEN SHOULD I SERVE IT?
For a sit-down dinner or a buffet
As an easy dessert for a crowd

HOW CAN I VARY IT?
Increase the strawberries and cut back on the blueberries and raspberries. Don't use fewer strawberries, though — they produce needed juice for the pudding.

Substitute 4 teaspoons vanilla extract for the orange liqueur.
Layer the pudding in stemmed goblets rather than a large dish.

WHAT SHOULD I SERVE WITH IT?
Grilled Chicken Breasts with Orange-Thyme Glaze (page 64)
Sear-Ahead Steaks or Salmon (page 66)

Chicken-Mushroom Crepes (page 108)

HOW FAR AHEAD CAN I MAKE IT?
The pudding is best made a day ahead.

WHAT ABOUT LEFTOVERS?
Leftover pudding can be refrigerated for 1 to 2 days.

SIMPLE, TENDER YELLOW CAKE—
AND FIVE VARIATIONS

Make this cake and you can have dessert for two gatherings. There's enough batter for one large 13-by-9-inch cake. But if your party's for eight or fewer, split the batter in half and make two smaller cakes. You can even make two different cakes: bake an upside-down cake in one pan, for example, and bake the remaining batter in another pan for a plain yellow cake. Double-wrap the second cake and squirrel it away in the freezer. The next time you need dessert, serve cake number two with sugared berries or peaches and whipped cream. Or split it into two layers and spread the bottom layer with jam or marmalade, then frost or glaze the cake.

Serve this cake with the optional Mixed Berry Compote or with sugared fresh fruit of your choice. Top the cake with ice cream or sweetened whipped cream (1 cup heavy cream, 1 tablespoon sugar, and 1 teaspoon vanilla extract).

MAKES ONE 13-BY-9-INCH CAKE, SERVING 12 TO 15, OR TWO 9-INCH LAYERS (SQUARE OR ROUND), EACH SERVING 8 OR 9

WHEN SHOULD I SERVE IT?

For any occasion, casual or formal

For large buffets or small dinners (the small cakes serve 8 or 9 each; the large serves 12 to 15)

When you need a slice-and-serve, no-assembly dessert

WHAT SHOULD I SERVE WITH IT?

Cake's a great way to end just about any meal!

HOW FAR AHEAD CAN I MAKE IT?

The plain cakes can be double-wrapped in plastic and stored at room temperature for 1 day or frozen for 1 month.

The upside-down cakes can be made the day before serving.

The frosted cakes can be assembled 3 hours before serving.

The Mixed Berry Compote (page 258) can be covered and refrigerated for 3 to 4 hours.

2½   cups all-purpose flour

¼   cup cornstarch

4   teaspoons baking powder

½   teaspoon salt

1   cup milk

3   large eggs

2   teaspoons vanilla extract

1   cup (2 sticks) unsalted butter, very soft

2   cups sugar

MIXED BERRY COMPOTE (OPTIONAL)

1   package (16 ounces) frozen strawberries, thawed and crushed

¾   pound mixed fresh berries (blueberries, raspberries, and/or blackberries)

6   tablespoons sugar

Adjust oven rack to lower-middle position and heat oven to 350 degrees. Coat a 13-by-9-inch baking pan or two 9-inch square or round baking pans with cooking spray. Line pan bottom(s) with parchment or waxed paper, spray again, and dust with flour.

Mix flour, cornstarch, baking powder, and salt in a large bowl. Mix milk, eggs, and vanilla in a 2-cup Pyrex measuring cup or small bowl.

With an electric mixer, beat softened butter into dry ingredients, first on low and then increasing speed to medium, until mixture forms pebble-size clumps. Add one third of milk mixture and beat on low speed until smooth. Add remaining milk mixture in 2 stages, beating on medium speed until batter is just smooth. Add sugar and beat until just incorporated, about 30 seconds.

Pour batter into prepared cake pan(s). Bake until a cake tester or toothpick inserted into center comes out clean, 35 to 40 minutes for the smaller cakes and about 40 minutes for the 13-by-9-inch size. Set pan(s) on a wire rack and cool for 5 minutes.

Run a knife around pan perimeter and invert cake(s) onto rack. Cool completely.

TO MAKE OPTIONAL COMPOTE: Mix frozen and fresh berries with sugar in a bowl.

To serve, cut cake into squares or wedges. Serve with berry compote, if desired.

TENDER LEMON CAKE

MAKES ONE 13-BY-9-INCH CAKE, SERVING 12 TO 15, OR TWO 9-INCH LAYERS (SQUARE OR ROUND), EACH SERVING 8 OR 9

This cake requires nothing more than a dusting of confectioners' sugar. Serve it unadorned or with a scoop of good vanilla ice cream or lemon sorbet.

Mix 2 teaspoons finely grated lemon zest into the sugar before adding it to batter. Just before serving, dust cake with confectioners' sugar.

MOIST, TENDER SPICE CAKE

SERVES 12 TO 15

Add 2 teaspoons ground ginger, 1 teaspoon ground cinnamon, ½ teaspoon ground nutmeg, ½ teaspoon ground allspice, and ½ teaspoon ground cloves to dry ingredients. Substitute 2 cups packed dark brown sugar for granulated sugar.

YELLOW CAKE WITH RASPBERRY FILLING AND LEMON CREAM CHEESE FROSTING

SERVES 9 IF MADE WITH A SQUARE LAYER, 8 TO 10 IF MADE WITH A ROUND LAYER

- 1   package (8 ounces) cream cheese, softened
- 4   tablespoons (½ stick) unsalted butter, softened
- ¾   cup jarred lemon curd
- 1   9-inch round or square Simple, Tender Yellow Cake layer (page 257)
- ½   cup raspberry jam

Beat cream cheese and butter in a medium bowl with an electric mixer until smooth. Beat in lemon curd until light and fluffy.

Split cake into 2 layers with a serrated knife. Place bottom layer on a serving plate, and spread with jam. Place top layer over jam and frost top and sides with cream cheese frosting. Cover loosely with plastic wrap until ready to serve.

YELLOW CAKE WITH ORANGE-MARMALADE FILLING AND CHOCOLATE GLAZE

SERVES 9 IF MADE WITH A SQUARE LAYER, 8 TO 10 IF MADE WITH A ROUND LAYER

- 1   cup heavy cream
- 8   ounces bittersweet chocolate, cut into small pieces
- 1   9-inch round or square Simple, Tender Yellow Cake layer (page 257)
- ½   cup orange marmalade

Combine cream and chocolate in a 1-quart Pyrex measuring cup or microwave-safe bowl and microwave, uncovered, on high power until cream is hot enough to melt chocolate, about 2 minutes; whisk to make a smooth glaze. Or heat in a small heavy saucepan over low heat, stirring, until chocolate is melted and glaze is smooth.

Split cake into 2 layers with a serrated knife. Place bottom layer on a wire rack, set over a plate, and spread with marmalade. Place top layer over marmalade. Pour glaze over top and smooth it around sides. Transfer cake to a serving plate.

APPLE OR PINEAPPLE UPSIDE-DOWN CAKE

MAKES ONE 9-INCH SQUARE CAKE, SERVING 9, PLUS AN EXTRA 9-INCH PLAIN SQUARE OR ROUND LAYER

3	tablespoons unsalted butter
½	cup packed dark brown sugar
1	teaspoon ground cinnamon
1	crisp apple (such as Granny Smith), peeled, cored, and thinly sliced, or 8 pineapple rings, halved
	Batter for Simple, Tender Yellow Cake (page 257)

Heat oven to 350 degrees. Spray a 9-inch square pan with vegetable cooking spray. Cut a sheet of parchment large enough to line bottom and opposite two sides to prevent sticking. Place in pan and spray with cooking spray. Coat another 9-inch pan, square or round, with cooking spray. Line pan bottom with parchment or waxed paper, spray again, and dust with flour.

Heat butter, brown sugar, and cinnamon in a small saucepan, stirring occasionally, until foamy. Pour into square prepared pan, and arrange fruit over sugar mixture.

Prepare batter as directed. Pour half batter over fruit and the rest into second pan. Bake until a toothpick or tester inserted into center comes out clean, about 35 minutes for plain cake and 40 minutes for upside-down cake.

Cool upside-down cake for about 2 minutes, plain cake for a few minutes longer, before running a knife around perimeter of pan and inverting cake onto a wire rack. Remove parchment, cool completely, and cover with plastic wrap until ready to serve.

Following recipes on page 259, fill and frost plain cake layer or double-wrap, freeze, and reserve for another use.

LEMON-RASPBERRY TRIFLETTES

These elegant and eye-catching desserts can be assembled in about half an hour. For a striking presentation, layer the dessert in large wineglasses.

SERVES 8

½   cup raspberry-flavored liqueur, such as Chambord
¼   cup cream sherry
2   packages (3 ounces each, about 48 total) ladyfingers, split, or 12 slices firm white sandwich bread (such as Pepperidge Farm), crusts removed, each slice cut into four 1-by-3½-inch strips
1   jar (10–12 ounces) lemon curd
½   teaspoon finely grated lemon zest
2   cups heavy cream
2   half pints (about 6 ounces each) raspberries

Mix liqueur and sherry in a small bowl. Brush both sides of the split ladyfingers with mixture, and line sides of eight stemmed goblets with ladyfingers rounded side out.

Place lemon curd in a small bowl and whisk to loosen it, then whisk in zest.

WHEN SHOULD I SERVE IT?
When you want a fancy-looking dessert
For small or large parties
When you need a do-ahead dessert

HOW CAN I VARY IT?
Substitute strawberries for raspberries.

WHAT SHOULD I SERVE WITH IT?
Really Good Lasagna (page 35)
Chicken-Mushroom Crepes (page 108)
Beef Tenderloin with Cracked Black Pepper Coating and Red Wine–Thyme Pan Sauce (page 86)

HOW FAR AHEAD CAN I MAKE IT?
The triflettes can be covered with plastic wrap and refrigerated for up to 8 hours.

WHAT ABOUT LEFTOVERS?
Though the berries will soften, the triflettes are fine the next day.

Beat heavy cream to soft peaks in a large bowl. Measure 1½ cups whipped cream and stir into lemon curd.

Place 5 or 6 raspberries in each of the goblets. Spoon a generous 2 tablespoons lemon curd mixture over each portion of berries, and spoon a generous 2 tablespoons whipped cream over lemon mixture. Repeat layering with another portion of raspberries and remaining lemon curd mixture and whipped cream. Top with remaining raspberries. Refrigerate to let flavors meld, about 1 hour, before serving.

MOLTEN CHOCOLATE CAKES WITH SUGAR-COATED RASPBERRIES

These decadent, oozy flourless cakes are drop-dead terrific and even easier than brownies. They are baked in paper liners in a muffin tin, so you don't have to worry about having matching ramekins. That also means you don't have to unmold the cakes— just lift them from the muffin pan and set on the dessert plates. And since the cakes bake for only 8 minutes, you can pop them into the oven when you're clearing the main course and making coffee.

Use extra-large baking cups for the cakes. These liners extend above the muffin cups, making it easy to lift the baked cakes from the pan. If your baking cups are foil-lined, remove the foil layer and reserve for another use, or discard.

16	tablespoons (2 sticks) unsalted butter
1⅓	cups (8 ounces) chocolate chips or semisweet chocolate, cut into small chunks
5	large eggs
½	cup sugar, plus a little more for coating raspberries
	Pinch of salt
4	teaspoons all-purpose flour
1	half pint (about 6 ounces) raspberries

Adjust oven rack to middle position and heat oven to 450 degrees. Line 8 cups of a muffin tin (with ½-cup-capacity cups) with extra-large paper liners (they should extend above cups to facilitate removal; if papers are foil-lined, remove foil layer). Coat papers with vegetable cooking spray.

Melt butter and chocolate in a medium heatproof bowl set over a pan of simmering water, stirring occasionally until smooth; remove from heat.

With an electric mixer, beat eggs, sugar, and salt in another medium bowl until sugar dissolves. Beat egg mixture, then flour, into chocolate.

Divide batter among muffin cups. Bake until batter puffs but centers are not set, 8 to 10 minutes. Let stand in tin for 5 minutes. Meanwhile, flick raspberries with a little water and roll in sugar to coat.

Carefully lift cakes from tin and transfer to dessert plates, removing paper liners. Top each cake with sugared berries and serve.

WHEN SHOULD I SERVE IT?
For a nice sit-down dinner
When you want a fancy dessert that's fast

ANY SHORTCUTS?
Don't bother peeling off the papers. When the cakes come out of the oven, just let them rest for a second, then lift them onto the plates and top with the berries.

HOW CAN I VARY IT?
For Passover, substitute unsalted margarine for the butter and ground matzo for the flour.

WHAT SHOULD I SERVE WITH IT?
One of the stews (pages 48–53)
Butterflied Cornish Hens with Apricot-Pistachio Dressing (page 76)
Beef Tenderloin with Cracked Black Pepper Coating and Red Wine–Thyme Pan Sauce (page 86)

HOW FAR AHEAD CAN I MAKE IT?
The batter can be made 1 week ahead and refrigerated; return to room temperature 1 hour before baking.

MERINGUE CAKE WITH RASPBERRIES AND WHIPPED CREAM

SERVES 8 TO 10

Light, crisp meringues are one of those French delicacies that are surprisingly simple. Once you've made them, you'll wonder why you didn't add them to your repertoire sooner. Just beat sugar, cornstarch, and egg whites to marshmallow-cream consistency and smear into free-form rectangles on a parchment-lined baking sheet. Pop them into a hot oven, then turn off the oven, turn on the oven light, and leave them overnight. (The oven light will provide enough heat to continue drying the meringues after the oven has cooled down.) The next day, spread them with whipped cream and top with berries.

The meringues should be crisp, not taffylike. If you find that they have not dried thoroughly after their night in the oven, peel them from the parchment, set the rectangles directly on the oven rack, and turn the oven to 170 degrees. At that temperature, they can continue to dry for hours: check them at your leisure.

1 cup confectioners' sugar

1/2 cup plus 1 tablespoon granulated sugar

1 tablespoon cornstarch

4 large egg whites, at room temperature

1/2 teaspoon cream of tartar

2 cups heavy cream

1 teaspoon vanilla extract

2 half pints (about 6 ounces each) raspberries

Adjust oven rack to lower-middle position and heat oven to 500 degrees. Crumple a sheet of parchment paper large enough to line a rimmed baking sheet about 18 by 12 inches (crumpling paper will prevent meringues from sticking); smooth it out again, and line pan with it.

Whisk confectioners' sugar, 1/2 cup granulated sugar, and cornstarch in a small bowl; set aside.

Beat egg whites and cream of tartar with an electric mixer on medium speed in a large bowl until they turn from foamy to white and beaters just start to leave a trail. On low speed, add sugar mixture 1 heaping tablespoon at a time. Increase speed to medium-high and beat to the consistency of marshmallow cream, 2 to 3 minutes longer.

Lightly flick water droplets over parchment. Spoon half of meringue into 2 or 3 mounds down one long side of pan, and use an offset or rubber spatula to smooth meringue into a rectangle 12 to 13 inches long and about 5 inches wide. Repeat with remaining meringue on other side of pan.

Set meringues in oven. Immediately turn off oven and turn on oven light. Let dry overnight (do not open oven door).

Remove meringues from oven and carefully set a large wire rack or cookie sheet over meringues. Invert, peel off parchment, and turn right side up. (It's okay if some edges chip.)

Whip cream to soft peaks in a large bowl, beating in remaining 1 tablespoon sugar and vanilla.

To assemble, set a meringue rectangle on a large serving platter. Spread with half the cream and sprinkle with half the berries. Top with remaining meringue rectangle, cream, and berries. Refrigerate to let meringue soften slightly, 30 minutes to 2 hours. Slice and serve.

WHEN SHOULD I SERVE IT?

When you want a simple yet striking dessert

When dessert needs to be completely do-ahead

For spring and summer entertaining

For festive events, including Christmas

ANY SHORTCUTS?

Buy individual meringue shells, available at many bakeries and gourmet stores. Fill them with the whipped cream and sprinkle with the raspberries.

HOW CAN I VARY IT?

Use a 1-pound bag of frozen raspberries. The taste will be similar, but because the juices will bleed onto the cream, your dessert will not be as beautiful.

Make it with nondairy whipped topping for Passover.

WHAT SHOULD I SERVE WITH IT?

Butterflied Cornish Hens with Apricot-Pistachio Dressing (page 76)

Beef Tenderloin with Cracked Black Pepper Coating and Red Wine–Thyme Pan Sauce (page 86)

Roast Rack of Lamb with Vinegar-Mint Pan Sauce (page 93)

Chicken-Mushroom Crepes (page 108)

Salmon Cucumber Salad with Sour Cream–Dill Dressing (page 192)

Crab-Stuffed Artichokes (page 150; or substitute shrimp for the crab)

HOW FAR AHEAD CAN I MAKE IT?

Once they are completely dried, the meringues can be wrapped in foil and stored in a cool, dry place for up to 1 month.

The dessert can be assembled up to 2 hours before serving; any longer, however, and the meringues will soften too much.

ORANGE PUDDING CAKES WITH MARMALADE DRIZZLE

If you keep instant flour in your pantry (it ensures lump-free batter), you may not even have to shop to make this dessert. The ingredients are so basic, but the results are almost magical.

Make a batter and bake it in custard cups—30 minutes later, you've got two desserts in one: pudding on top, cake on the bottom. These are delicious drizzled with an impromptu sauce made with orange marmalade to carry the theme, lemon juice to cut the sweetness, and liqueur to give it some kick.

2	tablespoons unsalted butter, very soft
3/4	cup sugar
1 1/2	teaspoons finely grated orange zest
4	large eggs, separated
1/4	cup instant (quick-mixing) flour, such as Wondra
1/4	cup fresh orange juice (from 1 large orange)
2	tablespoons fresh lemon juice (from 1 lemon)
1	cup milk

DRIZZLE

6	tablespoons orange marmalade
2	tablespoons orange-flavored liqueur
2	tablespoons fresh lemon juice

Heat oven to 325 degrees. Coat eight 6-ounce custard cups with vegetable cooking spray; set them in two 9-inch square or round baking pans. Bring about 1 1/2 quarts water to a boil.

Whisk butter, 1/2 cup sugar, and zest in a large bowl until smooth. Whisk in egg yolks, then whisk in flour until smooth. Whisk in orange juice, lemon juice, and then milk.

With an electric mixer, beat egg whites in a medium bowl until foamy. Gradually beat in remaining 1/4 cup sugar, beating until whites hold a firm peak. Fold whites into batter until just smooth.

Divide batter among custard cups. Place baking pans on oven rack, then carefully pour enough boiling water into each pan to come halfway up sides of custard cups. Bake until cake tops are golden and spring back when pressed lightly, about 25 minutes.

Remove pans from oven and let cakes stand in water until just warm, about 15 minutes. Remove custard cups from pans and let stand for about 5 minutes to firm up.

MEANWHILE, TO MAKE DRIZZLE: Mix marmalade, liqueur, and lemon juice in a small bowl.

Place a dessert plate over each custard cup and invert cake onto plate. Spoon drizzle over cakes, and serve.

LEMON PUDDING CAKES

Substitute lemon zest for orange zest, omit orange juice, and use ¼ cup fresh lemon juice in all. Proceed as directed, omitting marmalade drizzle.

WHEN SHOULD I SERVE IT?

In spring, winter, and fall

At a dinner party for no more than eight (unless you've got lots of custard cups)

When there's not much time to prepare dessert

WHAT SHOULD I SERVE WITH IT?

One of the stews (pages 48–53)

Butterflied Cornish Hens with Apricot-Pistachio Dressing (page 76)

Rosemary-Scented Roast Pork Loin Stuffed with Roasted Garlic, Dried Apricots, and Cranberries with Port Wine Sauce (page 83)

Sear-Ahead Steaks or Salmon (page 66)

HOW FAR AHEAD CAN I MAKE IT?

You can prepare the batter, up to beating the egg whites, up to 2 hours ahead; cover and refrigerate.

The baked pudding cakes can sit in the warm water in the turned-off oven (with the light on to provide a little additional heat) for up to

2 hours. (In that case, there's no need to let them stand for 5 minutes before unmolding.)

The orange marmalade drizzle can be made 3 to 4 hours ahead.

WHAT ABOUT LEFTOVERS?

Leftover pudding cakes are delicious. If you want them warm, pop them into the microwave for several seconds. They're also good cold.

SIMPLE STRAWBERRY SHORTCAKES

When it comes to strawberry shortcake, biscuits rule. The ones for this shortcake are crisp yet delicate—and foolproof. You grate frozen butter into the dry ingredients, stir in the milk and egg, and then press the dough into a ball. You don't need a rolling pin or special cutter to form the biscuits: you just pat the dough into a rectangle and cut it into squares with a knife. There's no rerolling of scraps, so all the shortcakes are equally attractive and tender.

For a fruit topping that's fresh, wonderfully juicy, and economical, use a mix of fresh and frozen berries.

SERVES 6

BISCUITS

2	cups all-purpose flour
½	teaspoon salt
1	tablespoon baking powder
5	tablespoons sugar
8	tablespoons (1 stick) unsalted butter, frozen
1	large egg
½	cup cold half-and-half

BERRIES

1	package (16 ounces) frozen strawberries, thawed and crushed
¾	pound fresh strawberries, hulled and sliced
6	tablespoons sugar

WHIPPED CREAM

1	cup heavy cream, chilled
1	tablespoon sugar
1	teaspoon vanilla extract

TO MAKE BISCUITS: Adjust oven rack to lower-middle position and heat oven to 425 degrees.

Mix flour, salt, baking powder, and 3 tablespoons sugar in a medium bowl. Grate butter on coarse holes of a box grater into dry ingredients; toss to coat.

Beat egg in a small bowl, then mix in half-and-half. Pour into flour mixture, and toss with a fork to form large clumps. Lightly press clumps into a ball.

Turn dough out onto a lightly floured work surface and press into a 7½-by-5-inch rectangle. Cut into 6 squares. Place squares 1 inch apart on a baking sheet and sprinkle tops with remaining 2 tablespoons sugar.

Bake until golden brown, 12 to 14 minutes. Cool for 5 minutes on a wire rack.

MEANWHILE, TO MAKE BERRIES: Mix crushed and fresh berries with sugar in a bowl.

TO MAKE WHIPPED CREAM: Beat cream to soft peaks, gradually adding sugar, then vanilla.

TO ASSEMBLE: Split biscuits, and place bottoms on plates. Spoon a portion of berries over each bottom, place a dollop of whipped cream on berries, and top with biscuit caps. Serve immediately.

WHEN SHOULD I SERVE IT?

In spring, summer, and early fall, whenever good berries are available

For small or large gatherings (the recipe multiplies easily, but for larger batches, you may want to grate the frozen butter in a food processor)

For elegant or casual dinners

HOW CAN I VARY IT?

Substitute an equal amount of frozen and fresh raspberries, blackberries, or blueberries for the strawberries.

WHAT SHOULD I SERVE WITH IT?

Sear-Ahead Steaks or Salmon (page 66)

Easy Baked Risotto (page 72)

Butter-Roasted Lobster Tails (page 90)

Roast Rack of Lamb with Vinegar-Mint Pan Sauce (page 93)

Chicken-Mushroom Crepes (page 108)

Salmon Cucumber Salad with Sour Cream–Dill Dressing (page 192)

Crab-Stuffed Artichokes (page 150; or substitute shrimp for the crab)

HOW FAR AHEAD CAN I MAKE IT?

The dough squares, without the sugar topping, can be covered loosely with plastic wrap and refrigerated for 3 to 4 hours before baking.

The sugared berries can be refrigerated for 3 to 4 hours.

The whipped cream can be covered and refrigerated for 3 hours.

WHAT ABOUT LEFTOVERS?

Leftover biscuits can be warmed in a 350-degree oven or split, buttered, and broiled for breakfast.

PERFECTLY SIMPLE
PUMPKIN CHEESECAKE

Looking for a traditional Thanksgiving dessert but don't want to make a piecrust? Try this cheesecake. It doesn't even require a springform pan. Baking the cake in a shallow baking pan means that the filling sets quickly and therefore will not crack, eliminating the need for a water bath. Line the pan with whole graham crackers and spread with melted butter and sugar for a super-simple crust. No grinding crackers into crumbs, mixing, or tamping the crumbs into the pan.

SERVES 12 TO 15

If garnishing the cheesecake with toasted pecans, toast them on a small baking sheet in a 325-degree oven until fragrant, about 10 minutes. To garnish it with candied pecans, follow the recipe for Candied Almonds (page 177), substituting pecan halves for the slivered almonds.

6	tablespoons (³/₄ stick) unsalted butter
¹/₄	cup granulated sugar
7–8	whole graham crackers
1	can (15 ounces) 100% pure pumpkin (not pie filling)
1³/₄	cups packed dark brown sugar
1	teaspoon ground ginger
¹/₂	teaspoon ground cinnamon
¹/₈	teaspoon ground nutmeg
¹/₈	teaspoon ground allspice
4	large eggs
1¹/₂	pounds cream cheese, softened
1	container (16 ounces) sour cream
1	teaspoon vanilla extract
	Toasted or candied pecans for garnish (optional; see above)

Adjust oven rack to middle position and heat oven to 375 degrees.

Heat butter and granulated sugar in a small saucepan until butter has melted. Meanwhile, line a 13-by-9-inch baking pan with a sheet of heavy-duty foil, leaving an overhang on two long sides to facilitate removal of cheesecake from pan.

Arrange graham crackers over pan bottom, cutting final few with a serrated knife as necessary to fit. Pour butter mixture over crackers and spread evenly with a rubber spatula. Bake until butter-sugar mixture starts to harden, about 7 minutes. Remove from oven, and reduce oven temperature to 300 degrees.

Meanwhile, combine pumpkin, 1¼ cups brown sugar, and spices in a medium saucepan and heat over medium-high heat, stirring occasionally, until mixture is sputtery hot. Transfer to a bowl with a spoon.

Process eggs in a blender on high speed until thoroughly mixed. With motor running, slowly add pumpkin mixture and puree until smooth. Add cream cheese 1 block at a time, and puree until smooth.

Pour pumpkin mixture over crust. Bake until filling is set but still jiggly at center, about 35 minutes.

Meanwhile, mix sour cream, remaining ½ cup brown sugar, and vanilla in a bowl.

Remove cheesecake from the oven, pour sour cream mixture evenly over top, and spread carefully so top is completely covered. Return to oven and bake until topping is set, about 5 minutes longer. Cool to room temperature, then refrigerate.

When ready to serve, run a knife around perimeter at the two short ends of pan to loosen cake. Use foil handles to pull cheesecake from pan, and cut into squares. Garnish with pecans, if desired, and serve.

WHEN SHOULD I SERVE IT?
When you want an easy but irresistibly rich fall or winter dessert for a crowd
For a casual lunch or supper

ANY SHORTCUTS?
To soften the cream cheese quickly, remove the blocks from their packaging and microwave one at a time on high until soft, about 30 seconds.
Omit the sour cream layer.

WHAT SHOULD I SERVE WITH IT?
Boneless Coq au Vin (page 42)
Simple Cassoulet (page 44)
One of the stews (pages 48–53)
Butterflied Cornish Hens with Apricot-Pistachio Dressing (page 76)
Twin Turkeys with Rich Pan Gravy (page 78)
Rosemary-Scented Roast Pork Loin Stuffed with Roasted Garlic, Dried Apricots, and Cranberries with Port Wine Sauce (page 83)

Chicken-Mushroom Crepes (page 108)

HOW FAR AHEAD CAN I MAKE IT?
The cheesecake can be refrigerated, covered with plastic, for up to 2 days.

WHAT ABOUT LEFTOVERS?
Though the crust will soften, the cheesecake will be good for 4 or 5 days.

CHOCOLATE OR LEMON TART

Making a homemade chocolate or lemon tart can be as simple as picking up a box of frozen puff pastry and either a bar of good chocolate and a half-pint of heavy cream or a couple jars of lemon curd.

SERVES 12

Remove the pastry sheet from the package so it thaws quickly. It will be ready to roll out in about 15 minutes, making it possible to prepare these desserts shortly before guests arrive. Because it is rich, one tart serves a small crowd.

1 sheet frozen Pepperidge Farm Puff Pastry (from a 17.3-ounce box), thawed but still cold

Rich Chocolate Filling or Lemon Curd Filling (recipes follow)

1 cup heavy cream, whipped to soft peaks

1 half pint (about 6 ounces) raspberries (optional)

Adjust oven rack to lower-middle position and heat oven to 425 degrees.

Roll pastry sheet out on a lightly floured work surface to a 12-inch square. Fit into a 9-inch fluted tart pan with a removable bottom, making sure not to stretch pastry. Trim excess pastry by pressing down around perimeter of pan with tip of your thumb. Prick pastry all over with a fork. Spray bottom of a 9-inch Pyrex pie plate with vegetable cooking spray and place in tart pan to keep pastry from puffing excessively.

Bake until crisp and golden brown, 20 to 22 minutes. Remove pie plate; cool tart shell completely on a wire rack.

Pour chocolate filling into tart shell or spread curd in shell. Let chocolate tart sit for 2 hours to allow filling to set; lemon tart may be served immediately.

To serve tart, slice and garnish with whipped cream and berries, if desired.

RICH CHOCOLATE FILLING

MAKES ENOUGH FOR ONE 9-INCH TART

8   ounces semisweet chocolate, cut into
     small pieces
1   cup heavy cream
2   large egg yolks

Combine chocolate and cream in a 1-quart Pyrex measuring cup or small microwave-safe bowl and microwave on high power until cream is hot enough to melt chocolate, about 2 minutes; whisk until smooth. Or heat in a small heavy saucepan, stirring, until chocolate is melted and mixture is smooth; remove from heat.

Whisk egg yolks in a small bowl, then slowly add 1 cup chocolate mixture to yolks, whisking constantly to keep eggs from curdling. Whisk chocolate-egg mixture back into remaining chocolate.

LEMON CURD FILLING

MAKES ENOUGH FOR ONE 9-INCH TART

2   jars (10–12 ounces each) lemon curd
1   teaspoon grate lemon zest

Spoon curd into a medium bowl. Stir or whisk in zest.

WHEN SHOULD I SERVE IT?
 For both casual and elegant dinners
 For a large group

HOW FAR AHEAD CAN I MAKE IT?
 The chocolate tart can be made 1 day ahead, covered, and refrigerated. Return to room temperature before serving.

The lemon tart can be made 2 hours ahead.

APPLE CROSTATA

When the occasion calls for apple pie but you don't have time to make dough for a crust, try this rustic fruit tart. Cooking the apples first keeps them from releasing too much liquid when they're spooned over the puff pastry, so it stays crisp. The stewed apples must be cooled before using, but if you spread them out on a large baking sheet, they'll cool in minutes. (Set that sheet in the freezer, and they'll be cold by the time you've thawed the pastry and rolled it out.)

SERVES 6 TO 8

Top apple crostata as you would apple pie—with ice cream or lightly sweetened whipped cream.

3   tablespoons unsalted butter

2   pounds crisp apples (such as Granny Smith), peeled, cored,
      and sliced ¼ inch thick

1   pound juicy, soft-textured apples (such as McIntosh), peeled, cored,
      and sliced ¼ inch thick

½   cup plus 1 tablespoon sugar

1   sheet frozen Pepperidge Farm Puff Pastry (from a 17.3-ounce box),
      thawed but still cold

1   large egg white, beaten

Melt butter in a large (12-inch) skillet over medium-high heat. Add apples and ½ cup sugar, cover, and cook until apples release their liquid, about 5 minutes. Remove lid and cook, stirring frequently, until juicy apples fall apart and juices thicken to a thin syrup, about 5 minutes. Pour onto a large rimmed baking sheet to cool.

Adjust oven rack to lowest position and heat oven to 400 degrees. Line a large cookie sheet with parchment paper.

Roll puff pastry sheet out on a lightly floured work surface to a 10-by-16-inch rectangle. Slide onto cookie sheet.

Spread apples over pastry, leaving a 2-inch border. Fold pastry edges over apples, then unfold corners and pleat so that dough is not a double thickness. Brush pastry border with egg white and sprinkle with remaining 1 tablespoon sugar.

Bake until golden brown, 25 to 30 minutes. Serve warm or at room temperature.

WHEN SHOULD I SERVE IT?

Whenever you'd serve an apple pie

WHAT SHOULD I SERVE WITH IT?

Any fall or winter beef, pork, or poultry dinner

HOW FAR AHEAD CAN I MAKE IT?

The stewed apples can be refrigerated in an airtight container for up to 2 days.

The crostata can be baked 2 hours, but no more, before serving.

WHAT ABOUT LEFTOVERS?

Although the pastry will get a little soggy, the crostata will be good, kept covered at room temperature, for a day or two.

DRINKS

ZIPPY BLOODY MARYS

I like my bloody Marys strong but not stiff. These are spicy without being too hot. Set out the pepper sauce bottle for those who want more heat. For the virgin version, leave out the vodka. Make a pitcher each of bloody and virgin Marys so you don't have to spike individual drinks.

MAKES ABOUT 12 DRINKS

2   quarts tomato juice

1   cup vodka

¼   cup fresh lemon juice (from 2 lemons)

3   tablespoons prepared horseradish

2   tablespoons rice wine vinegar

2   teaspoons Worcestershire sauce

1   teaspoon hot red pepper sauce

1   teaspoon salt

1   teaspoon celery seeds

½   teaspoon garlic powder

Mix all ingredients in a large pitcher. Refrigerate until ready to serve.

WHEN SHOULD I SERVE IT?
For brunch
For a small or large group—it's easy to halve or multiply the recipe
For all seasons

WHAT SHOULD I SERVE WITH IT?
My Big Fat Greek Frittata (page 100)
Easy Savory Strata (page 102)
Orange Cream Cheese Strata with Cranberries and Walnuts (page 106)
Chicken-Mushroom Crepes (page 108)

HOW FAR AHEAD CAN I MAKE IT?
All the ingredients except the lemon juice can be combined in the pitcher the night before the party; add the lemon juice when you're ready to serve.

SPARKLING COOLERS

These colorful, attractive coolers are a not-too-sweet alternative for those who don't care for the spiked stuff.   **MAKES 8 DRINKS**

SPARKLING LIMEADE

1   can (12 ounces) frozen limeade
     concentrate (not thawed)
1¹/₂ quarts (48 ounces) seltzer water, chilled
     Lime wedges for garnish

SPARKLING CRANBERRY JUICE

1   can (12 ounces) frozen cranberry juice
     concentrate (not thawed)
1¹/₂ quarts (48 ounces) seltzer water, chilled

SPARKLING ORANGE JUICE

1   can (12 ounces) frozen orange juice
     concentrate (not thawed)
1¹/₂ quarts (48 ounces) seltzer water, chilled

SPARKLING LEMONADE

1   can (12 ounces) frozen lemonade
     concentrate (not thawed)
1¹/₂ quarts (48 ounces) seltzer water, chilled

Mix concentrate and seltzer in a large pitcher and stir to blend. Or add about 3 tablespoons concentrate to each glass and top off with about ³/₄ cup seltzer water. Serve, with garnish, if using.

WHEN SHOULD I SERVE IT?
For intergenerational gatherings
For picnics and other outdoor parties

HOW CAN I VARY IT?
Any fruit juice concentrate can be turned into a sparkling cooler — try apple juice, grape juice, mixed berry, or pineapple.

WHAT SHOULD I SERVE WITH IT?
Serve it before any of the main courses, casual or refined, in this book.

HOW FAR AHEAD CAN I MAKE IT?
Because they're made with seltzer (and because they're so easy), these should be mixed only at the last minute.

SPARKLING WINE COCKTAILS

MAKES 6 DRINKS

For special occasions, champagne is usually my drink of choice—but not when I've invited twenty-odd friends and relatives over to celebrate. Then sparkling wine cocktails are my solution. They look festive and taste wonderful, at a fraction of the cost of champagne.

When buying the sparkling wine, make sure it's dry—select brut wine. Despite its name, extra-dry is actually sweeter than brut (demi-sec is sweeter than extra-dry).

Like champagne, a sparkling wine cocktail should be served well chilled. Move the bottles from the refrigerator to the freezer ten to fifteen minutes before serving. (Don't forget them, or you'll end up with semi-frozen sparkling wine, which flows unstoppably, like slow-moving lava.)

Flavoring of choice (recipes follow)
1   bottle (750-milliliter) inexpensive dry (brut) sparkling wine, well chilled

Add selected flavoring, and any garnish, to six champagne flutes. Holding each flute at an angle, with tip of bottle resting just inside flute, fill, turning glass straight up as it is filled. Serve immediately.

WHEN SHOULD I SERVE IT?
For festive brunches, lunches, or dinners
Year-round

WHAT SHOULD I SERVE WITH IT?
Serve before any brunch, lunch, or dinner

CLASSIC SPARKLING WINE COCKTAIL

Sugar cubes are located with other sugars in the baking aisle of supermarkets.

6 sugar cubes, each soaked with 8–12 drops aromatic bitters, such as Angostura (1 per glass)

KIR ROYALE

2 tablespoons crème de cassis (1 teaspoon per glass)

KIR IMPERIALE

2 tablespoons Chambord or other raspberry-flavored liqueur (1 teaspoon per glass)
6 fresh or frozen raspberries for garnish (optional)

FRENCH 75

2 tablespoons Cognac (1 teaspoon per glass)

MOCK BELLINI

6 tablespoons peach schnapps (1 tablespoon per glass)
6 fresh, frozen, or canned peach slices for garnish (optional)

GRAND SPARKLING WINE

6 tablespoons Grand Marnier, Torres orange liqueur, or Cointreau (1 tablespoon per glass)
6 orange peel twists for garnish (optional)

GIN (OR YOUR CHOICE) AND TONIC

MAKES 8 DRINKS

More important than the quality of the gin is the quality of the tonic. Schweppes tonic in the little 10-ounce glass bottles is my mixer of choice. Bombay Sapphire is my favorite brand of gin.

Good ice matters too. Forget the shaved stuff. It melts too quickly and dilutes the drink. Use big cubes instead (and insulated glasses if you like).

There is no such thing as a good gin and tonic without fresh lime, which should flavor the rim of the glass as well as the drink. If your guests don't like gin, offer them vodka, rum, or even tequila tonics.

Ice cubes
1 large lime, cut into 8 chunks
½ bottle (½ liter) gin (or your favorite vodka, rum, or tequila), stored in the freezer
4 10-ounce bottles tonic water, chilled

Fill eight 12-ounce glasses with ice cubes. Rub each glass rim with a lime chunk, then squeeze juice over ice. Add 2 ounces gin (or other liquor) to each glass. Top each with tonic water and serve immediately.

WHEN SHOULD I SERVE IT?
Since these are individually mixed drinks, they are better for smaller parties.

WHAT SHOULD I SERVE WITH IT?
Oven-Barbecued Pulled Pork Sandwiches or Carnitas (page 17)

Shish Kebabs (page 56)
Mixed Grill with Tandoori Flavorings (page 62)
Grilled Chicken Breasts with Orange-Thyme Glaze (page 64)
Sear-Ahead Steaks or Salmon (page 66)

Butter-Roasted Lobster Tails (page 90)
Roast Rack of Lamb with Vinegar-Mint Pan Sauce (page 93)

INSTANT FROZEN MARGARITAS

I used to make a very simple margarita—equal parts tequila, orange liqueur, and lime juice. It was good, but by the time I had served a couple of rounds, no one cared about dinner. My new formula is even simpler to make (using frozen limeade concentrate saves a lot of time) and less potent, so everyone's ready to sit down and enjoy a lively dinner after cocktail hour.

MAKES 8 DRINKS

- 8 cups ice cubes
- 1 can (12 ounces) frozen limeade concentrate
- 1½ cups tequila
- ¼ cup Cointreau or other orange-flavored liqueur
  Margarita salt or kosher salt for rims of glasses (optional)
- 6 lime half slices, plus extra wedges if salting rims of glasses

Place 4 cups ice cubes in a blender. Add half the limeade concentrate, ¾ cup tequila, and 2 tablespoons Cointreau. Blend at high speed until almost smooth. Pour into a pitcher and place in the freezer. Repeat with remaining ingredients.

If salting glass rims, pour a layer of salt onto a small plate, moisten each glass rim with lime juice, and dip in salt. Pour frozen margaritas into glasses, garnish with lime, and serve.

WHEN SHOULD I SERVE IT?
At casual dinners and buffets, especially in summer
For a crowd—they can be made ahead by the pitcher

WHAT SHOULD I SERVE WITH IT?
Chicken Chili—Red or White (page 13)
Oven-Barbecued Pulled Pork Sandwiches or Carnitas (page 17)
Grown-Up Sloppy Joes (page 22)
Grilled Chicken Breasts with

Orange-Thyme Glaze (page 64)
Sear-Ahead Steaks or Salmon (page 66)

HOW FAR AHEAD CAN I MAKE IT?
The margaritas can be made up to 3 hours ahead and kept in the freezer.

COSMOPOLITANS (OR MARTINIS) BY THE PITCHER

MAKES 6 DRINKS

The key to these drinks is very cold good vodka and very cold glasses. If you have room, chill the glasses in the freezer; if not, fill them with ice water while you make the drinks. Just before filling the glasses, dump the ice water and give them a good shake.

If you don't have martini glasses, serve these in any small wide-mouthed, stemmed glasses.

- ¼ cup fresh lime juice (from 2 limes), plus extra half slices for garnish
- 2 teaspoons sugar
- 4 cups ice cubes
- 1½ cups vodka, chilled
- ½ cup cranberry juice

Mix lime juice and sugar in a Pyrex measuring cup or small bowl until sugar dissolves. Drop ice into a pitcher. Add lime juice mixture, vodka, and cranberry juice and stir until well chilled. Strain into another pitcher and set in the freezer until ready to serve.

Pour drinks into martini glasses. Garnish with lime slices and serve.

WHEN SHOULD I SERVE IT?
Since they can be made by the pitcher, these are good for both small dinner parties and, as long as the glasses hold out, large buffets.

When you want a do-ahead drink —then just pour

HOW CAN I VARY IT?
Make Martinis by the Pitcher (facing page) or, for a nonalcoholic version, Bug Juice (facing page).

WHAT SHOULD I SERVE WITH IT?
Serve before any fun, festive dinner, especially during the warmer months.

HOW FAR AHEAD CAN I MAKE IT?
You can make these several hours before the party and keep in the freezer.

GIN OR VODKA MARTINIS BY THE PITCHER

Stir 1½ cups cold good gin (such as Bombay Sapphire) or vodka (such as Absolut) and ¼ cup dry vermouth with the ice. (Omit lime, sugar, and cranberry juice.) Store in freezer. When serving, garnish each drink with one of the following: a twist of lemon, a pickled cocktail onion (or strips of Pickled Pink Onions, page 127), a cornichon, a few capers, 1–2 cracked Spanish olives, 1–2 large pimiento-stuffed olives or peperoncini, or any pickled vegetable.

BUG JUICE

MAKES 8 DRINKS

Here's a look-alike nonalcoholic version of the Cosmopolitan.

1   can (12 ounces) frozen limeade concentrate
½   cup cranberry juice
1   bottle (64 ounces) ginger ale, chilled
    Dark raisins and marshmallows for garnish (optional)

Add limeade concentrate and cranberry juice to pitcher of ice and stir to blend. Stir in ginger ale, and serve, adding a few raisins and marshmallows, if desired, to each glass.

A PITCHER OF MOJITOS

While this Cuban libation feels especially appropriate for the warmer months, I serve mojitos (mo-*hee*-tos) year-round, especially with Asian- or Indian-style appetizers. Since the taste reminds many people of a mint julep, you can also serve these on Derby Day.

MAKES 8 DRINKS

2 cups ice cubes, plus extra for serving

8 large mint sprigs, plus 8 smaller sprigs for garnish

⅓ cup sugar

1 cup fresh lime juice (from 4–6 limes)

2 cups white rum

8 dashes aromatic bitters, such as Angostura

1 liter club soda, chilled

Drop ice into a large pitcher and add large mint sprigs, sugar, and lime juice. Beat mint against ice with a wooden spoon to bruise it. Add rum and bitters. Strain, if desired, into another pitcher. Store in freezer until ready to serve.

To serve, fill eight 12-ounce glasses with ice, and add rum mixture to come about two thirds of the way up each glass. Top off with club soda, garnish with fresh mint sprigs, and serve immediately.

WHEN SHOULD I SERVE IT?
For casual dinners and buffets
When you're on a budget — white rum is very reasonably priced
When you want a do-ahead drink

WHAT SHOULD I SERVE WITH IT?
Chicken Chili — Red or White (page 13)
Oven-Barbecued Pulled Pork

Sandwiches or Carnitas (page 17)
Grown-Up Sloppy Joes (page 22)
Mixed Grill with Tandoori Flavorings (page 62)
Grilled Chicken Breasts with Orange-Thyme Glaze (page 64)
Sear-Ahead Steaks or Salmon (page 66)

HOW FAR AHEAD CAN I MAKE IT?
The mojito base can be made up to 2 hours ahead and kept in the freezer.

WHAT ABOUT LEFTOVERS?
If you strain out the mint, leftover mojito base can be stored in the freezer for 1 week or more.

MILK PUNCH

This punch is lighter in calories and texture than eggnog, and it's much simpler to make. I serve it during the holiday season, either in the late afternoon or after dinner. A friend of mine calls it an adult milkshake.

MAKES 12 DRINKS

1½   cups dark rum
¾   cup brandy
3   tablespoons vanilla extract
1½   cups sugar
3   quarts whole milk
   Ground nutmeg for garnish

Combine rum, brandy, and vanilla in a large pitcher and stir in sugar until dissolved. Stir in milk. Freeze until very cold or even slushy, at least 4 hours.

To serve, pour into glasses and sprinkle with nutmeg.

WHEN SHOULD I SERVE IT?
   For small or large gatherings of adults — the recipe multiplies easily, and the punch stores well
   As a pleasant end to a fall or winter dinner
   As a summer dessert, with cookies
   As part of the dessert table at an open house

WHAT SHOULD I SERVE WITH IT?
   Boneless Coq au Vin (page 42)
   Simple Cassoulet (page 44)
   One of the stews (pages 48–53)
   Butterflied Cornish Hens with Apricot-Pistachio Dressing (page 76)
   Twin Turkeys with Rich Pan Gravy (page 78)
   Sear-Ahead Steaks or Salmon (page 66)

   Rosemary-Scented Roast Pork Loin Stuffed with Roasted Garlic, Dried Apricots, and Cranberries with Port Wine Sauce (page 83)

HOW FAR AHEAD CAN I MAKE IT?
   The punch is best made at least 4 hours ahead.

WHAT ABOUT LEFTOVERS?
   The punch can be frozen in a covered container for up to 1 month.

MULLED CIDER

To keep the cider warm and make pouring easier, transfer it to the carafe of an automatic drip coffeemaker and turn on the machine.

MAKES A GENEROUS GALLON; SERVES 12 TO 16

4 cinnamon sticks

2 teaspoons allspice berries

2 teaspoons whole cloves

Zest of 1 orange, removed with a vegetable peeler

1 gallon apple cider

1½ cups brandy (optional)

Combine spices, orange zest, and 1 cup water in a small saucepan and bring to a boil. Reduce heat and simmer until cinnamon sticks start to unfurl and spices release their flavor, about 15 minutes. Remove from heat.

Pour cider into a Dutch oven or large pot. Add spice mixture to cider and bring just to a simmer over low heat. Turn off heat.

To serve, pour about 2 tablespoons brandy, if desired, into each mug. Ladle in hot cider and serve.

WHEN SHOULD I SERVE IT?

During fall and winter

At both small and large gatherings — the recipe easily halves or multiplies

Since the drink can be spiked or not, it works well at gatherings with both drinkers and nondrinkers.

WHAT SHOULD I SERVE WITH IT?

Creamy Baked Macaroni and Cheese (page 32)

Boneless Coq au Vin (page 42)

Simple Cassoulet (page 44)

One of the stews (pages 48–53)

Butterflied Cornish Hens with Apricot-Pistachio Dressing (page 76)

Rosemary-Scented Roast Pork Loin Stuffed with Roasted Garlic, Dried Apricots, and Cranberries with Port Wine Sauce (page 83)

Beef Tenderloin with Cracked Black Pepper Coating and Red Wine–Thyme Pan Sauce (page 86)

Twin Turkeys with Rich Pan Gravy (page 78)

HOW FAR AHEAD CAN I MAKE IT?

Because it makes the house smell good, simmer the spices up to several hours before dinner; but don't heat the cider until the last minute.

WHAT ABOUT LEFTOVERS?

With the spices strained out, the cider will keep, refrigerated, for 2 weeks.

INDEX

Note: page numbers in *italics* refer to photographs.

A

almond-cherry scones, 232

almonds, toasted, and mustard sauce, creamed green beans with, 200–201

almonds, toasted, glazed, 177

ambrosia, grapefruit-orange, 234, *235*

appetizers and first courses. *See also* soups (first course)

    appetizer bar, *125*, 126–27

        breads and chips for, 123–24

        spreads for, 122–23

        toppings for, 126

    big bowl of garlicky mussels or clams, 152, *153*

    butter-roasted lobster tails, *89*, 90–91

    cheddar puffs with scallions and cayenne, 131–32, *133*

    chips

        baked pita triangles, 124

        fried corn tortilla triangles, 123–24

        fried wonton rectangles, 124

        golden toast rounds, 124

    coconut shrimp with sweet-and-sour orange sauce, 142–44, *143*

    crab-stuffed artichokes, 150–51

    curried popcorn, 116

    easy baked risotto, 72–75, *74*

    easy butternut squash ravioli with rosemary oil, *147*, 148–49

    fresh goat cheese on flatbread with grapes and rosemary oil, 130

    lacy cheddar crisps, 118, *119*

    pastry triangles with mushroom–goat cheese filling, 137

    pastry triangles with spinach and feta, 136–37

    perfect deviled eggs, 120–21

    pickled pink deviled eggs, 121

    potato crisps with smoked salmon and herbed cream cheese, 128, *129*

    quesadillas for a crowd, 138–39

        with bacon and chive-onion cream cheese, 139

        with crab, scallions, and cream cheese, 139

        with goat cheese, olives, and red onions, 139

        with shrimp, feta, and scallions, 139

        with spicy cheese and scallions, 139

        with zucchini, green chiles, and string cheese, 139

    quick marinated olives, 117

    ricotta-filled ravioli, 149

    roasted buttery pecans, 115

    slow-roasted cumin-garlic shrimp with lemon-cilantro yogurt, 145–46

    spicy Asian lettuce cups, 140–41

    spreads

        feta, oregano-flavored, 122

        hummus, 123

        olive, with lemon and thyme, 122

        sun-dried tomato, with fresh basil, 123

        white bean, with garlic and rosemary, 123

    vegetable egg rolls with lime-ginger dipping sauce, 134–35

apple(s)

    crostata, 278–80, *279*

    paste, curried, 59

    roasted, with caramel sauce, 254

    upside-down cake, 261

apricot-pistachio dressing, butterflied Cornish hens with, 76–77

apricot-prune sauce with Moroccan spices, 41

artichoke(s)

    crab-stuffed, 150–51

    quarters, parsleyed, for appetizer bar, 127

    sauce, lemon, with garlic and parsley, 41

asparagus, broiled or grilled, 195

asparagus, orange-glazed, 196, *197*

B

bacon and chive-onion cream cheese, quesadillas with, 139

banana–cinnamon chip mini muffins, 228–29

bars, s'more, 236–37

basil-buttermilk dressing, 182–83

bean(s). *See also* chickpeas; green bean(s)

coffee mascarpone sauce, frozen tiramisu with, 250–52, *251*

compote, mixed berry, 258

cookies, saucer-size oatmeal, 238–40, *239*

corn

and black beans, chicken soup with, 7

muffins, moist, savory, 226–27

quick white chicken chili with hominy, 15–16, *16*

salad, fresh, with cabbage and bell peppers, 184

soup, creamy, with cumin and cayenne, 159

Cornish hens, butterflied, with apricot-pistachio dressing, 76–77

cosmopolitans by the pitcher, 288

couscous with chickpeas and carrots, 215

crab, scallions, and cream cheese, quesadillas with, 139

crab-stuffed artichokes, 150–51

cranberry(ies)

dried, blue cheese, and toasted pecans, baby greens, romaine, and iceberg lettuce with, 174, *175*

juice, sparkling, 283

-orange scones, 232

sauce, just-right, with ginger and orange, 222

saucer-size oatmeal cookies, 238–40, *239*

and walnuts, orange cream cheese strata with, 106–7

cream cheese

chive-onion, and bacon, quesadillas with, 139

crab, and scallions, quesadillas with, 139

herbed, and smoked salmon, potato crisps with, 128, *129*

lemon frosting, yellow cake with raspberry filling and, 259

orange strata with cranberries and walnuts, 106–7

perfectly simple pumpkin cheesecake, 274–75

crepes, chicken-mushroom, 108–11, *110*

crostata, apple, 278–80, *279*

croutons, 172

cucumber(s)

mango gazpacho, 164

pineapple gazpacho, 164

salmon salad with sour cream–dill dressing, 192–93, *193*

watermelon gazpacho, 164

year-round classic gazpacho, 162–64, *163*

cumin vinaigrette, 178–79

curd, lemon, 277

curried apple paste, 59

curried chicken soup with chickpeas and cauliflower, 7

curried popcorn, 116

curried tomato soup, quick, 161

D

desserts. *See also* cake(s)

apple crostata, 278–80, *279*

berry bread pudding, 256

chocolate or lemon tart, 276–77

frozen tiramisu with coffee mascarpone sauce, 250–52, *251*

grapefruit-orange ambrosia, 234, *235*

hot-fudge brownie sundaes, 244–45

instant strawberry ice cream, 248, *249*

lemon-raspberry triflettes, 262–63, *263*

perfectly simple pumpkin cheesecake, 274–75

roasted peaches (or pears, plums, or apples) with caramel sauce, 254, *255*

saucer-size oatmeal cookies, 238–40, *239*

simple strawberry shortcakes, 272–73

s'more bars, 236–37

sorbet- or ice cream–filled crisp cinnamon cups, 246–47

tortilla sundaes with minted mango salsa, 241–43, *242*

turtle fondue (with or without the pot), 253

dressings. *See also* vinaigrettes

Asian, 181

basil-buttermilk, 182–83

creamy American, 181

orange-cumin, 181

salsa verde, 181

sour cream–dill, 192–93

drinks

bug juice, 289

cosmopolitans (or martinis) by the pitcher, 288–89

gin or vodka martinis by the pitcher, 289

gin (or your choice) and tonic, 286

instant frozen margaritas, 287

milk punch, 291

mulled cider, 292, *293*

pitcher of mojitos, 290

sparkling coolers, 283

cranberry juice, 283

lemonade, 283

limeade, 283

orange juice, 283

sparkling wine cocktails, 284–85

classic, 285

French 75, 285

grand, 285

kir imperiale, 285

red sauce for, 27

white sauce for, 28

plums, roasted, with caramel sauce, 254

popcorn, curried, 116

popovers, bake-ahead, 224–25

pork. *See also* sausage(s)

    carnitas, 20, *21*

    loin, rosemary-scented, stuffed with roasted gar-
lic, dried apricots, and cranberries with port
wine sauce, *82,* 83–85

    my big fat Greek frittata, *99,* 100–101

    one stew, many variations, 48–53, *51*

        with bell peppers and olives, 52–53

        with southwestern flavorings, 52

        with tomatoes and chickpeas, 53

        with tomatoes, rosemary, and white beans, 53

    oven-barbecued, 17–19

    pulled, sandwiches, *18,* 20

    quesadillas with bacon and chive-onion cream
cheese, 139

    shish kebabs, 56–60, *57*

    simple cassoulet, 44–47, *46*

    spicy Asian lettuce cups, 140–41

port wine sauce with blue cheese, 69

potato(es). *See also* sweet potato(es)

    cake, crisp, 208

    crisps with smoked salmon and herbed cream
cheese, 128, *129*

    gratin with garlic and thyme, 211

    mashed, garlic, 207

    mashed, make-ahead, 206–7

    new, roasted, salad, with olives, red onions, and
creamy vinaigrette, 185–86, *186*

    new, smashed, 209

    red, roasted, 210

    soup, creamy, rosemary-scented, 159

    and wild mushroom soup, pureed, 160

prune-apricot sauce with Moroccan spices, 41

puddings, bread

    berry, 256

    easy savory strata, 102–5, *103*

    orange cream cheese strata with cranberries and
walnuts, 106–7

puddings, Yorkshire, bake-ahead, 224–25

pumpkin cheesecake, perfectly simple, 274–75

punch, milk, 291

Q

quesadillas for a crowd, 138–39

    with bacon and chive-onion cream cheese, 139

    with crab, scallions, and cream cheese, 139

    with goat cheese, olives, and red onions, 139

    with shrimp, feta, and scallions, 139

    with spicy cheese and scallions, 139

    with zucchini, green chiles, and string cheese, 139

R

raspberry(ies)

    berry bread pudding, 256

    filling and lemon cream cheese frosting, yellow
cake with, 259

    -lemon triflettes, 262–63, *263*

    mixed berry compote, 258

    sugar-coated, molten chocolate cakes with,
264–66, *265*

    and whipped cream, meringue cake with, 267–68

ravioli, easy butternut squash, with rosemary oil, *147,*
148–49

ravioli, ricotta-filled, 149

rice

    and chicken soup, classic, 7

    coconut, 217

    easy baked risotto, 72–75, *74*

    lemon, 217

    Parmesan, 217

    risotto cakes, 75

    saffron, 217

    yellow, with green peas, 216–17

risotto, easy baked, 72–75, *74*

risotto cakes, 75

rosemary oil, easy butternut squash ravioli with, *147,*
148–49

rutabaga soup, creamy, with paprika and thyme, 159

S

saffron rice, 217

salad dressings. *See* dressings; vinaigrettes

salads

    baby greens, romaine, and iceberg lettuce with
blue cheese, toasted pecans, and dried cranberries, 174, *175*

    baby spinach, with shaved Parmesan and garlic
vinaigrette, 170–71

    Boston lettuce and baby spinach, 176–77

    Caesar, chopped, 172–73

    carrot, with cumin vinaigrette, 178–79

    corn, fresh, with cabbage and bell peppers, 184

    four slaws, 180–81

    green bean–cherry tomato, with basil-buttermilk
dressing, 182–83

    mixed green, with fresh herbs, 168–69

    parsley, with capers and cornichons, 88

    pear halves with blue cheese and toasted nuts,
166–67

stuffing, classic bread, with sausage, 221
sundaes, hot fudge brownie, 244–45
sundaes, tortilla, with minted mango salsa, 241–43,
    242
sweet potato(es)
    soup, creamy, with ginger and nutmeg, 157
    stew with Indian flavors, 52
    twice-baked, 212–14, *213*

T

tart, chocolate or lemon, 276–77
tiramisu, frozen, with coffee mascarpone sauce,
    250–52, *251*
tomato(es)
    Bolognese-style sauce, 36
    cherry, –green bean salad with basil-buttermilk
        dressing, 182–83
    cherry, sautéed, with garlic and basil, 202, *203*
    and chickpeas, stew with, 53
    cooked red sauce, 27
    plum, slow-roasted, with pesto-flavored crumbs,
        204
    really good lasagna, *34*, 35–37
    red sauce for pizza, 27
    soup, quick curried, 161
    sun-dried, spread with fresh basil, 123
    white beans, and rosemary, stew with, 53
    year-round classic gazpacho, 162–64, *163*
    zippy bloody Marys, 282
    and zucchini, chicken tortellini soup with, 7
tortellini soup, chicken, with zucchini and tomatoes,
    7
tortilla(s). *See also* quesadillas
    carnitas, 20, *21*
    corn, triangles, fried, 123–24
    sundaes with minted mango salsa, 241–43, *242*
triflettes, lemon-raspberry, 262–63, *263*
tuna salad, Niçoise-style, with white beans and
    olives, *189*, 190–91
turkey(s)
    Bolognese-style sauce, 36
    grown-up sloppy joes, 22–23
    really good lasagna, *34*, 35–37
    spicy Asian lettuce cups, 140–41

twin, with rich pan gravy, 78–81, *80*
turnips, carrots, and peas, classic stew with, 50
turnip soup, creamy, with paprika and thyme, 159

V

vegetable(s). *See also specific types*
    egg rolls with lime-ginger dipping sauce, 134–35
    shish kebabs, 56–60, *57*
    soup, creamy, and many variations, 155–59, *158*
vinaigrettes, 168–69
    creamy, 185–86
    cumin, 178–79
    garlic, 170–71
    red onion–caper, 187–88

W

walnuts, toasting, 166
walnuts and cranberries, orange cream cheese strata
    with, 106–7
watercress and smoked salmon salad with red
    onion–caper vinaigrette, 187–88
watermelon gazpacho, 164
wine, sparkling, cocktails, 284–85
    classic, 285
    French 75, 285
    grand, 285
    kir imperiale, 285
    kir royale, 285
    mock bellini, 285
wonton rectangles, fried, 124

Y

yogurt
    lemon-cilantro, slow-roasted cumin-garlic shrimp
        with, 145–46
    seasonal fruit parfaits, 97–98
Yorkshire puddings, bake-ahead (or popovers),
    224–25

Z

zucchini
    green chiles, and string cheese, quesadillas with,
        139
    and tomatoes, chicken tortellini soup with, 7